S0-CFU-795

Families, Schools, and the Adolescent

Connecting Research, Policy, and Practice

Families, Schools, and the Adolescent

Connecting Research, Policy, and Practice

EDITED BY

NANCY E. HILL and RUTH K. CHAO

Foreword by Jacquelynne Eccles

Teachers College, Columbia University
New York and London

Published by Teachers College Press, 1234 Amsterdam Avenue, New York, NY 10027

Library of Congress Cataloging-in-Publication Data

Families, schools, and the adolescent : connecting research, policy, and practice /
    edited by Nancy E. Hill and Ruth K. Chao ; foreword by Jacquelynne Eccles.
        p. cm.
    Includes bibliographical references and index.
    ISBN 978-0-8077-4995-1 (pbk. : alk. paper)
    ISBN 978-0-8077-4996-8 (hardcover : alk. paper)
    1. Middle school teaching—United States. 2. High school teaching—United
States. 3. Teenagers—Education—United States. 4. Teenagers and adults—
United States. 5. Teacher-student relationships—United States. 6. Parent-
teacher relationships—United States. 7. Motivation in education—United
States. I. Hill, Nancy E. II. Chao, Ruth K.
    LB1623.5.F36   2009
    371.19'2—dc22   2009015337

ISBN 978-0-8077-4995-1 (paper)
ISBN 978-0-8077-4996-8 (hardcover)

Printed on acid-free paper
Manufactured in the United States of America

16   15   14   13   12   11   10   09   8   7   6   5   4   3   2   1

Contents

**PART II—Facing the Challenges:
Feasibility of Parental Involvement During Adolescence**

Foreword

I
T IS AN HONOR TO WRITE THE FOREWORD for this book. Drs. Hill and Chao have given us an exceptionally broad and comprehensive set of chapters that analyze and illuminate a wide spectrum of issues related to family and school relations during adolescence. This book could not have come at a better time. We have a new president who is committed to reviving the American public education system and is willing to take bold action to accomplish this goal. Youth today, and their families, are facing an increasingly complex, changing, and opaque world—a world that is quite different from the world in which the parents of these youth grew up. Schools and families face an extraordinary task of preparing today's youth for a world that is changing at a dizzying pace. None of us know the kinds of jobs that will be available and the kinds of skills that will be needed and most marketable when today's youth mature and enter the labor market. It is commonly believed that our youth must be prepared to change occupations several times over their life course. These challenges make the importance of a high quality K–12 and college education more important than ever. These challenges also make the need for well developed social and cognitive skills—as well as social, intellectual, and cultural capital—more essential than ever.

And yet for many youth, particularly those in under-resourced neighborhoods and communities, the quality of education they are offered is often minimal at best. In addition, many youth are growing up in fractionated and highly mobile neighborhoods, making the accumulation of social capital quite challenging for both the youth themselves and their families. Finally, today's youth must make it through the educational pipeline despite the omnipresent prevalence of a diverse, easily accessible, and very attractive array of distractions that pull them away from a strong engagement with their own education. As Hillary Clinton reminded us years ago, it will "take a village" to help today's youth make it successfully through their adolescent years, as well as to prepare them to meet the challenges they will face as they move from their adolescence and through their adult lives. We must find a way to work as a community to bring our youth safely through their education and to ensure that they have learned or acquired the wide range of social, emotional, intellectual, and technical skills they will need to succeed in the world economy of the 21st century. To accomplish these goals, families, schools, and neighborhoods will have to work together closely to make sure each adolescent has the resources, guidance, and support she or he needs to move successfully through adolescence and then to transition successfully into adulthood. There needs to be a strong sharing of information and a powerful co-ordination of services and experiences.

I want to thank Drs. Hill and Chao for the rich tapestry of information they have gathered together on how we can meet these goals. The authors of the many chapters provide us with numerous insights into how we can move forward to increase the quality of family-school relations in many different types of neighborhood and community settings. The information will be of great use to teachers, parents, community workers, and youth activity directors and personnel. The authors also offer excellent guidance for researchers and scholars about where to go next. We are fortunate to have this book to help us create the strongest village we can for our youth's education and development.

—Jacquelynne Eccles

Acknowledgments

C OMPLETION OF THIS BOOK WOULD NOT have been possible without the generous support of Duke University's Arts and Sciences Research Council, Program in Education, Department of Psychology and Neuroscience, and the Center for Child and Family Policy. In addition, grants supporting this work were received from the National Science Foundation, the American Psychological Association's Committee on Children, Youth, and Families, and the American Psychological Association's Board of Directors. With the support from these entities, we convened a 2-day conference at Duke University's Sanford Institute of Public Policy on July 20–21, 2006, to present and debate research, theories, programs, and policies to enhance family–school relationships and, ultimately, school achievement among middle and high school students. The conference was attended by more than 150 teachers, principals, parents, state and local policymakers, researchers, and students. This book is the culmination of discussion and analysis that took place during the conference.

The contributors wish to thank the following people for their support: Harris Cooper, Ph.D., Kenneth A. Dodge, Ph.D., Timothy Strauman, Ph.D., and Erika Hanzely-Layko of Duke University, and Mary Campbell, Annie Toro, and Gabrielle McCormick of the American Psychological Association.

Families, Schools, and the Adolescent

Connecting Research, Policy, and Practice

Introduction

Background in Theory, Practice, and Policy

NANCY E. HILL
RUTH K. CHAO

FAMILIES AND TEACHERS ALIKE SEEK SOLUTIONS to building better working relationships in order to increase the chances that adolescents will reach their academic and social potential. Although families and school personnel share a desire for students to succeed, they often are perplexed about how to effectively collaborate and support achievement, especially as students move into middle and high school. The transition to middle school is marked by declines in achievement levels and engagement in school (Barber & Olsen, 2004; Eccles, 2004; Gutman & Midgley, 2000), even as the importance and long-term implications of achievement increase. Further, students have many teachers, making it harder for parents to connect and get information. Teachers instruct a large number of students over the course of the day, making it impossible to build relationships with each parent or family. The strategies that parents and teachers used in elementary school are no longer effective or harder to implement now that students are teenagers. Although teens may resist involvement from parents, parental involvement can have enormous benefits for adolescents' school achievement and emotional development (Hill & Tyson, 2009). This book will help parents, teachers, and other school personnel to identify the most effective ways in which parents can remain involved in their teens' education as they move into middle and high school. The strategies presented in this book are based on research with families and adolescents from a wide range of backgrounds, and they will broaden our thinking about the most effective and developmentally appropriate ways for families to support achievement.

Research from a variety of perspectives has documented the benefits of parental involvement in education, including those of community (Smith et al., 1997), developmental (Grolnick & Slowiaczek, 1994; Hill et

al., 2004), and school psychologists (Christenson, 2004), along with economists (Jimenez & Sawada, 1999; McMillan, 2000), sociologists (Epstein &
Sanders, 2002; Lareau, 2003), and education scientists (Brain & Reid, 2003;
Greene & Tichenor, 2003). Each of these perspectives addresses the issue
of family involvement in education from a unique viewpoint and thereby
often focuses on only part of the phenomenon. Further, some teachers,
school personnel, and parents figure out what works but do not have a
context for sharing this information with others or determining whether
their strategies might work for other schools and families. Often policies
and programs designed to increase parental involvement in education are
established without the full benefit of the combined knowledge gained
through research, experiences of practitioners, and needs of parents and
students, reducing the effectiveness of policies and the likelihood that research will inform policy and practice effectively. This book provides research, policy, and practice agendas to contribute to our understanding of
the unique and collaborative roles of families and schools in supporting
adolescents' achievement

The authors of the chapters in this book identify, through research, the
best ways in which families and schools can work independently and together to improve academic achievement for adolescents. This book has
two goals. First, the focus is on adolescence because little is known about
developmentally appropriate ways in which parents can and should be
involved in their middle and high school students' education (Hill & Taylor, 2004). Several theories have been proposed over the years that suggest
ways to be involved in one's children's schooling during the elementary
years (Epstein, 1987; Grolnick & Slowiaczek, 1994). These theories even
explain why these strategies work for elementary school students (Epstein
& Sanders, 2002; Hill & Craft, 2003). However, middle schoolers and teenagers are different, and the strategies parents used to effectively engage in
their elementary-school-aged students' education do not work as well for
adolescents. To date, researchers and policymakers often apply elementary school theories to middle and high school students without considering all of the ways adolescents are different from elementary-school-aged
children and all of the ways that middle and high schools are different
from elementary schools (Hill & Taylor, 2004). Developmentally appropriate and effective strategies for middle and high school students need to be
identified to support adolescents' achievement.

Second, the American school population is becoming increasingly diverse, ethnically and economically. For example, in 2001–02, almost 40%
of all students enrolled in public schools in the United States were ethnic
minorities (National Center for Education Statistics [NCES], 2003). This
ranged from an average of 63% ethnic minorities in large and midsized

cities to 36% in suburban and 21% in rural areas (NCES, 2003). For urban areas in California and for cities like New York and Washington, DC, as many as 86% of students are ethnic minorities (NCES, 2005). Cultural backgrounds and values shape beliefs about parental involvement in education, levels of involvement, and the ways in which parental involvement in education shapes achievement (Hill, in press; Hill et al., 2004; Hill & Craft, 2003; Lareau, 2003). Therefore, it is imperative to consider such diversity in order to effectively understand the types of parental involvement in education that are most important for adolescents.

FAMILY–SCHOOL RELATIONSHIPS: WHAT DO WE MEAN?

Generally, family–school relationships, or parental involvement in education, have been defined as collaborations among families, teachers, and schools to help students succeed in school (Epstein, 1987). Some have defined parental involvement as "parents' work with schools and with their children to benefit their children's educational outcomes and future success" (Hill et al., 2004, p. 1491). Federal policies, such as the No Child Left Behind Act (NCLB), define it as "the participation of parents in regular, two-way and meaningful communication involving student academic learning and other school activities" (107th Congress, 2002, section 9101, paragraph 32). Although these definitions form the basis of our understanding of parental involvement, each branch of learning or field of study defines parental involvement from its own unique perspective. Similarly, policies define it in their own ways as well.

Researchers within the field of *economics* often define parental involvement collectively across parents within schools and school districts, rather than as strategies individual families use. For example, "collective parental pressure" on the school, through PTAs or parental monitoring of the school, positively influences school quality and performance, even after taking into account differences across schools or school districts on parental and community characteristics (McMillan, 2000). Collective utilization of school choice may impact school climate and in turn school performance (Epple & Romano, 1998). In addition, collective influence, such as voting on school board members and school district budgets, affects school level academic outcomes (Jimenez & Sawada, 1999; Nechyba, McEwan, & Older-Aguilar, 1999). Increasing the instructional quality of one student raises the instructional quality for other students in the class or school (McMillan, 2000). From the perspective of economists, not all parents need to be involved—just enough to improve the school, instruction, or school performance.

Researchers from the fields of *sociology* and *developmental psychology* most often consider the individual family and student, rather than the collective efforts of a group of parents. Common across the major theories of parental involvement used by sociologists and psychologists are involvement at school (e.g., volunteering), involvement at home (e.g., helping with homework), and communication between school and families (Epstein, 1987; Epstein & Sanders, 2002; Grolnick & Slowiaczek, 1994). Other theories include the school's roles in educating parents on health, safety, nutrition, and methods for disciplining children and parents' involvement in school governance (Epstein, 1987; Epstein & Sanders, 2002). Also, parental involvement is characterized by three dimensions: *behavioral involvement*, reflecting actions that parents take, including volunteering at school, assisting with homework, and communications between home and school; *cognitive/intellectual stimulation*, reflecting things that parents provide or expose their children to, such as extracurricular activities, current events, and intellectual materials; and *personal involvement*, reflecting parents' attitudes about school, its utility and importance, expectations for achievement, and enjoyment of learning (Grolnick & Slowiaczek, 1994).

Developmental psychologists tend to focus on individual students' learning processes and achievement outcomes, and the role of their families in shaping these. For example, parental involvement influences achievement motivation, the extent to which students feel that they are capable of mastering academic work, students' perceptions of their competence in academics, students' focus, and their behavior at school, which in turn increases academic outcomes (Chao, 2000; Hill et al., 2004; Ibenez, Kuperminc, Jurkovic, & Perilla, 2004). Sociologists, on the other hand, tend to examine macro-processes such as school policies, and the influences of demographic variables such as the influence of families' economic resources and knowledge about or experience with the educational process (i.e., social and cultural capital) on the amount and type of parental involvement and the ways in which it affects achievement outcomes (Dika & Singh, 2002; Jordan & Plank, 2000; Lareau & Horvat, 1999; McNeal, 1999; Reay, 1999).

Whereas psychologists and sociologists often focus on the parents' perspective, *education scientists* focus on the teachers' roles and perspectives on parental involvement in education. Although the responsibility for initiating and coordinating parental involvement often is placed on teachers, they frequently are not trained in how to involve parents, including holding productive meetings with parents, especially those involving sensitive matters (MacDonald, 1991), and managing parents as classroom and school volunteers (Brain & Reid, 2003; Wallace, Shin, Bartholomay, & Stahl, 2001). Moreover, teachers' anxiety with regard to dealing with difficult parents has been documented (Fielstein & Phelps, 2001; Joseph & Burnaford, 1994). Integrating families' and teachers' perspectives will bridge these disparities in expectations and lead to more effective programs and policies.

Each field of study reflects a different focus and perspective, and often a different level of analysis of the relationship between parental involvement in education and student achievement. In this book, these definitions and perspectives are expanded upon and integrated as they apply to adolescents from diverse ethnic and socioeconomic (SES) backgrounds. To provide a framework for the book, hallmarks of adolescent development and the structural aspects of middle and high schools are outlined below.

ADOLESCENT DEVELOPMENT

Adolescence is marked by biological, cognitive, and social changes. These developmental changes interact and coincide with school transitions and with an increase in the long-term implications of decisions and course selections during middle and high school.

Biological Changes in Adolescent Development

Puberty, with its associated hormonal fluctuations, is the most significant biological change during adolescence. Triggered by hormones, adolescents experience the largest growth spurt they will experience in their lifetimes outside of infancy. There is increasing evidence that hormone levels and fluctuations impact mood and behavior, including aggression, anxiety, depression, and vacillation between elation and depression (Arnett, 1999; Buchanan, Eccles, & Becker, 1992). The biological changes of pubertal development interact with pubertal timing (e.g., early or later entry into puberty) to affect adolescents' behavior, mental health, and mood, which in turn influence engagement in school and interactions with peers (Simmons & Blythe, 1987). Early pubertal development places girls at increased risk for anxiety, depression, and risky behavior, whereas early development for boys seems advantageous for their self-image and mental health. School transitions often coincide with pubertal development, and early-developing girls have the most difficulty adjusting to school transitions (Simmons & Blythe, 1987).

Changes in Cognitive Development During Adolescence

Adolescence also brings changes in brain and cognitive development. It is during adolescence that synaptic connections in the brain are reorganized and mylenization increases (Wigfield, Byrnes, & Eccles, 2006), improving mental processes and decisionmaking (Keating, 2004). Associated with these changes in brain functioning, information processing becomes more efficient, and working memory and deductive reasoning increase, along with abstract-thinking abilities (Keating, 2004; Moshman, 1998). These cognitive abilities lead to increased negotiating skills, ability to make sound judgments, emotional maturity, and self-regulation (Richards, Miller, O'Donnell, Wasserman, & Colder, 2004).

The Development of Identity, Self, and Autonomy

Also marking the period of adolescence is the development of identity, independence, and autonomy (Erikson, 1968), which builds on adolescents' increased cognitive skills. Adolescents negotiate and integrate a wide variety of experiences, roles, beliefs, and interests into a coherent identity and manage it privately and publicly (i.e., self-image/popularity). Often as a result of identity development, adolescence, while focused on redefining self, self-image, and self-concept, is also a time of heightened self-consciousness, self-focus, and concerns about competence (Wigfield et al., 2006). Adolescents' concerns about being looked at, laughed at, and talked about by peers and friends peak during adolescence (Abe & Suzuki, 1986; Rutter, Graham, Chadwick, & Yule, 1976; Simmons & Blythe, 1987). Although at times the source of concern and anxiety, friendships and relationships with peers facilitate identity development and affirm self-image (Hamm & Faircloth, 2005; Kuperminc, Blatt, Shahar, Henrich, & Leadbeatter, 2004), which is particularly salient as the peer group increases in size and diversity. Adolescents often conform to friends' academic attitudes, thereby impacting engagement and achievement.

Classic theories of identity development point to the need for independent exploration and distancing from family (Erikson, 1968; Marcia, 1966). As part of adolescents' desire for independence from parental control, they often challenge parents' authority in certain areas of their lives (Smetana, Campione-Barr, & Daddis, 2004). This increase in autonomy and independence is especially salient in Western cultures (Arnett, 1999) and often impedes parents' ability to maintain involvement at school.

Renegotiating Family Relationships

Along with cognitive and social development, family roles and parent–adolescent relationships are renegotiated (Collins & Laursen, 2004). Parents and adolescents spend much less time together, as teens spend more time with friends and peers. Rather than the more hierarchical authority that parents held with their elementary-school-aged children, a discussion-based decisionmaking style is more characteristic of parents and adolescents (Fuligni & Eccles, 1993). In addition, there is increased parent–adolescent conflict. Compared with childhood, both the frequency and intensity of conflict increase (Arnett, 1999). Although often noted as a painful aspect of parent–adolescent relations, moderate levels of conflict are associated with more-adaptive developmental outcomes (Adams & Laursen, 2001). Despite the increased distancing and conflict between parents and adolescents, parents remain an important and significant resource for adolescents (Grotevant, 1998; Steinberg, 2001; Steinberg & Silk, 2002). They are second only to friends in closeness and support (Laursen & Williams, 1997) and remain the primary source for information about adolescents' future goals (e.g., Jodl, Michael, Malanchuck, Eccles, & Sameroff, 2001).

Academic Achievement in Adolescence

Despite adolescents' enhanced thinking and reasoning skills, academic achievement often declines across middle and high school (Barber & Olsen, 2004; Gutman & Midgley, 2000). As teens become more self-conscious and comparative, their self-confidence declines, as do their motivation and engagement in school. Identifying ways in which parents, as adolescents' strongest and most committed advocates, can work with schools to enhance adolescents' academic outcomes is imperative in order for adolescents to reach their potential and realize their dreams.

STRUCTURAL DIFFERENCES BETWEEN ELEMENTARY AND SECONDARY SCHOOLS

Structural challenges within middle and high schools undermine parents' ability to remain effectively involved in their adolescents' education and to work productively with schools (Epstein & Sanders, 2002). First, these schools are larger and more complex than elementary schools, making it difficult for parents to figure out how to become involved. Second, teachers instruct many more students than do elementary school teachers, making it difficult for teachers to develop productive relations with each student's family. Third, because students have multiple teachers, there is rarely a single person who can provide a holistic assessment of how an adolescent is doing. Fourth, parents receive much less guidance from middle and high schools about how to be involved. Finally, as academic material becomes increasingly complex, many parents may not be able to assist or feel comfortable assisting their teens with schoolwork.

FEDERAL POLICIES AND PROGRAMS
PERTAINING TO FAMILY–SCHOOL RELATIONS

Despite the challenges to developing productive family–school relations during middle and high school, there are several federal policies that mandate parental involvement in education. One of the most prominent is the No Child Left Behind Act (NCLB), which discusses expectations for parental involvement in five areas: (1) local educational agency policy; (2) school parental involvement policy; (3) policy involvement; (4) shared responsibilities for high student performance; and (5) building capacity for involvement (107th Congress, 2002). Local educational agencies (i.e., school districts) are required to develop written policies outlining expectations for parental involvement, including details on how the agency will assist schools in parental involvement efforts, coordinate parental involvement across other programs (e.g., Head Start), and annually evaluate the policies. Further, parents are to be included in deciding how allotted parental involvement funds are used. Similarly, each school is expected to create a parental involvement policy with parents. Parents and schools are to agree on the shared responsibilities for student achievement. Schools are required to hold an annual meeting for parents regarding their involvement in education and ensure that these meetings are open to all parents. Finally, schools are expected to provide training for parents, make information available to parents in their language, pay for expenses related to involvement activities, and conduct in-home conferences for parents who cannot attend meetings (107th Congress, 2002).

Although NCLB mandates family–school relationships, their implementation and evaluation are managed at the state level and vary widely in quality and effectiveness. Schools and school districts may be more or less sensitive to the needs of families. For example, in school districts with a large number of immigrants, families may be uncomfortable speaking English or participating in meetings. Moreover, because parental involvement programs do not have funding for evaluations (107th Congress, 2002), the status of parental involvement in education throughout the nation remains largely unknown. Each year, schools report adequate yearly progress (AYP) on children's achievement (National Title I Director's Conference, 2003). Interestingly, however, this progress report focuses on students' test scores and does not incorporate other important aspects of learning specified in NCLB, such as parental involvement in education. Because of the focus on accountability, NCLB may inadvertently set parents and teachers up to monitor or blame one another, rather than collaborate.

Other federal programs that aim to involve parents in their children's education and that affect middle and high schools include those under the Individuals with Disabilities Education Act (IDEA). The IDEA maintains that parental involvement is crucial in special education, across elementary, middle, and high school. Parental consent is required for special education testing, and parents are involved in their child's educational placement and in developing the child's Individualized Education Program (IEP). The IDEA also mandates that parents be given the opportunity to attend any meetings regarding their child. Moreover, an amendment of the IDEA specifies that "the majority of the members on the State Advisory Panel must be parents of children with disabilities or individuals with disabilities" (Office of Special Education Program, 2002). Parental involvement in education is well integrated in the IDEA, with parents participating at a variety of levels. While NCLB aims to increase parental involvement in education, the IDEA appears to be most successful in incorporating parents in their children's education.

Federal policies aimed at involving parents in their children's education provide some guidelines as to what this involvement should entail. However, most do not address the developmental stage of students by providing specific guidelines that recognize adolescents' development and changing family relationships and fit the structural changes of middle and high schools. This book identifies developmentally appropriate and effective strategies for families and schools and informs research, programs, and policies.

ABOUT THIS BOOK

There are two Parts to this book. The first, "Staying with Families Through Secondary School: Broadening the Scope for Effective Parental Involvement," builds on the developmental needs and assets of adolescence. Its six chapters identify parental involvement strategies that are most effective in enhancing achievement for middle and high school students. In addition, the chapters broaden the conceptualization of appropriate outcomes. Beyond grades and test scores, they pinpoint markers of academic success that are developmentally appropriate and are important predictors of adolescents' achievement, including outcomes that better reflect the resources students need in order to succeed in the less structured and more self-directed contexts in which adolescents find themselves after high school, including work and college. Chapter 1, by Kathleen V. Hoover-Dempsey, Christa L. Ice, and Manya C. Whitaker, outlines the factors that change, shape, and motivate parents' involvement as their children move into middle school, and proposes effective parental involvement strategies. Chapter 2, by James L. Rodríguez, identifies how characteristics of the community and school context shape the relationship between families and schools and the effect on achievement. Chapter 3, by Nancy E. Hill, Diana F. Tyson, and Lea Bromell, focuses on middle school and identifies strategies that reflect academic socialization (which often are not included in theories of family–school relations) among African American, Latino, and European American families as key factors that promote achievement. Chapter 4, by Nathan Jones and Barbara Schneider, provides empirical evidence that the most influential parental involvement strategies for high school students are not those that take place at school, but the types of interactions families engage in at home. Similarly, Belkis Suazo deCastro and Sophia Catsambis, in Chapter 5, find that involvement outside of school is most influential on academic outcomes, especially the broader range of outcomes. Moreover, their chapter demonstrates that these findings are generalizable across four ethnic groups. And finally in Chapter 6, to determine whether the strategies identified for adolescents are beneficial, Ruth K. Chao, Akira Kanatsu, Nicole Stanoff, Inna Padmawidjaja, and Christine Aque tested traditional, elementary-school-based strategies against developmentally appropriate strategies, longitudinally, for Asian American and European American high school students. Further, because cross-ethnic/SES comparisons only partly account for diversity, they examined within-group variation based on national origin (among Asians) and generational status. The chapters in the first Part consistently identify a set of effective strategies for parental involvement that works for adolescents, and test the generalizability across ethnic, immigrant, and socioeconomic status.

The second Part of the book, "Facing the Challenges: Feasibility of Parental Involvement During Adolescence," identifies the unique challenges of building relationships between families and schools and provides some solutions, especially for middle and high schools. Each chapter focuses on a different level, beginning with the family and then moving to schools and communities. Chapter 7, by Jelani Mandara, focuses on the parent and family level in describing workshops for parents that provide them with the knowledge and information necessary to enhance their adolescents' chances for academic success. Chapter 8, by Suzanne M. Bouffard, moves to the level of the school by outlining the challenges teachers experience in maintaining communication with families. The chapter describes how technology can bridge the gap between families and schools in a way that fits with the developmental needs of adolescents.

Moving to interactions between schools, Chapter 9, by Robert Crosnoe, focuses on the types of linkages between schools and families that enhance adolescents' success at the transition from middle to high school, and how they may serve as the most effective points for policy interventions. The final chapter in this Part, Chapter 10, addresses the broader level of policies and programs by focusing on the roles of the government, community, and school districts. In it, Holly Kreider and Suzanne M. Bouffard present the "complementary framework," involving linkages among community organizations, businesses, schools, and families, as a rubric for integrating resources across families, schools, and communities to support academic achievement for adolescents. Building these linkages across community agencies and families may engage all stakeholders in the educational process. This set of chapters focuses on strengthening the bridges across the key entities that support adolescents' achievement (i.e., families, schools, communities, and government).

In the conclusion, Ruth K. Chao and Nancy E. Hill integrate the research presented across all the chapters in this book and provide recommendations for families and for policies. Emerging from the work presented in this book are four types of strategies that are developmentally appropriate for middle and high school students and that families can use to support achievement during adolescents. These developmentally appropriate strategies are consistently supported by research presented throughout this book and are culturally inclusive. The conclusion describes these four strategies and also highlights developmentally appropriate, culturally sensitive policy solutions that have been identified throughout the book. In total, this book provides research, policy, and practice agendas that contribute to our understanding of the unique and collaborative roles of families and schools in supporting adolescents' achievement.

REFERENCES

107th Congress. (2002). Public Law 107-110, The No Child Left Behind Act of 2001. Retrieved May, 2006, from http://www.ed.gov/policy/elsec/leg/esea02/107-110.pdf

Abe, K., & Suzuki, T. (1986). Prevalence of some symptoms in adolescence and maturity: Social phobias, anxiety symptoms, episodic illusions and ideas of reference. *Psychopathology, 19*(4), 200–205.

Adams, R., & Laursen, B. (2001). The organization and dynamics of adolescent conflict with parents and friends. *Journal of Marriage and the Family, 63*(1), 97–110.

Arnett, J. J. (1999). Adolescent storm and stress, reconsidered. *American Psychologist, 54*(5), 317–326.

Barber, B. K., & Olsen, J. A. (2004). Assessing the transitions to middle and high school. *Journal of Adolescent Research, 19*(1), 3–30.

Brain, K., & Reid, I. (2003). Constructing parental involvement in an education action zone: Whose need is it meeting? *Educational Studies, 29*(2–3), 292–305.

Buchanan, C. M., Eccles, J. S., & Becker, J. B. (1992). Are adolescents the victim of raging hormones? Evidence for activational effects of hormones on moods and behavior at adolescence. *Psychological Bulletin, 111*(1), 62–107.

Chao, R. K. (2000). Cultural explanations for the role of parenting in the school success of Asian American children. In R. W. Taylor & M. C. Wang (Eds.), *Resilience across contexts: Family, work, culture, and community* (pp. 333–363). Mahwah, NJ: Erlbaum.

Christenson, S. L. (2004). The family–school partnership: An opportunity to promote the learning competence of all students. *School Psychology Review, 33*(1), 83–104.

Collins, W. A., & Laursen, B. (2004). Parent–adolescent relationships and influences. In R. M. Lerner & L. Steinberg (Eds.), *Handbook of adolescent psychology* (2nd ed., pp. 331–361). Hoboken, NJ: Wiley.

Dika, S. L., & Singh, K. (2002). Applications of social capital in educational literature: A critical synthesis. *Review of Educational Research, 72*(1), 31–60.

Eccles, J. S. (2004). Schools, academic motivation, and stage-environment fit. In R. M. Lerner & L. D. Steinberg (Eds.), *Handbook of adolescent psychology* (2nd ed., pp. 125–153). Hoboken, NJ: Wiley.

Epple, D., & Romano, R. (1998). Competition between public and private schools, vouchers, and peer group effects. *American Economic Review, 88*(1), 33–63.

Epstein, J. L. (1987). Toward a theory of family–school connections: Teacher practices and parent involvement. In K. Hurrelmann, F. X. Kaufmann, & F. Losel (Eds.), *Social intervention: Potential and constraints* (pp. 121–136). Berlin: de Gruyter.

Epstein, J. L., & Sanders, M. G. (2002). Family, school, and community partnerships. In M. H. Bornstein (Ed.), *Handbook of parenting: Vol. 5. Practical issues in parenting* (2nd ed., pp. 407–437). Mahwah, NJ: Erlbaum.

Erikson, E. H. (1968). *Identity, youth, and crisis.* New York: Norton.

Fielstein, L., & Phelps, P. (2001). *Introduction to teaching.* Belmont, CA: Wadsworth/Thomson Learning.

Fuligni, A. J., & Eccles, J. S. (1993). Perceived parent–child relationships and early adolescents' orientation toward peers. *Developmental Psychology, 29*(4), 622–632.

Greene, P. K., & Tichenor, M. S. (2003). Parents and schools: No stopping the involvement for parents particularly. *Childhood Education, 70*(1), 113–131.

Grolnick, W. S., & Slowiaczek, M. L. (1994). Parents' involvement in children's schooling: A multidimensional conceptualization and motivation model. *Child Development, 65*(1), 237–252.

Grotevant, H. S. (1998). Adolescent development in family contexts. In W. Damon & N. Eisenberg (Eds.), *Handbook of child psychology: Social, emotional, and personality development* (5th ed., Vol. 3, pp. 1097–1150). New York: Wiley.

Gutman, L. M., & Midgley, C. (2000). The role of protective factors in supporting the academic achievement of poor African American students during the middle school transition. *Journal of Youth and Adolescence, 29*(2), 223–248.

Hamm, J., & Faircloth, B. S. (2005). Peer context of mathematics classroom belonging in early adolescence. *Journal of Early Adolescence, 25*(3), 345–366.

Hill, N. E. (in press). Culturally-based worldviews, family processes, and family-school interaction. In S. Christenson & A. Reschly (Eds.), *The handbook on school-family partnerships for promoting student competence.* New York: Routledge/Taylor Francis

Hill, N. E., Castellino, D. R., Lansford, J. E., Nowlin, P., Dodge, K. A., Bates, J. E., & Pettit, G. (2004). Parent academic involvement as related to school behavior, achievement, and aspirations: Demographic variations across adolescence. *Child Development, 75*(5), 1491–1509.

Hill, N. E., & Craft, S. A. (2003). Parent–school involvement and school performance: Mediated pathways among socioeconomically comparable African American and Euro-American families. *Journal of Educational Psychology, 95*(1), 74–83.

Hill, N. E., & Taylor, L. C. (2004). Parental school involvement and children's academic achievement: Pragmatics and issues. *Current Directions in Psychological Science, 13*(4), 161–164.

Hill, N. E., & Tyson, D. F. (2009). Parental involvement in middle school: A meta-analytic assessment of the strategies that promote achievement. *Developmental Psychology, 45*(3), 740–763.

Ibenez, G. E., Kuperminc, G. P., Jurkovic, G., & Perilla, J. (2004). Cultural attributes and adaptations linked to achievement motivation among Latino adolescents. *Journal of Youth and Adolescence, 33*(6), 559–568.

Jimenez, E., & Sawada, Y. (1999). Do community-managed schools work? An evaluation of El Salvador's EDUCO program. *The World Bank Economic Review, 13*(3), 415–441.

Jodl, K. M., Michael, A., Malanchuck, O., Eccles, J. S., & Sameroff, A. (2001). Parents' roles in shaping early adolescents' occupational aspirations. *Child Development, 72*, 1247–1265.

Jordan, W. J., & Plank, S. B. (2000). Talent loss among high-achieving poor students. In M. G. Sanders (Ed.), *Schooling students placed at risk: Research, policy and practice in the education of poor and minority adolescents* (pp. 83–108). Mahwah, NJ: Erlbaum.

Joseph, P., & Burnaford, G. (1994). *Images of schoolteachers in twentieth century America.* New York: St. Martin's Press.

Keating, D. P. (2004). Cognitive and brain development. In R. M. Lerner & L. D. Steinberg (Eds.), *Handbook of adolescent psychology* (2nd ed., pp. 45–84). Hoboken, NJ: Wiley.

Kuperminc, G. P., Blatt, S. J., Shahar, G., Henrich, C., & Leadbeatter, B. J. (2004). Cultural equivalence and cultural variance in longitudinal associations of young adolescent self-identification and interpersonal relatedness to psychological and school adjustment. *Journal of Youth and Adolescence, 33*(1), 13–30.

Lareau, A. (2003). *Unequal childhoods: Class, race, and family life.* Berkeley: University of California.

Lareau, A., & Horvat, E. M. (1999). Moments of social inclusion and exclusion: Race, class, and cultural capital in family–school relationships. *Sociology of Education, 72*(1), 37–53.

Laursen, R. W., & Williams, V. (1997). Perceptions of interdependence and closeness in family and peer relationships among adolescents with and without romantic partners. In S. Shulman & W. A. Collins (Eds.), *Romantic relationships in adolescence: Developmental perspectives* (pp. 3–20). San Francisco: Jossey-Bass.

MacDonald, R. A. (1991). *Handbook of basic skills and strategies for beginning teachers.* New York: Longman.

Marcia, J. E. (1966). Development and validation of ego identity status. *Journal of Personality and Social Psychology, 3*(5), 551–558.

McMillan, R. (2000). Competition, parental involvement, and public school performance. In J. R. Hines (Ed.), *National tax association proceedings* (pp. 150–155). Washington, DC: National Tax Association.

McNeal, R. B. (1999). Parental involvement as social capital: Differential effectiveness on science achievement, truancy, and dropping out. *Social Forces, 78*(1), 117–144.

Moshman, D. (1998). Cognitive development beyond childhood. In D. Kuhn & R. S. Siegler (Eds.), *Handbook of child psychology: Cognition, perception, and language* (Vol. 2, pp. 947–978). New York: Wiley.

National Center for Education Statistics. (2003). *Overview of public elementary and secondary schools and districts: School year 2001–2002.* Retrieved July 12, 2005, from www.nces.ed.gov/pubs2003/overview03/table_11.asp

National Center for Education Statistics. (2005). *The condition of education, 2005.* (NCES 2005-094). Washington, DC: U.S. Government Printing Office.

National Title I Director's Conference. (2003). No Child Left Behind, Accountability and AYP. Retrieved May, 2006, from http://www.ed.gov/admins/lead/account/ayp203/accountabilityayp03.pdf

Nechyba, T., McEwan, P., & Older-Aguilar, D. (1999). The impact of family and community resources on student outcomes: An assessment of the international literature with implications for New Zealand. Duke University, Durham, NC.

Office of Special Education Program. (2002). Module 9: Parent and student participation in decision-making in background text. *IDEA Amendments of 1997 Curriculum.* Retrieved April, 2006, from http://www.nichcy.org/trainpkg/traintxt/9txt.htm

Reay, D. (1999). Linguistic capital and home–school relationships: Mothers' interactions with their children's primary school teachers. *Acta Scoiologica, 42*(2), 159–168.

Richards, M. H., Miller, B. V., O'Donnell, P. C., Wasserman, M. S., & Colder, C. (2004). Parental monitoring mediates the effects of age and sex on problem behaviors among African American urban young adolescents. *Journal of Youth and Adolescence, 33*(3), 221–233.

Rutter, M., Graham, P., Chadwick, O., & Yule, W. (1976). Adolescent turmoil: Fact or fiction? *Journal of Child Psychology and Psychiatry, 17*(1), 35–56.

Simmons, R. G., & Blythe, D. A. (1987). *Moving into adolescence: The impact of pubertal change and school context.* New York: de Gruyter.

Smetana, J. G., Campione-Barr, N., & Daddis, C. (2004). Longitudinal development of family decision making: Defining healthy behavioral autonomy for middle class African American adolescents. *Child Development, 75*(5), 1418–1434.

Smith, E. P., Connell, C. M., Wright, G., Sizer, M., Norman, J. M., Hurley, A., et al. (1997). An ecological model of home, school, and community partnerships: Implications for research and practice. *Journal of Educational & Psychological Consultation, 8*(4), 339–360.

Steinberg, L. (2001). We know some things: Adolescent–parent relationships in retrospect and prospect. *Journal of Adolescent Research, 11*, 1–19.

Steinberg, L., & Silk, J. S. (2002). Parenting adolescents. In M. H. Bornstein (Ed.), *Handbook of parenting: Vol. 1. Children and parenting* (2nd ed., pp. 103–134). Mahwah, NJ: Erlbaum.

Wallace, T., Shin, J., Bartholomay, T., & Stahl, B. (2001). Knowledge and skills for teachers supervising the work of paraprofessionals. *Exceptional Children, 67*(4), 520–533.

Wigfield, A., Byrnes, J. P., & Eccles, J. S. (2006). Development during early and middle adolescence. In P. A. Alexander & P. H. Winne (Eds.), *Handbook of educational psychology* (2nd ed., pp. 87–113). Mahwah, NJ: Erlbaum.

PART I

Staying with Families Through Secondary School

Broadening the Scope for Effective Parental Involvement

1

"We're Way Past Reading Together"

Why and How Parental Involvement in Adolescence Makes Sense

KATHLEEN V. HOOVER-DEMPSEY
CHRISTA L. ICE
MANYA C. WHITAKER

INTEREST IN THE ROLE OF PARENTAL INVOLVEMENT[1] in adolescents' schooling has grown markedly in recent years. Investigators have offered evidence of its beneficial effects for student learning. These include, for example, increased positive beliefs about one's ability to learn; stronger skills for learning, such as goal setting, planning, and monitoring one's progress; and stronger attentiveness to learning in the classroom. In part because of these developments, parental involvement also has been linked to stronger performance on summary measures of achievement, such as school grades and standardized tests in varied subjects (e.g., Catsambis, 2001; Epstein & Van Voorhis, 2001; Fan & Chen, 2001; Hill & Craft, 2003; Jeynes, 2007; Krieder, Caspe, Kennedy, & Weiss, 2007; Rodriguez, 2002). A small but growing body of research has suggested at the same time that adolescents *want* parental involvement and believe that parents should be involved in their education (e.g., Deslandes & Cloutier, 2002; Xu, 2002), albeit in forms that often differ from those appropriate with younger students.

Despite evidence of its beneficial effects, parental involvement generally declines as students move into the middle and high school years (Eccles et al., 1993; Spera, 2005). Reasons include normative developmental changes during adolescence (e.g., adolescents' growing sense of personal identity and autonomy; accompanying shifts in family roles and relation-ships) (Eccles et al., 1993; Falbo, Lein, & Amador, 2001) as well as changes in school structure and school expectations that accompany the transitions to middle and high school (e.g., a focus on more independent work and more advanced curricula; lower levels of trust and interaction between parents and schools) (Adams & Christenson, 2000; Barber & Olsen, 2004; Eccles et al., 1993; Roeser, Eccles, & Sameroff, 2000).

In this chapter, we discuss a theoretical model of the parental involve-ment process and related research as they inform understanding of the causes and consequences of parental involvement in adolescents' educa-tion. The model begins in parents' motivations for becoming involved; moves through the involvement activities they choose and the learn-ing mechanisms they employ during involvement, as well as students' perceptions of their involvement; and concludes with consideration of involvement's influence on student learning outcomes, both proximal (student attributes that enhance learning) and distal (summary indicators of student achievement). Following this discussion, we offer broad recom-mendations for school support of developmentally appropriate parental involvement during the adolescent years.

A MODEL OF THE PARENTAL INVOLVEMENT PROCESS

Hoover-Dempsey and Sandler (1995, 1997) offered a theoretical model of the parental involvement process, which was refined as informed by subsequent work (e.g., Green, Walker, Hoover-Dempsey, & Sandler, 2007; Walker et al., 2005) and related research, some of which is highlighted below. Grounded in the revised model (Figure 1.1), we examine specific questions about parental involvement during adolescence: Why do par-ents become involved in adolescents' education? What does develop-mentally appropriate involvement look like and how does it work during adolescence? What key learning outcomes are influenced by parental in-volvement during adolescence?

Why Parents Become Involved (Model Level 1)

The model suggests that parents become involved in their teens' edu-cation because personal motivators (role construction and efficacy) sug-gest that they *should* be involved, contextual constructs (invitations from school, teachers, and adolescent) *invite* involvement, and life context vari-ables (skills, knowledge, time, and energy; family culture; and school re-sponses thereto) *allow or support* involvement.

Figure 1.1. Model of the Parental Involvement Process (as adapted from Hoover-Dempsey & Sandler, 1995, 1997; Hoover-Dempsey et al., 2005)

Level 5

Student Achievement (Varied Summary Measures)

Level 4

Student Proximal Learning Beliefs and Skills, for example

| Beliefs About Oneself as a Learner | Personal Motivations for Learning | Personal Skills for Effective Learning (e.g., Planning, Goal Setting, Paying Attention in Class) | Personal Confidence About Asking Teachers for Help |

Level 3

(Mediated by) Student Perceptions of Parents' Involvement, for example

| Parents' Encouragement of Student's Learning, Education | Parents' Modeling of Learning Interest, Skills, and Behaviors | Parents' Reinforcement for Learning (e.g., Positive Attention, Praise) | Parents' Teaching Activities Related to Student's Schoolwork |

Level 2

Supports for Student Learning Offered by Parents During Involvement Activities, for example

| Parents' Encouragement of Student's Learning Efforts, Work, and Accomplishments | Parents' Modeling of Interest in Learning, Learning Skills, and Behaviors | Parents' Reinforcement of Student's Learning Efforts and Schoolwork | Parents' Teaching Activities with Student Related to Schoolwork |

Level 1.5

Parental Involvement Forms, for example

| Expression of Values, Aspirations, Expectations for Student's Education | Involvement Activities at Home | Communications with Teachers and School | Involvement Activities at School |

Level 1

| **Personal Motivators** | **Parents' Perceptions of Invitations to Involvement** | **Family Variables Influencing Involvement Decisions** |

| Parental Role Construction for Involvement | Parental Efficacy for Helping the Student Succeed in School | General Invitations from School | Specific Invitations from Teachers | Specific Invitations from Student | Parental Knowledge and Skills | Parental Time and Energy | Family Culture |

Personal motivators: Role construction and self-efficacy for involvement. Parents become involved in part because they hold an active role construction for involvement (i.e., they believe they are *supposed* to be involved in their adolescents' education). These role beliefs and behaviors are socially constructed over time, based on parents' personal experiences with schools, the expectations of relevant social groups (e.g., family, school, community), and interactions with others considered by parents to be knowledgeable about schooling (Biddle, 1986; Hoover-Dempsey & Sandler, 1997). Several investigators have noted role construction's contributions to parental involvement during adolescents' schooling; Deslandes and Bertrand (2005), for example, found role construction to be a significant predictor of involvement among parents of young adolescents, as did Green and colleagues (2007; see also Grolnick, Benjet, Kurowski, & Apostoleris, 1997; Sheldon, 2002). Similar findings have been reported for older adolescents as well (e.g., Chrispeels & Rivero, 2001; Simon, 2004; Trevino, 2004).

The model suggests that parents also are motivated to become involved by a sense of efficacy for helping students succeed in school. Sense of efficacy is related in part to the parent's assessment of personal knowledge and skills pertinent to the goals of involvement, but is grounded fundamentally in a personal belief that using his or her pertinent knowledge and skills will make a positive difference in the student's achievement of those goals (Bandura, 1989, 1997; Hoover-Dempsey & Sandler, 1997). As with role construction, sense of efficacy for involvement is socially constructed, and developed in personal experiences of successful involvement, observation of similar others' successful involvement, and verbal persuasion by important others about the likely success of one's efforts (e.g., Bandura, 1997; Hoover-Dempsey & Sandler, 1997). Bandura, Barbaranelli, Caprara, and Pastorelli (1996) reported that parents with stronger efficacy for promoting middle schoolers' academic success were more likely than those with lower sense of efficacy to encourage their teens' interest in academic work and to monitor their schoolwork and behavior (see also Green et al., 2007; Grolnick et al., 1997). Shumow and Lomax (2002) reported similar links between parents' sense of efficacy and their involvement in middle and high school students' education.

School-based motivators: Invitations from the school, teacher, and student. General invitations from the school emerge in well-developed school practices that welcome, value, and respect parents as critical participants in students' educational success (Adams & Christenson, 2000; Griffith, 2001; Hoover-Dempsey et al., 2005). The success of such invitations has been identified, for example, in examination of school-wide practices that support school-based involvement among ethnic minority and immigrant families in the middle and high school years (Lopez, Sanchez, & Hamilton, 2000; see also Scribner, Young, & Pedroza, 1999) and in studies of invitations to school events focused on helping adolescents' families support students' learning and success (e.g., Simon, 2004).

Specific invitations to involvement from teachers also have been found to predict parental involvement across the middle and high school years (e.g., Epstein & Van Voorhis, 2001; Green et al., 2007; Simon, 2004). The power of such invitations emerges in part from teachers' recognition and valuing of parents' contributions to student learning (Adams & Christenson, 2000) and in part from teachers' responsiveness to parents' wishes for *specific* involvement suggestions that will support students' learning (Hoover-Dempsey, Bassler, & Burow, 1995). Consistent with these observations, Balli, Demo, and Wedman (1998) reported that a combination of specific teacher and student requests for parental involvement in middle schoolers' homework yielded strong parental responses and high homework completion rates.

Specific requests from students for parental involvement are also quite powerful in prompting parents' active engagement in student learning processes. Student invitations may be implicit (e.g., parents respond to students' learning difficulties with increased parent–teacher communication or support and monitoring of students' work) (Hoover-Dempsey et al., 2001; Xu & Corno, 2003) or explicit (e.g., direct requests from the student or as prompted by teachers for specific support for assignments and learning tasks) (Balli et al., 1998; Gonzalez, Andrade, Civil, & Moll, 2001; Van Voorhis, 2003). Both types of student requests have been identified as strong predictors of involvement among parents of younger adolescents in school-based activities and home-based help with schoolwork (Deslandes & Bertrand, 2005; Green et al., 2007).

Personal factors: Skills and knowledge, time and energy, family culture. Parents' life context variables also influence their involvement decisions. Such circumstances include parents' perceptions of the specific skills and knowledge they can bring to involvement as their teens move into middle and high school (e.g., Grolnick, Kurowski, Dunlap, & Hevey, 2000; Hoover-Dempsey et al., 1995). This variable appears most likely to influence parents' motivations for becoming involved when specific involvement requests incorporate the use of skills and knowledge that a parent believes she or he has (and, as suggested earlier in discussion of parents' sense of efficacy for involvement, when the parent believes that using his or her knowledge and skill will in fact contribute to the student's learn-ing). Similarly, parents whose time and energy are bound up in multiple family or employment responsibilities may struggle to make time for school-based involvement, but nonetheless focus regularly after getting home on checking up on their middle or high schoolers' homework for the day (e.g., Clark, 1983; Gutman & McLoyd, 2000; Scribner et al., 1999; Weiss et al., 2003). Finally, elements of family culture in various commu-nities (e.g., language differences; limited understanding of school expec-tations for involvement) also influence parents' ideas about and choices of involvement activities (e.g., Clark, 1983; Garcia Coll et al., 2002; Moll, Amanti, Neff, & Gonzalez, 1992). Critically important are findings that barriers to parents' active engagement in student learning often are ad-dressed successfully by schools' positive and explicit efforts to engage respectfully with families and offer a wide variety of opportunities and suggestions for family support of student learning that are consistent with parents' life circumstances (e.g., Gonzalez et al., 2001; Hoover-Dempsey et al., 2005; Simon, 2004).

The Nature of Parental Involvement
(Model Levels 1.5, 2, and 3)

The model suggests next that parents who choose to become involved select varied forms of involvement and engage varied learning mecha-nisms in the course of involvement. It suggests also that the influence of parents' involvement activities depends in part on how students perceive those efforts and activities. Student perceptions take on particular impor-tance in adolescence as developmental issues (e.g., a press toward person-al autonomy, a focus on peer relationships) cause many to lower reliance on parental help and become more exacting in preferences for involve-ment when it does occur.

Forms of involvement (Level 1.5). Parental involvement has been defined in many ways, ranging from home-based support of student learning, to traditional school-based activities, to much broader understandings of the term, including parents' involvement in school governance (e.g., Epstein, 1992) and collaborative efforts to link family needs with community-based services and resources (e.g., Lopez, Scribner, & Mahitivanichcha, 2001). While an understanding of the many ways in which diverse families sup-port students' school learning is often critical to productive family–school relationships, we focus here on a sample of involvement forms examined most frequently in the literature.

Parents' expressed *goals, values, expectations, and aspirations* for students' educational attainments—often reflecting personal, familial, and culturally grounded hopes for students' current and future well-being—have been positively related to adolescents' learning, goals for education, and achievement (e.g., Catsambis, 2001; Fan & Chen, 2001; Trevino, 2004). *Home-based involvement activities* also have been positively related to adolescents' motivation to achieve and learning outcomes (e.g., Clark, 1983; Rodriguez, 2002; Simon, 2004). Such activities often include parental efforts in the context of everyday family life to support, motivate, monitor, or discuss student schoolwork and progress. *Parent–teacher–school communications* also occur in many forms (e.g., written notes, phone calls, email, formal or informal conferences and discussions) and often play an important role in supporting student progress, especially when schools meet the language needs of all families and when feedback and continued discussion are routinely available. Parents' *school-based involvement* (e.g., attending school programs, volunteering—the parental activities generally most visible to school personnel) offers opportunities to enhance parents' and teachers' knowledge of students and student progress, as well as opportunities to offer suggestions for enhancing student learning. These occur especially when school-based interactions are characterized by mutual respect in support of student learning (e.g., Adams & Christenson, 2000; Chrispeels & Rivero, 2001).

Across these varied forms of involvement, we note the critical importance of family and school understanding that developmentally appropriate manifestations of involvement appropriate during childhood often change markedly as students move into and through adolescence. Home-based support of student learning, for example, which may have included parents' help with learning specific skills in childhood (e.g., math, reading), often shifts as students move into adolescence to support that responds to specific student requests and to broader suggestions for organizing learning projects, encouragement of the student's efforts and perseverance, and suggesting alternative sources of help as the parent hears or perceives that the student may need such help with specific tasks. Similarly, school-based involvement most often shifts from direct parental presence with the child at school to less visible forms of support as the student moves into adolescence (e.g., attending student athletic or arts programs, bringing refreshments for a team on a field day, offering help and advice as needed at home rather than in school or in the presence of peers). Across such developmentally grounded changes in parental involvement activities, adolescents' learning success continues to be well served by family support for students' productive engagement in school learning tasks, but

in ways that clearly respect adolescents' emerging sense of personal identity, exploration of autonomy, and focus on peer relationships.

   Learning mechanisms engaged during involvement (Level 2). The learning mechanisms engaged by parents in the course of involvement are
particularly important because they offer insight into *how* parents' involvement influences student learning outcomes. While many learning
mechanisms may be engaged by families, those included in the model
represent a sample familiar to many parents and schools. Each offers
benefits for adolescents as they engage with the increasingly complex
learning tasks presented by middle school and high school curricula.
Importantly, however, the potential effectiveness of any learning mechanism engaged in the course of involvement in adolescents' learning
is greatest when families and schools suggest and implement specific
manifestations of varied learning mechanisms that are respectful of and
responsive to students' changing developmental needs and capabilities
across adolescence.

   Parental *encouragement* includes parents' explicit, positive support for
student activities related to school tasks and learning (Martinez-Pons,
1996). Use of the mechanism may be particularly helpful with adolescents,
as it often allows involvement, support, and engagement with minimal
intrusiveness, an important issue in parenting adolescents (Pomerantz,
Grolnick, & Price, 2005). Parental encouragement has been related to a
variety of adolescent attributes and accomplishments important to school
learning (e.g., increased school engagement, successful transitions to
middle and high school) (Grolnick et al., 2000; Steinberg, Lamborn, Dornbusch, & Darling, 1992).

   Parental *modeling* is also an important learning mechanism often engaged in the course of involvement. Bandura (1997) suggests that parents
serve as particularly important models of behaviors and values important to learning across childhood and adolescence (e.g., asking questions; expressing interest; demonstrating varied attitudes, strategies,
and learning behaviors linked to effective learning) (see also Gutman &
McLoyd, 2000; Martinez-Pons, 1996). Modeling may be particularly important during adolescence, when students often are introduced to (and
expected to engage in) learning tasks that are unfamiliar or complex, or
seem far removed from students' developmental priorities or personal
interests (Bandura, 1997; Xu, 2004). Because modeling can be and often
is demonstrated by parents in the course of daily life—and may be engaged in nonintrusive ways—it can be particularly useful in supporting
adolescents' school learning.

Reinforcement is grounded in theory suggesting that behavior patterns are developed and maintained when they are consistently associated with desired consequences (Skinner, 1989). Applied to parental involvement, theory suggests that parents' use of positive reinforcement increases the likelihood that students will develop and use reinforced behaviors and skills in varied learning situations. The effectiveness of reinforcement in adolescence is particularly dependent on parents' use of developmentally appropriate strategies (e.g., offering genuine praise for strong effort in learning, for effective engagement in school tasks and activities, and for strong or improved learning performance; showing genuine interest in students' opinions and accomplishments; responding positively and specifically to students' initiation of discussions of school issues, peer relationships, assignments, etc.). When so used, parental reinforcement has been linked to adolescents' mastery orientation, success in complex learning tasks, and stronger overall achievement (Bandura, 1997; Ginsburg & Bronstein, 1993). These findings stand in contrast to those observed when parents use less developmentally appropriate reinforcements with their adolescents (e.g., offering external rewards for learning has been negatively associated with mastery orientation and achievement among young adolescents) (e.g., Ginsburg & Bronstein, 1993). Parents' use of developmentally appropriate reinforcement is also consistent with adolescents' expressed interest in parents' responsiveness to their learning successes (Deslandes & Cloutier, 2002; Xu, 2002).

Parental *instruction* related to learning tasks may be indirect, involving discussion of task demands or alternative approaches to organizing work, shared thinking about task-appropriate learning strategies, and support of self-regulatory skills (Ginsburg & Bronstein, 1993; Hoover-Dempsey et al., 2001). Direct instruction involving factual, procedural, or conceptual learning may include parental help in structuring learning tasks, support in refining learning strategies, or joint review of student work (Hoover-Dempsey et al., 2001). In general, adolescents' developmental press toward personal competence and autonomy, teachers' focus on personal responsibility for learning in middle and high school, and the limits of many parents' content or procedural expertise in more advanced courses suggest that indirect forms of parental instruction often may be most feasible, appropriate, and effective during adolescence.

Adolescents' perceptions of parents' involvement activities (Level 3). Grounded in evidence that adolescents' perceptions of events in their environments mediate the influence of those events on their behavior and learning (e.g., Bandura, 1997; Grolnick, Ryan, & Deci, 1991), the model suggests that the influence of parental involvement on student learning is dependent in part on how adolescents perceive that involvement. While parents' and adolescents' perceptions of events in which they both participate are often positively correlated (e.g., Grolnick & Slowiaczek, 1994), their perceptions also may vary due to differences in cognitive abilities, interests, and goals; in addition, they may vary as a function of qualities characterizing the parent–adolescent relationship, as well as the meanings ascribed to parents' involvement activities by the family's broader culture (Mandara, 2006; Pomerantz et al., 2005; Xu & Corno, 2003). In general, parental involvement seems most likely to support adolescents' learning when it is perceived as nonintrusive and respectful of developmental needs for increasing autonomy and independence (e.g., Pomerantz et al., 2005).

The Outcomes of Parental Involvement During Adolescence (Model Levels 4 and 5)

The model suggests that the most direct outcomes of parental involvement include the development of varied student attributes, skills, and learning strategies (proximal learning outcomes), which students may then use in support of performance and achievement (distal learning outcomes, such as grades and test scores).

Proximal learning outcomes (Level 4). Although several student learning attributes are influenced by parental involvement, the model suggests that students' academic self-efficacy, intrinsic motivation, self-regulatory knowledge and skills, and social self-efficacy for seeking help from knowledgeable others are among the most important of these proximal outcomes. Proximal learning outcomes are particularly important for adolescents, in part because they offer critical support for student learning and development across the middle and high school years, when students typically experience much less individual attention from teachers than is generally true across the elementary years. Students moving into the adolescent years, thus, often bear increased personal responsibility for communicating their needs in relation to learning and for seeking help from knowledgeable others as needed (e.g., Eccles et al., 1993). The (continued) development of these proximal learning attributes in adolescence is also quite important because they are among the attributes that continue to be important as adolescents encounter the many new learning demands that often emerge in young adulthood and across the life span.

Academic self-efficacy is grounded in personal beliefs about one's ability to use one's skills effectively in learning (Bandura, 1997; Ryan

& Patrick, 2001). Parental involvement has been linked to the development of academic self-efficacy, and self-efficacy in turn has been linked to improved school performance among adolescents (e.g., Bandura et al., 1996; Grolnick et al., 2000). Self-efficacy development also has been linked to other important learning attributes that are influenced by parental involvement and supportive of student achievement (e.g., attributions about the causes of academic success, mastery goal orientation, academic aspirations) (Bandura et al., 1996; Ginsburg & Bronstein, 1993; Gonzalez, Doan Holbein, & Quilter, 2002). *Intrinsic motivation*—students' interest in learning more for its own sake than for the extrinsic rewards it may bring—also is influenced by parental involvement (e.g., Bronstein, Ginsburg, & Herrera, 2005; Gonzalez-DeHass, Willems, & Doan Holbein, 2005; Steinberg et al., 1992). Variations in motivation for learning, in turn, have been linked to varied patterns of achievement (Bronstein et al., 2005; Eccles et al., 1993). Parental support for the development of intrinsic motivation may be especially important in adolescence, as students report perceiving that middle and high school work often lacks intrinsically motivating qualities (Xu, 2004; see also Bronstein et al., 2005).

Student *self-regulatory skills and knowledge* encompass a wide-ranging set of cognitions, metacognitions, and behaviors that support student learning across childhood and adolescence (e.g., planning, goal setting, self-monitoring, evaluation, and adjustment of learning strategy use) (Ryan & Patrick, 2001; Zimmerman, 1986). Parents' involvement often supports the development of self-regulatory skills; in turn, students' use of self-regulatory skills supports their own learning and achievement (e.g., Bandura et al., 1996; Gonzalez-DeHass et al., 2005). *Social self-efficacy for relating to teachers* also functions as an important proximal outcome of effective parental involvement. Grounded in self-efficacy theory (Bandura, 1997), this construct reflects student beliefs that seeking help from teachers and other knowledgeable persons will support learning. This ability to ask for help when needed is an important attribute of high-achieving students, and personal confidence in this area often characterizes successful students (Roeser, Midgley, & Urdan, 1996).

Distal learning outcomes (Level 5). The model suggests finally that varied summary measures of achievement constitute the longer term or distal goal of parental involvement in student learning. It also suggests that parents' influence on student achievement occurs most often through their support of students' proximal learning attributes, which students then engage in day-to-day classroom learning activities and in summary assessments of school learning.

POLICY IMPLICATIONS

Grounded in the theoretical model and review of related research, we offer selected recommendations here for program and policy directions as schools and communities take steps to support effective parental involvement in adolescent education.[2] Such involvement, when developmentally appropriate and targeted to supporting the growth and development of student learning attributes that enable and support student achievement, holds the promise of increased school success in educating adolescents.

First, policymakers should take steps to ensure that everyone engaged in the parental involvement process—families, students, schools, and communities—know and understand that developmentally appropriate and well-supported parental involvement during the middle and secondary school years promises substantial contributions to adolescents' development of the learning attributes and skills that are critical to their school success and achievement. Schools' and families' long-term commitment to active parental support for adolescent learning are also quite likely to benefit from policy-supported efforts to ensure that both families and schools have direct access to accurate information about (1) parents' ongoing contributions to students' school success throughout adolescence and (2) steps that schools, districts, and communities may take to communicate and disseminate this information in terms that all families are able to understand.

Second, policy-supported efforts by schools, families, and communities to develop productive home–school collaborations focused on supporting all adolescents' learning success are likely to benefit substantially from an integrated systemic focus—including schools, district, and communities—on developing community-appropriate actions that will support families' motivations for becoming involved. For example, both parents' role construction for involvement and their sense of efficacy for helping their adolescents succeed in school are socially constructed and therefore open to coordinated influence by schools, school systems, and relevant community organizations. Similarly, evidence suggests that invitations to family members' productive involvement in adolescents' education—general invitations conveyed in a welcoming school climate, specific invitations and suggestions from students' teachers, as well as specific invitations from students—exert substantial influence on parents' decisions about becoming involved. Further, all participants' efforts to suggest, offer, and support parental involvement opportunities and activities that take families' life circumstances and culture into careful account are also likely to support families' decisions to become actively involved in supporting their adolescents' education.

Third, policymakers and program developers should understand that schools', families', and family–school partnerships' effective support of adolescent learning will benefit substantially from specific knowledge of the proximal student learning attributes that are the specific targets of involvement activities. Clear articulation and understanding of the specific goals toward which actions are to be directed, offer a critical foundation for the development of specific strategies, actions, and evaluation plans to be engaged in supporting and monitoring students' development of these learning attributes. Information should include clear and easily comprehensible summaries of (1) theoretically and empirically based knowledge regarding the targeted student learning attributes, (2) information about specific ways in which families, schools, and family–school partnerships may support the development of these learning attributes across adolescence, and (3) information about specific ways in which these student learning attributes contribute, in turn, to adolescents' learning success and achievement.

Fourth, policymakers, program developers, families, and schools should understand that families' and family–school partnerships' effective support of adolescents' learning is most likely to be realized when schools' activities and practices reflect explicitly positive attitudes regarding families' essential roles in adolescent learning, when they incorporate specific suggestions for family support of student learning, and when they focus on developing family–school relationships grounded in mutual trust and a commitment to giving and receiving information about student learning and progress. The reality that schools often hold more power in the educational process than do many of the families they serve also makes it critical that schools take the initiative—repeatedly if necessary, and as informed by experience—in offering specific, family-friendly invitations and involvement suggestions that promise support for adolescents' learning and fit families' life contexts and cultures.

CONCLUSION

The promise of parental involvement in supporting and enhancing adolescents' school success warrants strong support by policymakers, educators, families, and communities. The benefits to *schools* in accessing the power of family hopes for their adolescents' learning and school success—through explicit, developmentally appropriate, family-friendly invitations and opportunities for involvement that supports students' learning outcomes (proximal and distal)—are great. The benefits to *families* in realizing hopes for their students' learning success across childhood and adolescence as they implement involvement strategies that promise long-term developmental and educational benefits for their children are also great. Similarly, the benefits to *adolescent learning* to be derived from school and family commitment to engaging theoretically grounded, empirically supported, and developmentally appropriate involvement strategies in support of student learning are in themselves most notable. Within a broad societal context that values the developmental and educational success of its children and adolescents, commitment by all participants to effective support of student learning across childhood and adolescence seems nothing less than essential.

NOTES

We gratefully acknowledge support for portions of this work from the Institute for Education Sciences (formerly Office for Educational Research and Improvement), U.S. Department of Education (*Parental Involvement: A Path to Enhanced Achievement*, 2001–2004, No. RR305T01673-02; see Hoover-Dempsey, K. V., & Sandler, H. M. (2005). *Final Performance Report for OERI Grant # R305T010673: The Social Context of Parental Involvement: A Path to Enhanced Achievement*. Presented to Project Monitor, Institute of Education Sciences, U.S. Department of Education, March 22, 2005). Many thanks also to Katherine W. Shepard of the Peabody Family–School Partnership Lab at Vanderbilt University.

1. We use the terms *parent* and *family* interchangeably in discussing parental involvement in adolescents' education. We mean by both terms any family, extended family, or surrogate family members who play a primary role in supporting adolescents' school learning and success. Similarly, we use the terms parental *involvement* and *engagement* interchangeably in discussing parents' activities and behaviors intended to support students' school learning and achievement.

2. For more specific suggestions about steps schools may take to support effective parental involvement, see Hoover-Dempsey et al. (2001, 2005).

REFERENCES

Adams, K. S., & Christenson, S. L. (2000). Trust and the family–school relationship: An examination of parent–teacher differences in elementary and secondary grades. *Journal of School Psychology, 38*(5), 447–497.
Balli, S. J., Demo, D. H., & Wedman, J. F. (1998). Family involvement with children's homework: An intervention in the middle grades. *Family Relations, 47*(2), 149–157.
Bandura, A. (1989). Human agency in social cognitive theory. *American Psychologist, 44*(9), 1175–1185.
Bandura, A. (1997). *Self-efficacy: The exercise of control.* New York: W.H. Freeman.

Bandura, A., Barbaranelli, C., Caprara, G. V., & Pastorelli, C. (1996). Multifaceted impact of self-efficacy beliefs on academic functioning. *Child Development, 67*(3), 1206–1222.

Barber, B. K., & Olsen, J. A. (2004). Assessing the transitions to middle and high school. *Journal of Adolescent Research, 19*(1), 3–30.

Biddle, B. J. (1986). Recent developments in role theory. *Annual Review of Sociology, 12*, 67–92.

Bronstein, P., Ginsburg, G. S., & Herrera, I. S. (2005). Parental predictors of motivational orientation in early adolescence: A longitudinal study. *Journal of Youth and Adolescence, 34*(6), 559–575.

Catsambis, S. (2001). Expanding knowledge of parental involvement in children's secondary education: Connections with high school seniors' academic success. *Social Psychology of Education, 5*(2), 149–177.

Chrispeels, J., & Rivero, E. (2001). Engaging Latino families for student success: How parent education can reshape parents' sense of place in the education of their children. *Peabody Journal of Education, 76*(2), 119–169.

Clark, R. (1983). *Family life and school achievement: Why poor black children succeed or fail*. Chicago: University of Chicago Press.

Deslandes, R., & Bertrand, R. (2005). Motivation of parent involvement in secondary-level schooling. *The Journal of Educational Research, 98*(3), 164–175.

Deslandes, R., & Cloutier, R. (2002). Adolescents' perception of parental school involvement. *School Psychology International, 23*(2), 220–232.

Eccles, J. S., Midgley, C., Wigfield, A., Buchanan, C. M., Reuman, D., Flanagan, C., & MacIver, D. (1993). Development during adolescence: The impact of stage-environment fit on young adolescents' experiences in schools and families. *American Psychologist, 48*(2), 90–101.

Epstein, J. L. (1992). School and family partnerships. In M. Aiken (Ed.), *Encyclopedia of educational research* (pp. 1139–1151). New York: Macmillan.

Epstein, J. L., & Van Voorhis, F. L. (2001). More than minutes: Teachers' roles in designing homework. *Educational Psychologist, 36*(3), 181–193.

Falbo, T., Lein, L., & Amador, N. A. (2001). Parental involvement in the transition to high school. *Journal of Adolescent Research, 16*(5), 511–529.

Fan, X., & Chen, M. (2001). Parental involvement and students' academic achievement: A meta-analysis. *Educational Psychology Review, 13*(1), 1–22.

Garcia Coll, C., Akiba, D., Palacios, N., Bailey, B., Silver, R., DiMartino, L., & Chin, C. (2002). Parental involvement in children's education: Lessons from three immigrant groups. *Parenting: Science & Practice, 2*(3), 303–324.

Ginsburg, G. S., & Bronstein, P. (1993). Family factors related to children's intrinsic/extrinsic motivational orientation and academic performance. *Child Development, 64*(5), 1461–1474.

Gonzalez, A. R., Doan Holbein, M. F. D., & Quilter, S. (2002). High school students' goal orientations and their relationship to perceived parenting styles. *Contemporary Educational Psychology, 27*(3), 450–470.

Gonzalez, N., Andrade, R., Civil, M., & Moll, L. (2001). Bridging funds of distributed knowledge: Creating zones of practices in mathematics. *Journal of Education for Students Placed at Risk, 6*(1–2), 115–132.

Gonzalez-DeHass, A. R., Willems, P. P., & Doan Holbein, M. F. (2005). Examining the relationship between parental involvement and student motivation. *Educational Psychology Review, 17*(2), 99–123.

Green, C. L., Walker, J. M. T., Hoover-Dempsey, K. V., & Sandler, H. M. (2007). Parents' motivations for involvement in children's education: An empirical test of a theoretical model of parental involvement. *Journal of Educational Psychology, 99*(3), 532–544.

Griffith, J. (2001). Principal leadership of parent involvement. *Journal of Educational Administration, 39*(2), 162–186.

Grolnick, W. S., Benjet, C., Kurowski, C. O., & Apostoleris, N. H. (1997). Predictors of parent involvement in children's schooling. *Journal of Educational Psychology, 89*(3), 538–548.

Grolnick, W. S., Kurowski, C. O., Dunlap, K. G., & Hevey, C. (2000). Parental resources and the transition to junior high. *Journal of Research on Adolescence, 10*(4), 465–488.

Grolnick, W. S., Ryan, R. M., & Deci, E. L. (1991). Inner resources for school achievement: Motivational mediators of children's perceptions of their parents. *Journal of Educational Psychology, 87*(4), 508–517.

Grolnick, W. S., & Slowiaczek, M. L. (1994). Parents' involvement in children's schooling: A multidimensional conceptualization and motivational model. *Child Development, 65*(1), 237–252.

Gutman, L. M., & McLoyd, V. C. (2000). Parents' management of their children's education within the home, at school, and in the community: An examination of African-American families living in poverty. *The Urban Review, 32*(1), 1–24.

Hill, N. E., & Craft, S. A. (2003). Parent–school involvement and school performance: Mediated pathways among socioeconomically comparable African American and Euro-American families. *Journal of Educational Psychology, 95*(1), 74–83.

Hoover-Dempsey, K. V., Bassler, O. C., & Burow, R. (1995). Parents' reported involvement in students' homework: Strategies and practices. *The Elementary School Journal, 95*(5), 435–450.

Hoover-Dempsey, K. V., Battiato, A. C., Walker, J. M., Reed, R. P., DeJong, J., & Jones, K. P. (2001). Parental involvement in homework. *Educational Psychologist, 36*(3), 195–209.

Hoover-Dempsey, K. V., & Sandler, H. M. (1995). Parental involvement in children's education: Why does it make a difference? *Teachers College Record, 97*(2), 310–331.

Hoover-Dempsey, K. V., & Sandler, H. M. (1997). Why do parents become involved in their children's education? *Review of Educational Research, 67*(1), 3–42.

Hoover-Dempsey, K. V., Walker, J. M. T., Sandler, H. M., Whetsel, D., Green, C. L., Wilkins, A. S., & Clossen, K. E. (2005). Why do parents become involved? Research findings and implications. *The Elementary School Journal, 106*(2), 105–130.

Jeynes, W. H. (2007). The relationship between parental involvement and urban secondary school student academic achievement: A meta-analysis. *Urban Education, 42*(1), 82–110.

Krieder, H., Caspe, M., Kennedy, S., & Weiss, H. (2007). *Family involvement makes a difference: Family involvement in middle and high school students' education* (Vol. 3).

Cambridge, MA: Harvard Family Research Project. Available at http://www. gse.harvard.edu/content/projects/fine/resources/research/adolescence/html

Lopez, G. R., Scribner, J. D., & Mahitivanichcha, K. (2001). Redefining parental involvement: Lessons from high-performing migrant-impacted schools. *American Educational Research Journal, 38*(2), 253–288.

Lopez, L. C., Sanchez, V. V., & Hamilton, M. (2000). Immigrant and native-born Mexican-American parents' involvement in a public school: A preliminary study. *Psychological Reports, 86*(2), 521–525.

Mandara, J. (2006). The impact of family functioning on African American males' academic achievement: A review and clarification of the empirical literature. *Teachers College Record, 108*(2), 206–223.

Martinez-Pons, M. (1996). Test of a model of parental inducement of academic self-regulation. *Journal of Experimental Education, 64*(3), 213–227.

Moll, L., Amanti, C., Neff, D., & Gonzalez, N. (1992). Funds of knowledge for teaching: Using a qualitative approach to connect homes and classrooms. *Theory Into Practice, 31*(2), 132–141.

Pomerantz, E. M., Grolnick, W. S., & Price, C. E. (2005). The role of parents in how children approach achievement: A dynamic process perspective. In A. J. Elliott & C. S. Dweck (Eds.), *Handbook of competence and motivation* (pp. 259–277). New York: Guilford Press.

Rodriguez, J. L. (2002). Family environment and achievement among three generations of Mexican-American high school students. *Applied Developmental Science, 6*(2), 88–94.

Roeser, R. W., Eccles, J. S., & Sameroff, A. J. (2000). School as context of early adolescents' academic and social-emotional development: A summary of research findings. *The Elementary School Journal, 100*(5), 443–471.

Roeser, R. W., Midgley, C., & Urdan, T. C. (1996). Perceptions of the school psychological environment and early adolescents' psychological and behavioral functioning in school: The mediating role of goals and belonging. *Journal of Educational Psychology, 88*(3), 408–422.

Ryan, A. M., & Patrick, H. (2001). The classroom social environment and changes in adolescents' motivation and engagement during middle school. *American Educational Research Journal, 38*(2), 437–460.

Scribner, J. D., Young, M. D., & Pedroza, A. (1999). Building collaborative relationships with parents. In J. D. Scribner & A. Paredes-Scribner (Eds.), *Lessons from high-performing Hispanic schools: Creating learning communities* (pp. 36–60). New York: Teachers College Press.

Sheldon, S. B. (2002). Parents' social networks and beliefs as predictors of parent involvement. *The Elementary School Journal, 102*(4), 301–316.

Shumow, L., & Lomax, R. (2002). Parental efficacy: Predictor of parenting behavior and adolescent outcomes. *Parenting: Science and Practice, 2*(2), 127–150.

Simon, B. S. (2004). High school outreach and family involvement. *Social Psychology of Education, 7*(2), 185–209.

Skinner, B. F. (1989). *Recent issues in the analysis of behavior*. Columbus, OH: Merrill.

Spera, C. (2005). A review of the relationship among parenting practices, parenting styles, and adolescent school achievement. *Educational Psychology Review, 17*(2), 125–146.

Steinberg, L., Lamborn, S. D., Dornbusch, S. M., & Darling, N. (1992). Impact of parenting practices on adolescent achievement: Authoritative parenting, school involvement, and encouragement to succeed. *Child Development, 63*(5), 1266–1281.

Trevino, R. E. (2004). Against all odds: Lessons from parents of migrant high-achievers. In C. Salinas & M. E. Franquez (Eds.), *Scholars in the field: The challenges of migrant education* (pp. 147–161). Charleston, WV: AEL.

Van Voorhis, F. L. (2003). Interactive homework in middle school: Effects on family involvement and science achievement. *The Journal of Educational Research, 96*(6), 323–338.

Walker, J. M. T., Wilkins, A. S., Dallaire, J. P., Sandler, H. M., & Hoover-Dempsey, K. V. (2005). Parental involvement: Model revision through scale development. *The Elementary School Journal, 106*(2), 85–104.

Weiss, H. B., Mayer, E., Kreider, H., Vaughan, M., Dearing, E., Hencke, R., & Pinto, K. (2003). Making it work: Low-income working mothers' involvement in their children's education. *American Educational Research Journal, 40*(4), 879–901.

Xu, J. (2002). Do early adolescents want family involvement in their education? Hearing voices from those who matter most. *School Community Journal, 12*(1), 52–72.

Xu, J. (2004). Family help and homework management in urban and rural secondary schools. *Teachers College Record, 106*(9), 1786–1803.

Xu, J., & Corno, L. (2003). Family help and homework management reported by middle school students. *The Elementary School Journal, 103*(5), 503–536.

Zimmerman, B. J. (1986). Becoming a self-regulated learner: What are the key sub-processes? *Contemporary Educational Psychology, 11*(4), 307–313.

2

Considering the Context of Culture

Perspectives in the
Schooling of Latino Adolescents
from the Classroom, Home, and Beyond

JAMES L. RODRÍGUEZ

INTEREST IN PARENTAL INVOLVEMENT PROGRAMS and school–community partnerships continues to increase in parallel with efforts to address the achievement gap. This is true specifically with regard to the education of various Latino populations. Interest in Latino parental involvement has mirrored research concerned with the nature and impact of home–school linkages for Mexican-origin children, adolescents, and families (Rodríguez, 2002; Stanton-Salazar, 2001; Suárez-Orozco & Suárez-Orozco, 1995; Valdés, 1996, Vásquez, Pease-Alvarez, & Shannon, 1994). Other researchers focused on the plight of ethnic minority adolescents have called for the study of the family context of ethnic minority adolescents, particularly as it relates to their education (Harrison, Wilson, Pine, Chan, & Buriel, 1990; National Research Council, 1993; Steinberg, 1996). However, researchers only recently have begun to explore ways to bridge the cultural discontinuities that can exist between the home and school experiences of Mexican-origin children and adolescents (Delgado-Gaitan, 1991; Valdés, 1996; Valenzuela, 1999). The disparities between the home and school experiences of Mexican-origin adolescents can be magnified by language differences, which impede communication among parents, students, and teachers. Furthermore, immigrant parents themselves may have limited educational experiences and may be unfamiliar with the education system in the United States (Suárez-Orozco & Suárez-Orozco, 1995; Valdés, 1996).

In her ethnography of 10 Mexican-descent families, Valdés (1996) points out that without an understanding of culturally driven variations in Mexican American family support systems for adolescents' education, intervention efforts may cause more long-term harm to immigrant families than any short-term benefits. Thus, it is critical to examine generational effects as they influence familial and educational processes. This is especially critical for Mexican-origin adolescents who are adapting to and within a school environment that is incongruent with their home environment, leading them to function between the two environments instead of within them.

This chapter examines the relationship between the home and school environments of Mexican American adolescents. A social ecological model is presented to explain the complex, dynamic, and interactive processes involved. The model serves to advance the examination of these processes for Mexican American adolescents and their families across school and community contexts. Findings from a study of Mexican American adolescents are presented to illustrate the utility of the model. Finally, this chapter discusses ways in which research, policy, and practice can promote linkages between families and schools in order to more effectively address the needs of Latino adolescents and their families. Particular attention will be given to family–school relations among U.S. Latino populations, taking into account the diversity of the populations while also being sensitive to their broad range of social and cultural experiences.

THEORIES AND MODELS
OF CONTEXT FOR ADOLESCENTS AND FAMILIES

Given the complexities of Latino adolescents' everyday experiences in school, home, and community contexts, the interactive dynamics between individuals within varying contexts are particularly salient. The impact of context on human development has been addressed theoretically and empirically dating back to Lewin's (1935) dynamic psychology and Bronfenbrenner's (1943) early work on social ecology. Bronfenbrenner's (1979, 1989) more recent work has emphasized the influence of culture and social status on the interactions between individuals within the various ecologies in which they live. Bronfenbrenner noted that the study of immigrant or ethnic minority groups must consider the personal and background characteristics of individuals.

In more recent years, the impact of context on adolescent development has become a focal point for researchers (Phelan, Davidson, & Yu, 1998). More specifically, theories and models have been developed to explore the impact of context on the psychological development and education of Latino adolescents. For the most part, these theories and models have focused on the type and nature of social interaction within different settings and the resulting impact on psychological development and education. Two theoretical models aimed at understanding the dynamics of Mexican- or Latino-origin adolescents and families in interaction with their community contexts provide a background for the social ecological model presented in this chapter.

A humanistic interaction model of human development initially was presented by Garza and Lipton (1982) and later was refined to specifically address acculturative processes among Mexican Americans (Garza & Gallegos, 1995). This model allows the examination of sociocultural factors associated with acculturative processes and the influence of such processes on individuals within varying contexts. While the model is not specific to parental involvement, its interactive quality provides an opportunity to consider the interplay among adolescents, families, and educators as they navigate the home, school, and community contexts.

Gilbert's (1980) community model incorporates historical, migratory, and political factors to describe how community context impacts individuals. Gilbert studied three Mexican American communities, located in separate California regions that were differentiated by social, economic, and political factors, and identified influential differences in the level of urbanity and Mexican American control of political and economic structures between the three communities that impacted their power, efficacy, and influence. Several interrelated factors were cited as explanations for these differences. In essence, the political, economic, and social status of Mexican Americans in each community was determined by the overall community context, which included not only the present Mexican American and European American communities, but also the historical legacies of those communities.

Overall, these models aim to capture the Mexican American experience as it is influenced at multiple levels of context. These models facilitate the examination of the dynamic nature of various contexts that are defined by multiple factors (i.e., sociocultural, economic, political, etc.). While these models are not focused specifically on parental involvement, they allow for its exploration and consideration within the broader frame of Mexican Americans navigating between home and school contexts.

A SOCIAL ECOLOGICAL MODEL
FOR THE STUDY OF LATINO ADOLESCENTS

The social ecological model presented in this chapter builds upon previous models and attempts to advance opportunities to engage in research that furthers the understanding of the psychological and educational development of Latinos. While the social ecological model can be applied more broadly, in this chapter it is focused on family–school relations and school involvement for Latino adolescents and families. In this social ecological model, social, political, economic, and cultural factors are described in relation to their impact on students' and family members' interactions at school and, ultimately, the psychological and educational development of adolescents. These factors are understood as they shape the larger school or community settings and, simultaneously, the dynamics within the home setting. Whereas most theories and research look only at individual families in relation to a monolithic "school setting," the proposed social ecological model highlights[1] how the characteristics and intersections of individuals with schools and their characteristics change the nature of family–school relationships and, ultimately, adolescents' outcomes.

Several salient school/individual defining factors that shape this interaction and that often have been missed in prior research include the following: (1) the numerical status of a group, (2) the social status of a group, (3) the amount of intergroup contact, and (4) the urbanity of an ecological/school setting. These defining factors can be used to understand the school and home contexts and to develop hypotheses concerning various processes, including family involvement within those contexts. In turn, behavioral, psychological, and educational processes within these contexts are impacted by interrelated mediating factors that may differ by context: cultural expression, empowerment, and opportunities. Together, the defining and mediating factors explain what the context is and how it impacts processes such family involvement. Figure 2.1 illustrates the defining and mediating factors by which the school context is understood and that explain the relationship between the ecological/school context and adolescents' psychological and educational outcomes.

The social ecological model and its defining and mediating processes will be described and illustrated later through a study of Mexican American adolescents at urban, rural, and rural border California high schools (Metro, Citrus, and Frontera High Schools, respectively),[1] which vary on the defining factors such as numerical status and urbanity. The theoretical model is used to understand findings for family involvement and educational outcomes for Mexican American adolescents.

Numerical and Social Status

Examinations of the impact of group status have been limited to studies of minority status, where minority status has been determined by membership in either an ethnic minority group or a numerical minority

Figure 2.1. Ecological Model of School/Community Context

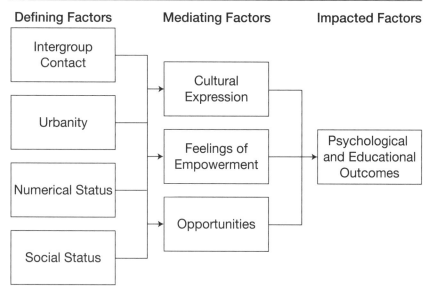

group. For the most part, the role of minority status in the psychological development of youth has been concerned primarily with the study of social identity (Ellemers, Doosje, Van Knippenberg, & Wilke, 1992) and ethnic identity formation (Smith, 1991). Research concerning the minority status of Mexican American adolescents has focused on ethnic identity (Rotheram-Borus, 1990, 1993) and acculturative stress (Saldana, 1995). Generally, this research has found that minority status in a given setting has greater impact on ethnic minorities than on individuals belonging to the cultural majority group (i.e., European Americans).

The first two defining factors of ecological/school context are the numerical and social statuses of a group. Numerical and social statuses are explained simultaneously because they are used to create a typology of ecological context. The numerical status of Mexican Americans within a given school is based on the proportion of Mexican American students in the entire school student population. For example, Mexican Americans at Frontera High School are the numerical and social majority since there are not significant numbers of students at the school who belong to other ethnic groups. However, sometimes numerical and social statuses are not interrelated. Mexican Americans at Citrus High School are the numerical majority, but not the social majority. Although European American students are not the numerical majority at this school (they are the 2nd largest group), they are the social majority because of their economic and political dominance within the school and community, as evidenced by leadership positions in student government, athletics, and club activities. At Metro High School, they are one of the two largest ethnic groups numerically but are a numerical minority relative to the entire school population. Within this model of school context, the numerical status of other ethnic groups within a school is also important. The most salient among these groups for understanding school culture is the size of the European American group, who are most often the dominant ethnic group and are considered to be the "mainstream." Table 2.1 provides an ethnic breakdown of adolescents at the three schools.

The second factor within this model of school context is social status. The social status of a group is determined by its ability to integrate itself within the school, to the point that its members can take part in determining the structure of the school context. Members of a social majority group can integrate themselves within the mainstream of the school or dictate what the mainstream within a school will be. Members of a social minority group will not have the same ability to integrate themselves within or determine the mainstream. Although the social status of a group may be related to its numerical status, social status also may be due to economic and political parameters. For example, a numerical minority group can have social majority status if it has high political and economic status, such as European Americans at Citrus High School, where they are over-represented in student governance and athletics. The result is a heightened perception of European American students converse with lowered perceptions for Mexican American students, which influence perceived

Table 2.1. Ethnic Breakdown by School

Ethnicity	Metro HS (n = 2,815)*	Citrus HS (n = 2,184)*	Frontera HS (n = 1,747)*
Mexican American	692	1,341	1,648
European American	574	480	21
Chinese American	240	44	30
Vietnamese American	356	35	0
Filipino	397	97	4
African American	193	47	5
Other Latino	114	38	17
Other	249	102	22

*Total student population.

Table 2.2. School/Community Characteristics

Characteristic	Metro HS (n = 692)*	Citrus HS (n = 1,341)*	Frontera HS (n = 1,648)*
Location	SF Bay Area	Central CA	Southern CA
Miles to Mexico	About 350	About 300	About 1
Urbanity	Urban	Rural	Border Rural
Crime Rate	Highest	High	Low
Gang Activity	High	High	Low
Group Proportion	Minority (25%)	Majority (60%)	Majority (95%)
Social Status	Minority	Minority	Majority

*Mexican American student population.

and real academic and social opportunities. Table 2.2 provides a summary of school and community characteristics that were used to determine numerical and social status for Mexican American adolescents at the three schools.

Intergroup Contact

A third defining factor that can be used to determine school context is the amount of contact between various groups. The frequency of intergroup contact, when it is possible, is impacted by a group's numerical and social statuses. This is especially true in urban school settings where school integration is attempted through busing, magnet schools, and school transfer programs. While no measures of intergroup contact were used in the study of the California high schools, it is possible to speculate the amount of intergroup contact at the three schools, given the availability of some basic data. For example, there is clearly little intergroup contact at Frontera High School, where 95% of the students are Mexican American, while it can be assumed there is more intergroup contact at the other two schools, where two or more ethnic groups are well represented.

Urbanity

A fourth defining factor to be considered when determining school context is the urbanity of the setting. In the past, social scientists have utilized primarily two categories of urbanity: rural and urban. In this social ecological model rural and border rural categories of urbanity also are included. The border rural category has been included specifically to take into account social ecological contexts along the United States–Mexico border. In this study, Frontera High School is in a border rural ecology, Citrus High School is in a rural ecology, and Metro High School is in an urban ecology.

While numerical status, social status, intergroup contact, and urbanity define the ecological/school context, the mediating factors explain how processes are shaped and influenced within each context. Taken together, defining and mediating factors provide an opportunity to hypothesize about contextual impacts on psychological and educational processes. The three mediating factors in the social ecological model (cultural expression, empowerment, and opportunities) are interrelated and are described briefly in the following paragraphs.

Cultural Expression

Cultural expression is the ability and propensity of an ethnic group to manifest or express culturally related behavior, values, and traditions. An ecological or school context may be relatively open or closed to the cultural expression of one or more ethnic groups. For example, an ethnically homogenous rural school where Mexican Americans are the numerical and social majority, such as Frontera High School, is more open to the expression of traditional Mexican values and practices, including the use of Spanish. This openness could be attributed to not only the group's numerical and social dominance, but also the isolation of the group and the lack of intergroup contact within the context. Contrary to the previous example, an ethnically diverse urban school such as Metro High School may be closed to the cultural expression of Mexican Americans if they are not the numerical or social majority and the amount of intergroup contact is high. Cultural expression can help explain Latino family involvement in schooling within a specific ecological/school context if we focus on Spanish language use as an example. If language is a barrier to family–school relations and involvement in schooling, the propensity for cultural expressiveness within a context via Spanish language use can promote or impede family–school relations and involvement.

Empowerment

Feelings of empowerment can be defined as the degree to which individuals feel enabled to act or participate. Empowerment is meant to imply more than the power held by individuals. It is meant to imply the potential of individuals who then decide to have and use power.

Feelings of empowerment are interrelated with cultural expressiveness and opportunities. For example, higher levels of cultural expressiveness may promote positive feelings of empowerment. Feelings of empowerment can be influenced by numerical and social statuses within an ecological/school context. If individuals' status is enhanced, their feelings of empowerment are raised. If their status becomes diminished, their feelings of empowerment are lowered. The effect of numerical and social statuses on Mexican Americans' feelings of empowerment also is magnified depending on the amount and nature of intergroup contact. Particular aspects of family–school relations and family involvement can be promoted by feelings of empowerment. For example, in ecological/school contexts where family members feel empowered, they are more likely to approach and engage with teachers and other school personnel to advocate for their adolescent.

Opportunity

Finally, the opportunities, both perceived and real, available to individuals within an ecological/school context are influenced by the defining factors and are interrelated with cultural expression and empowerment. The definition of opportunities includes immediate opportunities such as participating in school sports and more distant opportunities such as attending college. An example of how opportunities might vary by context is the perceived and real employment opportunities in an urban context as opposed to a rural context. Numerical and social statuses within the rural setting also can increase the number of employment opportunities, while lower numerical and social statuses in an urban setting may lower the number of employment opportunities. Family–school relations and family involvement can be impacted by adolescent and family member perceptions of opportunities present within the context. For example, if parents perceive there are educational opportunities within the ecological/school context for their adolescent, they will be more likely to engage in the educational process.

As stated previously, defining factors can be used to determine the ecological/school context, and mediatory factors explain how processes are shaped and influenced within each context. Taken together, defining and mediating factors provide an opportunity to hypothesize about contextual impacts on psychological and educational processes. The utility of the social ecological model for understanding family involvement and educational outcomes across contexts is illustrated in the following summary of a study of adolescents at three California high schools.

USING THE MODEL:
A STUDY OF THREE CALIFORNIA HIGH SCHOOLS

Each of the three high schools in this study represents a different social ecology. A survey questionnaire was used that provided data for four family variables and two educational outcomes. Of the family variables, *family involvement* is the amount of school support students receive from family members and was determined by asking students about family participation in school-related events and activities such as meeting with teachers. *Family control* describes the decisionmaking and parameters for social and extracurricular activities. *Family monitoring* is the extent to which family members are aware of the extracurricular and social activities of students, such as where students spend their time after school. *Familism* is the strength and unity of the family unit. In addition to the family variables, findings for *self-reported grades* and *educational expectations* are presented. It was hypothesized there would be higher levels of family involvement and more positive educational outcomes reported at the border rural (Frontera) and rural (Citrus) schools, where Mexican American adolescents were the numerical majority. The study sample consisted of 3,681 Mexican American adolescents enrolled in 9th through 12th grades. There were 1,403 first-generation, 1,237 second-generation, and 1,017 third-generation adolescents (24 nonresponses). Also, there were 1,833 females and 1,837 males (11 nonresponses).

The study findings for three of the four family variables and for both of the educational outcome variables indicate school/ecological differences that generally support the previously mentioned hypothesis. Adolescents at the border rural school (Frontera) reported the highest levels of family involvement, family control, and family monitoring. Furthermore, family involvement at Frontera High School significantly differed from the levels reported at the two other high schools. Family control at Frontera significantly differed from reported levels at Metro, but not from levels reported at Citrus. Reported levels of family monitoring significantly differed between Frontera and the other two schools, but did not differ between Citrus and Metro High Schools. Familism was stable across the ecological/school contexts.

There was also a significant ecology/school effect for both self-reported grades and educational expectations. As hypothesized, the highest grades were reported at the border rural school (Frontera) and the lowest grades were reported at the urban school (Metro). Grades at the rural school (Citrus), were almost exactly the same as those reported at Frontera High School. As with self-reported grades, the highest educational expectations were reported at the border rural school (Frontera). Unlike grades, the lowest educational expectations were reported at the rural school (Citrus), with expectations at the urban school (Metro) falling between the border rural and rural schools.

These findings provide evidence of the utility of the social ecological model for understanding the dynamics of family involvement and educational outcomes among Mexican American adolescents. Figure 2.2 illustrates differences across the school ecologies.

RESEARCH ISSUES AND SUGGESTIONS FOR FUTURE RESEARCH

The findings provide evidence of the utility of the model for understanding familial and educational outcomes across contexts for Mexican American adolescents. The social ecological model also presents a number of research issues and opportunities to increase our understanding of familial and educational processes among Latino adolescents and families.

Figure 2.2. Differences in School Ecology

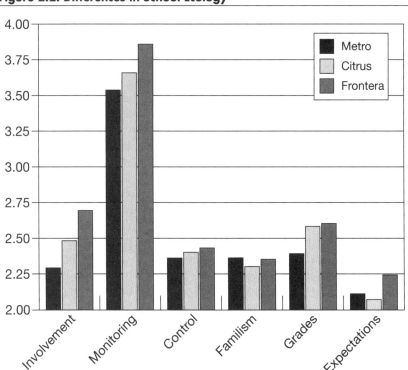

These include further refinement and utilization of the social ecological model. For example, not all four defining factors were captured by the study presented to illustrate the social ecological model. The three high schools were defined by numerical status and urbanity, but not by social status and intergroup contact. Ongoing conceptualization and the development of measures and methodologies are needed to determine social status and intergroup contact. Future research could develop and utilize quantitative and qualitative measures of social status and intergroup contact. Observation of the quality of interactions between adolescents of different ethnic backgrounds is as important as the presence of quantitative information on intergroup contact.

The findings presented and the model also raise research questions concerning the impact of school segregation and desegregation on Latino parental involvement and the educational attainment of Latino adolescents. The highest levels of parental involvement, grades, and educational expectations were reported at Frontera High School, where 95% of the students were Mexican American and by default were segregated from other ethnic groups. This is somewhat inconsistent with previous research that found a negative relationship between academic achievement and the concentration of Latino students within high schools (Donato, Menchaca, & Valencia, 1991; Espinosa & Ochoa, 1986) and more recent literature that has chronicled the historical patterns of inequity and achievement within segregated schools serving Latino students (Valencia, Menchaca, & Donato, 2002). These studies reported that Mexican American students in schools with higher concentrations of minority students, including mostly Mexican American schools, had lower academic achievement than Mexican American students in schools with lower concentrations of minority students. However, the schools in these earlier studies were primarily urban schools in large school districts. The mostly Mexican American school in this study was located in a small rural school district with a single public high school. Researchers could explore further the impact of segregation/desegregation (voluntary and involuntary), parental involvement, and educational attainment among Latino adolescents.

There is also an opportunity for researchers to apply the social ecological model beyond California and to examine regional differences for Mexican Americans and other Latino populations. The examination of Latino adolescents in California and elsewhere would provide further insight into the model's utility, allow further refinement of the defining factors, and increase understanding of contextual and individual factors that impact parental involvement and home–school linkages. Such research also would provide a more accurate assessment of the applicability of the model to the various Latino populations in the United States. It is also important to understand the model's robustness in explaining familial processes and parental involvement for immigrant and nonimmigrant Latino populations.

Finally, as part of the effort to understand the heterogeneity of Latinos within varying social ecological contexts, researchers should continue to explore sociocultural and familial processes in relation to parental involvement and educational outcomes. Efforts to study and understand these familial processes must be sensitive to the cultural tools that shape Latino families. Parental involvement in education among Latino families should be promoted, while leaving their structure, values, and cultural practices intact. Latino culture may, in part, provide buffers and coping mechanisms that promote the healthy adaptation and academic success of Latino adolescents.

IMPLICATIONS FOR EDUCATIONAL POLICY AND PRACTICE

The social ecological model and the illustrative study have implications for educational policy and practice in relation to parental involvement and education for Latino adolescents. On a broad level, there are implications for school segregation/desegregation policy. It is important to understand how the school and community ecologies might be impacted, perhaps differentially, by voluntary and involuntary segregation/desegregation. In many instances, school desegregation or integration is accomplished through student busing programs that can take students from one community and place them into an entirely different community. From a practical standpoint of distance, time, and transportation, busing students to disparate communities can create challenges for parental involvement. There is also a connection between segregation/desegregation policy and the No Child Left Behind Act, which provides for parental choice when schools repeatedly fail to meet standards. Large-scale parental choice can lead to voluntary segregation/desegregation depending on the particular school contexts.

Additionally, consideration should be given to the sociocultural and ecological contexts Latino adolescents and families navigate in their daily lives. Differences across contexts and sociocultural diversity among Latino populations may require multiple program models for parental involvement. As program models are conceptualized and developed, it is critical to consider the diversity within and between various Latino populations. Policies, funding, and programs at the federal, state, and local levels need to recognize and be responsive to contextual and sociocultural diversity among Latinos. Given contextual and sociocultural diversity, parental involvement programs and interventions for Latino adolescents and families must be culturally responsive in order to maximize their effectiveness. For example, previous research has established the importance of understanding generational differences for Latino and other immigrant populations (Buriel & De Ment, 1997; Rodríguez, 2002). As the heterogeneity within Latino populations is better understood, parental involvement programs should be sensitive to the specific characteristics of the group. Furthermore, parental involvement programs should incorporate mechanisms that utilize the group's strengths and operational contexts in order to more effectively meet the needs of adolescents and their families.

It is also important to consider other key players in the schooling process who impact the dynamics of the school context and educational processes such as parental involvement. There should be a focus on the recruitment and preparation of highly qualified teachers (as dictated by NCLB), school counselors, and administrators in order to better understand and more effectively serve Latino adolescents and their families. Federal, state, and local recruitment policies and efforts, for example, could focus on increasing the number of Latino teachers, who currently are underrepresented in the teaching force. Latino teachers can bring familiarity with contexts and group processes that can be utilized to bridge the home and school contexts. All teacher preparation programs must address parental involvement generally and incorporate research and models on Latino adolescents and families more specifically into their curricula. Professional development for experienced educators also must integrate emerging research and models for Latino parental involvement. Consideration of the recruitment, preparation, and ongoing professional development of educators is critical if parental involvement programs for Latino adolescents and their families are to be effective.

NOTE

1. Pseudonyms have been substituted for the actual names of the schools. The terms *school contexts* and *ecological settings* are used interchangeably in this chapter.

REFERENCES

Bronfenbrenner, U. (1943). A constant frame of reference for sociometric research. *Sociometry, 6*(4), 363–397.
Bronfenbrenner, U. (1979). *The ecology of human development*. Cambridge, MA: Harvard University Press.

Bronfenbrenner, U. (1989). Ecological systems theory. *Annals of Child Development, 6*, 187–249.

Buriel, R., & De Ment, T. (1997). Immigration and sociocultural change in Mexican, Chinese, and Vietnamese American families. In A. Booth, A. C. Crouter, & N. Landale (Eds.), *Immigration and the family: Research and policy on U.S. immigrants* (pp. 165–200). Mahwah, NJ: Erlbaum.

Delgado-Gaitan, C. (1991). Involving parents in the schools: A process of empowerment. *American Journal of Education, 100*(1), 20–46.

Donato, R., Menchaca, M., & Valencia, R. R. (1991). Segregation, desegregation, and integration of Chicano students: Problems and prospects. In R. R. Valencia (Ed.), *Chicano school failure and success: Research and policy agendas for the 1990s* (pp. 27–63). New York: Falmer Press.

Ellemers, N., Doosje, B. J., Van Knippenberg, A., & Wilke, H. (1992). Status protection in high status minority groups. *European Journal of Social Psychology, 22*(2), 123–140.

Espinosa, R., & Ochoa, A. (1986). Concentration of California Hispanic students in schools with low achievement: A research note. *American Journal of Education, 95*(1), 77–95.

Garza, R. T., & Gallegos, P. I. (1995). Environmental influences and personal choice: A humanistic perspective on acculturation. In A. M. Padilla (Ed.), *Hispanic psychology: Critical issues in theory and research* (pp. 3–14). Thousand Oaks, CA: Sage.

Garza, R. T., & Lipton, J. P. (1982). Theoretical perspectives on Chicano personality development. *Hispanic Journal of Behavioral Sciences, 4*(4), 407–432.

Gilbert, M. J. (1980). Communities within communities: Social structural factors and variation in Mexican American communities. *Hispanic Journal of Behavioral Sciences, 2*(3), 241–268.

Harrison, A. O., Wilson, M. N., Pine, C. J., Chan, S. Q., & Buriel, R. (1990). Family ecologies of ethnic minority children. *Child Development, 61*(2), 347–362.

Lewin, K. (1935). *A dynamic theory of personality.* New York: McGraw-Hill.

National Research Council, Commission on Behavioral and Social Sciences in Education. (1993). *Losing generations: Adolescents in high-risk settings.* Washington, DC: National Academy Press.

Phelan, P., Davidson, A. L., & Yu, H. C. (1998). *Adolescents' worlds: Negotiating family, peers, and school.* New York: Teachers College Press.

Rodríguez, J. L. (2002). Family support for academic achievement among three generations of Mexican American high school students. *Applied Developmental Science, 6*(2), 88–94.

Rotheram-Borus, M. J. (1990). Adolescents' reference-group choices, self-esteem, and adjustment. *Journal of Personality and Social Psychology, 59*(5), 1075–1081.

Rotheram-Borus, M. J. (1993). Biculturalism among adolescents. In M. E. Bernal & G. P. Knight (Eds.), *Ethnic identity: Formation and transmission among Hispanics and other ethnic minorities* (pp. 81–104). Albany: State University of New York Press.

Saldana, D. H. (1995). Acculturative stress: Minority status and distress. In A. M. Padilla (Ed.), *Hispanic psychology: Critical issues in theory and research* (pp. 43–54). Thousand Oaks, CA: Sage.

Smith, E. J. (1991). Ethnic identity development: Toward the development of a theory within the context of majority/minority status. *Journal of Counseling & Development, 70*(1), 181–188.

Stanton-Salazar, R. D. (2001). *Manufacturing hope and despair: The school and kin support networks of U.S.-Mexican youth.* New York: Teachers College Press.

Steinberg, L. (with Brown, B. B., & Dornbusch, S. M.). (1996). *Beyond the classroom: Why school reform has failed and what parents need to do.* New York: Simon & Schuster.

Suárez-Orozco, C., & Suárez-Orozco, M. (1995). *Transformations: Immigration, family life, and achievement motivation among Latino adolescents.* Stanford: Stanford University Press.

Valdés, G. (1996). *Con respeto: Bridging the distances between culturally diverse families and schools.* New York: Teachers College Press.

Valencia, R. R., Menchaca, M., & Donato, R. (2002). Segregation, desegregation, and integration of Chicano students: Old and new realities. In R. R. Valencia (Ed.), *Chicano school failure and success: Past, present, and future.* New York: Falmer Press.

Valenzuela, A. (1999). *Subtractive schooling: U.S.-Mexican youth and the politics of caring.* Albany: State University of New York Press.

Vásquez, O. A., Pease-Alvarez, L., & Shannon, S. M. (1994). *Pushing boundaries: Language and culture in a Mexicano community.* New York: Cambridge University Press.

3

Developmentally Appropriate Strategies Across Ethnicity and Socioeconomic Status

Parental Involvement During Middle School

NANCY E. HILL
DIANA F. TYSON
LEA BROMELL

ADOLESCENCE, ESPECIALLY MIDDLE SCHOOL, is a time that is marked by declines in academic achievement, especially in grades; declines in school engagement; and increases in school behavioral problems (Barber & Olsen, 2004; Gutman & Midgley, 2000). Concomitantly, it is during middle school that course selection and course track placement (e.g., college preparatory, vocational) begin to have long-term implications for educational and occupational attainment (Eccles & Harold, 1996). Although parents' expectations and aspirations for education remain high (Hill et al., 2004), their involvement in education declines, especially for volunteering at school, helping with homework, and communicating with teachers (Eccles & Harold, 1996; Hill & Taylor, 2004). Further, not only does the use of these strategies decline, but they become less effective in promoting achievement (Hill & Tyson, 2009). Paradoxically, whereas declines in parental involvement in education are deemed consistent with the emerging independence and autonomy that are hallmarks of adolescence, parents are hungry for information about how to best help their teens succeed in school and get into the best colleges or receive the best vocational training (Hill & Torres, in press; Lareau & Horvat, 1999).

As described in the introduction to this book, there is a need to identify strategies that are proven to promote academic success among middle and high school students. Current policies to promote achievement emphasize the role of families across elementary, middle, and high schools (e.g., NCLB). However, strategies that are known to work for teens and that account for their unique strengths and needs have not been identified. Existing frameworks that outline ways to be involved in children's education and work with schools are based on research with elementary students and families and work best in that context (Hill & Taylor, 2004). The unique developmental assets and needs of adolescents have not been considered in determining how parents can and should be involved in education and how middle school teachers and families can work together to benefit students. This chapter outlines ways in which current theories and policies can be broadened to be developmentally inclusive and presents the results of a program of research that has identified developmentally appropriate strategies for middle school students.

EXISTING PARENTAL INVOLVEMENT FRAMEWORKS

Over the past 2 decades, the amount of research on parental involvement in education has increased exponentially, with two common types of involvement identified and analyzed for effectiveness. These are *involvement at school*, which includes volunteering at school, visiting the school, and communicating with teachers and other school personnel, and *involvement at home*, which includes helping with and monitoring homework and providing educational experiences outside of school. Whereas the research with elementary students shows that these types of strategies are associated with higher levels of achievement (Fan & Chen, 2001), the evidence is mixed for middle school students. Some research finds that parental involvement in education remains positively associated with adolescents' achievement throughout middle and high school (Baker & Stevenson, 1986; Bandura, Barbaranelli, Caprara, & Pastorelli, 1996; Catsambis, 2001; Hill et al., 2004). Other research shows that parental involvement is either unrelated to achievement or even associated with lower levels of achievement (Balli, Wedman, & Demo, 1997; Bronstein, Ginsburg, & Herrera, 2005; Driessen, Smit, & Sleegers, 2005). Differences in the ways in which researchers define and measure parental involvement in education across studies may partially explain the inconsistent findings. However, other factors may impact the effectiveness of parental involvement for supporting achievement, including how welcoming the school is or feels to parents, the support teachers receive to work with parents and families, the resources families have to support achievement both at home and at school, and parents' knowledge about how the school functions (i.e., social capital). For example, if parents understand when and how students are placed into academic tracks and the implications of those track placements for getting into college, they will be in a better position to effectively prepare their teens for courses and to be effectively involved in course selection.

In a study that followed families from when their teens were in 7th grade until they were in 11th grade (i.e., across middle and high school), parental involvement in 7th grade was related to achievement in 9th grade and aspirations in 11th grade for parents who had a college education (Hill et al., 2004). Based on these findings, one could conclude that parental involvement still matters and matters in the same way as it does in elementary school. In contrast, for parents who did not have a college degree, parental involvement in 7th grade was directly and positively related to students' educational and occupational aspirations in 11th grade. However, surprisingly, parental involvement was *not* associated with improved school behavior or with academic performance. That is, these parents were effective in communicating their high expectations, but their involvement in their adolescents' education was not effective in improving school behavior and academic achievement—the prerequisites for reaching their aspirations. Whereas these parents were involved in ways that other parents were involved, including assisting with homework, attending PTA meetings, volunteering at school, and meeting with teachers, their involvement did not have the same "payoff" for their adolescents' achievement as it did for parents with college degrees.

One of the reasons there may be differences in parental effectiveness in supporting their teens' achievement between those parents with and without a college degree is that middle schools and high schools provide significantly less information to parents about how to be involved. Therefore, parents of middle and high school students are more dependent on their own knowledge about how schools function, what teens need in order to reach their goals, and how to help students who are having difficulties (Dika & Singh, 2002; Lareau, 1987; Stanton-Salazar & Dornbusch, 1995). One of the costs of not having identified effective ways for parents to be involved in their teens' education in middle school is that parents and schools fall back on the strategies that worked in elementary school, which often are shown to be less effective (e.g., volunteering at school). Parents with more experience with schooling and who understand the pathways between middle school and college access (e.g., have a college degree) may be engaged in their teens' education in ways that are not included in current theories and measures of involvement. These unmeasured or unidentified practices might explain the differences in effectiveness of parental involvement for college-educated parents compared with parents without a college degree. Identifying and labeling the practices that parents most need to engage in are not only the goals of this chapter and this book, but imperative so that such information can be communicated to all parents who are grappling with how to help their teens reach their goals.

Identifying strategies for parental involvement in education that work for middle school students, and broadening theories of involvement to include strategies that will help parents build upon teens' developmental needs and strengths, will go a long way toward supporting the educational and occupational attainment of middle-school-aged students from a broad range of backgrounds. This chapter presents research designed to identify strategies of parental involvement in education that are effective in middle schools and with young adolescents, who are trying out their burgeoning decisionmaking skills and autonomy.

THREE STEPS TO IDENTIFYING
DEVELOPMENTALLY APPROPRIATE STRATEGIES

To identify strategies of involvement that are appropriate for the families of adolescents, we engaged in three types of studies. The first was to determine whether firm conclusions can be reached from the existing research. Rather than placing emphasis on a single study, we conducted an analysis of all of the existing research on the influence of parental involvement in education and achievement in middle school to determine whether parental involvement in education was related to achievement. Further, we tested different types of parental involvement in education to identify the types of parental involvement that have the strongest impact on achievement (Hill & Tyson, 2009). Second, because of the increasing diversity of American schoolchildren and to ensure that any theories or recommendations for involvement are sensitive to the needs of families from diverse cultural backgrounds, we reviewed the existing literature on culturally based beliefs about parental involvement in education for the three largest ethnic groups in the United States (i.e., African Americans, Latinos, and European Americans) (Hill, in press; Hill & Torres, in press). Third, we listened to the voices of middle school students and their parents to identify the needs of middle school students from their perspectives and to identify novel strategies that are not included in the existing theories (Hill, Tyson, Bromell, & Flint, 2008). Again, we focused on the three largest ethnic minority groups in the United States—European Americans, African Americans, and Latinos, representing 75%, 12%, and 12% of the U.S. population, respectively (Greico & Cassidy, 2001).

Firm Conclusions from Existing Research—
A Meta-Analytic Assessment

The body of research on parental involvement in middle school is based on a variety of theories (e.g., general parenting theories, social capital, and social stratification) and methods, resulting in a literature that is disaggregated and inconsistent. The goal of this meta-analysis was to aggregate results across all existing studies in order to systematically determine whether and which types of parental involvement are consistently and significantly associated with achievement (Hill & Tyson, 2009). The benefits of a meta-analysis over a general review of the literature is that it creates a mathematical average of the strength (or meaningfulness) of the relation between parental involvement and achievement, while taking into account several factors that impact the quality of a study. Factors such as sample size, whether the sample was randomly selected and is representative of all middle school students, how well parental involvement and achievement were measured, and the quality of the statistics used, impact how much confidence can be placed in the findings of a study. A meta-analysis takes into account many of these characteristics of the study design and calculates the average strength of the relation between parental involvement and achievement, determines whether the relationship is strong enough to be meaningful, and determines whether one type of parental involvement has a stronger or more meaningful relationship than another. Three types of parental involvement in education were examined in this meta-analysis: (1) home-based involvement, (2) school-based involvement, and (3) academic socialization. Home-based and school-based involvement were of central concern because each is consistently highlighted in leading theories of parental involvement in education (see introduction). In addition, we examined parental involvement strategies that may have increased importance for adolescents, such as communication of parental expectations for and the value or utility of education, linking schoolwork to current events, fostering educational and occupational aspirations, discussing learning styles and strategies, and making preparations and plans for the future, which we call "academic socialization" (Hill & Tyson, 2009).

An exhaustive search of the literature to identify relevant studies included searches of the major databases that catalogue research study, such as PsychInfo, ERIC, Dissertation Abstracts International, and Sociological Abstracts; hand searches of major research journals; scans of reference lists of published papers for relevant articles; and the use of Social Science Citation Index to identify articles that cited seminal studies (see Hill & Tyson, 2009, for details). We found 50 different studies that examined the relation between parental involvement in education and achievement. Because studies often look at multiple types of involvement and multiple measures of achievement (e.g., grades and test scores), some studies provided multiple indicators of the relation between parental involvement and achievement. In total, across the 50 studies, we were able to use 127 correlations. A correlation is a numerical expression that indicates how strongly one construct (i.e., parental involvement) is related to another (i.e., achievement).

Using meta-analysis strategies that take into account the sample size and quality of the study and aggregate across studies, we found an overall positive relation between parental involvement in education and achievement for middle school students, confirming that parental involvement still matters for adolescents' achievement. We also identified which type of involvement in education (i.e., home-based, school-based, and academic socialization) is most strongly related to achievement. School-based involvement had small but positive effects on achievement, whereas home-based involvement was not associated with achievement. In contrast, academic socialization, defined as communicating expectations for and the value or utility of education, linking schoolwork to current events, fostering education and occupational aspirations, discussing learning styles and strategies, and making preparations and plans for the future, had the strongest and most positive influence on achievement. Therefore, *academic socialization emerged as a critical component* of parental involvement for middle school students.

Because home-based involvement is a key component of parental involvement, we examined the relation between home-based involvement and achievement more carefully. Some research has distinguished types of home-based involvement (e.g., structural and managerial; see Chapter 6). Further, among types of home involvement, homework help has been deemed controversial (Cooper, 1989). Indeed, in looking at the array of correlations between home-based involvement and achievement, there seemed to be multiple types of home-based involvement, with different associations with achievement. Because homework help may either accelerate or interfere with achievement, depending on the motives, strategies, and parent–adolescent relationship (Cooper, 1989, 2007; Wolf, 1979), homework help was compared with other types of home-based involvement. Homework help may undermine achievement when it interferes with students' autonomy, results in excessive parental pressure, or is not consistent with how materials are presented at school. In contrast, other types of involvement at home, such as providing educationally enriching activities, making books and other educational materials available, and taking adolescents to museums and other educational outlets, enhance achievement (Reynolds & Gill, 1994). As predicted, home involvement defined as homework help was associated with lower levels of achievement, whereas other types of home involvement were positively related to achievement. Overall, educationally enriching activities were positively related to achievement.

The clear conclusion from this meta-analysis of the existing research is that parental involvement in education remains important in supporting achievement during middle school. Further, a specific type of parental involvement in education, namely, academic socialization, has the strongest positive relation with achievement during middle school. Academic socialization builds on adolescents' developing autonomy, independence, and cognitive abilities and supports the internalization of achievement motivation and ability to make semi-autonomous decisions about their academic pursuits. Further, it is often not included in theories of parental involvement.

Despite these clear conclusions, one significant limitation in the existing literature is the lack of sufficient data to permit the examination of ethnic and cultural differences in beliefs about parental involvement in education, the types of parental involvement in education in which families from different ethnic groups engage, or the relations between parental involvement in education and achievement. However, parental involvement in education has different meanings and motivations across ethnic and economic groups, and the processes by which involvement shapes achievement differ (Hill, in press; Hill & Craft, 2003; Lareau & Horvat, 1999; Lynch & Stein, 1987). Because of differences in the extent to which parents are involved in education and the processes by which involvement influences achievement, the next section provides a summary of the theoretical work that may undergird ethnic differences in parental involvement.

Ethnic Differences in Beliefs and Processes

Families and school personnel hold assumptions about the ways students learn, the nature of the world for which students are being prepared, and sources of change and stability in children's development. More relevant for adolescents, these assumptions identify the ages at which adolescents should be responsible or independent, the appropriate balance between parental and peer influences, appropriate and desired adult roles for which adolescents should be prepared, and the content and conflicts to be grappled with as core components of identity development. These are world views, which are socialized within cultural systems and are considered part of the "natural and moral order" of a given culture (Goodnow,

2002; Hill, in press). Although many strive to be "culture free" or "color blind" in the United States, it is not possible to be truly culture free or color blind (Pollock, 2004). World views, which are held by everyone, are necessary to organize and make sense of the world and to interpret other people's actions (Sigel & McGillicuddy-DeLisi, 2002). Culture shapes world views and therefore shapes the interactions (and their interpretations) between families and schools.

Although schools often think of themselves as "neutral" cultural environments, objective in their teaching and learning styles, and even as embracing cultural diversity, American schools operate with implicit and explicit assumptions and with a specific world view. Whereas these assumptions may seem unbiased to some, they are embedded in the larger, mainstream American culture. American schools emphasize individual achievement, along with the promotion of self-esteem, self-expression and independence, while devaluing cooperation, interdependence, and conformity (Linney & Seidman, 1989). The emphasis on independent work, the development of the self as an individual, and one's "rights" as an individual heightens during adolescence as the development of the self and identity become salient. Whereas this emphasis seems "normal" and appropriate from the perspective of American schools, it conflicts with the cultural world views of many ethnic minority families in the United States (Hill, in press). Differences and similarities in world views and experiences between families and school personnel shape the effectiveness of these interactions. The impact of differences in cultural world views between families and schools is most poignant when examining the incongruence between home and school culture for ethnic minorities. Here, we review the cultural world views described in the literature for African American and Latino families. We focus on Latinos and African Americans because they are the largest ethnic minority groups in the United States. Further, teachers and schools have been shown to hold negative stereotypes or biases against Latino and African American students (Tenenbaum & Ruck, 2007).

African Americans

Although there is considerable diversity among African American families, including diversity in economic background; urban, suburban, and rural residence; religious and political beliefs, among other indicators, there are some commonalities based on ethnic background and experiences in the United States (Hill, Murry, & Anderson, 2005). In a survey of over 200 urban African American parents asking them to rank their goals for their children, obtaining a good education and securing a good job were ranked the highest (Hill & Sprague, 1999). This primacy of education remains, even though African American adolescents, on average, perform less well than do others. Although scholars debate whether African American culture maintains aspects of West African culture or the African roots in African American culture have been erased by slavery (Hill et al., 2005; Mitchell, 1975), culturally based experiences during the more than 4 centuries during which African Americans have been part of American society have resulted in some commonalities in beliefs about the nature of the world for which they are preparing their adolescents, in experiences with American schools and educational opportunities, and in culturally embedded ways of learning.

For good reason, African American parents often find that they are preparing their adolescents, especially their sons, for a world that is at times hostile toward them, will not always give them a fair chance, and may misinterpret their behavior unfavorably (Ferguson, 1998; Tyler, Boykin, Miller, & Hurley, 2006). African American parents often find they must prepare their adolescents to cope with and understand discriminatory experiences, while maintaining their sense of self and value of education (Hughes et al., 2006; Stevenson, Davis, & Abdul-Kabir, 2001). It is often within school contexts that African American parents experienced their first encounters with discrimination and where their adolescents will have their first encounters with discrimination.

African Americans, as an ethnic group, have experienced the most intense denigration of their educational opportunities and achievement motivation of any group in the United States (Cross, 2003). "Separate but unequal" schools resulted in the under-education of many African Americans, and desegregated schools increased the amount of discrimination experienced by African Americans. The implications of these experiences are heightened during middle school because early adolescence is a time when identity formation and peer conformity are at their most salient. These historical and contemporary experiences have resulted in a mistrust of school and teachers by many African American parents (Lareau, 1987; Ogbu, 1978).

In contrast to the independent style of achievement supported in American schools, African Americans tend to value collaborative learning styles, such as working together and sharing materials and information, and find that more is learned when working together than when working alone (Sankofa, Hurley, Allen, & Boykin, 2005). Further, a cultural value of expressiveness and movement (i.e., verve) means that African American adolescents often focus on multiple activities and circulate among and learn from several activities simultaneously (i.e., multitask) and are more likely to thrive in classes that permit nonlinear learning methods (i.e., multiple pathways to learning), which is different from the linear learning styles presented in most American classrooms (Sankofa et al., 2005). Consistent with the value of interdependence and cooperation, African American adolescents performed better academically when they worked collaboratively, compared with working independently (Boykin, Tyler, Watkins-Lewis, & Kizzie, 2006), and high-performing African American adolescents were rated more favorably by their peers when their methods of learning embraced collaborative, interdependent styles (Sankofa et al., 2005). These styles of learning and their cultural underpinnings often are misunderstood in American schools.

Latinos

The Latino population in the United States is extremely diverse, with families who draw cultural ties to more than 30 countries on three continents. Among these countries of origin, Latinos of Mexican descent are the largest subpopulation in the United States, constituting more than 60% of the Latino population (U.S. Census Bureau, 2006). The second largest subgroup of Latinos in the United States are those of Puerto Rican descent, constituting 9% of the Latino population. In line with the population figures, the majority of research on Latinos in the education system focuses on families of Mexican descent, although many studies do not distinguish their samples by country of origin (Hill & Torres, in press). Latinos, many of whom are immigrants, hold strong beliefs about the role of education for upward mobility and place high trust in the quality of the American school system to assist them in reaching their goals (Hill & Torres, in press). Despite valuing education and trusting American schools, their achievement lags behind others in the United States, with students whose families have been in the United States longer performing worse than recent immigrants (Rodríguez, 2002). Like African Americans, most Latino cultures place a value on cooperative, collaborative learning and interdependence. Further, many Latino cultures place a high value on social relationships and understanding oneself in relation to others. Therefore, forging relationships with school personnel should be easier. However, Latinos often feel disenfranchised from U.S. education systems, in part due to the incongruence between the culture of home and that of school.

Research finds that many Latino families define being well educated more broadly than do American schools. Whereas a good education, according to many Latinos, includes the academic and cognitive aspects that typically are consistent with U.S. definitions, it also encompasses aspects of one's character, such as being moral, responsible, respectful, and well behaved (Auerbach, 2006; Hidalgo, Pedraza, & Rivera, 2005). Latino parents often believe that they are most responsible for these latter aspects of education, which are the foundation for cognitive and academic development, whereas developing the cognitive and academic aspects of education are often believed to be the role of the school. Further, Latino cultures hold teachers and the profession of teaching in high regard (Jones, 2003; Yan & Lin, 2005). Whereas much of the research focuses on partnerships between families and schools, many Latino families find the notion of being "equal partners" foreign and uncomfortable (Correa & Tulbert, 1993).

Some Latino parents find that the values that are encouraged and developed at school contradict the values they wish to preserve at home, making it difficult at times for families to fully embrace the American school experience. For example, the United States' emphasis on individualism, individual rights, and the primacy of individual goals goes against many Latino cultures' value for and understanding of the self through relationships and promotion of the common good (Reese, 2002). Latino parents are often uncomfortable advocating for their rights as parents and accepting adolescents' demanding individual rights as they learned in school and from their peer group. Each of these differences in world views makes it challenging to develop and maintain partnerships with Latino families (Hill, in press).

Although much was gained from understanding these cultural frames and experiences and from identifying academic socialization as a key form of involvement, we had uncovered only part of the story. Therefore, we sought to listen to the voices of parents to find out how they supported academic achievement. Further, we listened to adolescents themselves to find out whether and how they wanted their parents to be involved in their educational pursuits. The preliminary results of this study are presented here.

Project Alliance/Projecto Alianzo:
Listening to the Voices of Teens and Parents

We conducted a series of focus groups with African American, European American, and Latino adolescents and their parents in a semiurban school district, with the purpose of identifying the goals parents have for maintaining involvement in their adolescents' education and effective strategies of involvement not found in extant theories (Hill et al., 2008). Separate focus groups were conducted with African American, Latino, and European American parents and adolescents. The sample was diverse economically, with annual family income ranging from less than $10,000 to greater than $100,000 and parental education levels ranging from a high school degree to graduate/professional degrees for African Americans and European Americans. The Latino sample had a somewhat lower average annual family income, ranging from $10,000 to $50,000, largely due to their immigrant status, and none of the parents had completed high school. Focus group discussions were recorded, transcribed, and coded by two independent coders who gleaned goals and strategies from the transcripts. One of the benefits of utilizing focus groups, over other research methodologies, is that the voices, experiences, and perspectives of parents and students are recorded without the constrictions of existing theories and measures. Further, focus groups are an effective method for learning about the population's values and styles of thinking (Vogt, King, & King, 2004). Focus groups are often desirable because interactions among participants about specific topics elicit a more in-depth discussion of the topic (Hughes & DuMont, 1993; Vogt et al., 2004).

Because it is both difficult and most of the time not appropriate for programs and policies to target a single ethnic group, we sought to identify strategies parents use to support their teens' education that were common across ethnic groups. The presentation of the results is organized around parental goals for maintaining involvement during middle school, followed by the strategies that adolescents and parents indicated were particularly important.

Goals for Involvement

All of the parents were motivated for their adolescents to succeed academically. They expressed a number of goals for maintaining involvement in their teens' education. For African American and Latino parents, the goals were more tightly focused on the utility and pragmatics of education, including ensuring their adolescents' academic success and managing their curriculum. For example, Latino parents indicated that they were involved to ensure that their adolescents were enrolled in advanced classes so that they would be able to take advantage of educational opportunities, which is consistent with prior research on Latino immigrant families' emphasis on the utility and value of education for upward mobility (Hill & Torres, in press). Similarly, African American parents indicated that they were involved because they were determined that their teens would beat the odds and be successful, and involvement that helped their adolescents stay focused was the only way to ensure that. They also wanted to use their involvement in their adolescents' education to increase their adolescents' understanding of the consequences and utility of schoolwork and to encourage and boost their confidence. In contrast, European American parents expressed more relational goals for their involvement, such as volunteering at school in order to know what their adolescents were experiencing during the day so as to facilitate conversation. They also talked about working "behind the scenes" at school, in order to set their adolescents up for success, by gathering information on teachers, courses, and extracurricular activities.

Effective Strategies

Parents and adolescents identified specific strategies that were effective or desirable. Strategies mentioned were itemized and then examined to identify those mentioned by all groups, by more than one ethnic group, and by both parents and teens. First, we present the common strategies across ethnicity. These are strategies that were mentioned by either all of the teen groups or all of the parent groups. Second, we present strategies that were confirmed across two of the three ethnic groups.

Common strategies across ethnicity. Not surprisingly, there were no strategies that were mentioned by both parents and teens from all three ethnic groups. However, five strategies were consistent across parent focus groups from all three ethnicities: (1) have family discussions about schooling and goals for schooling; (2) communicate expectations for graduation and educational attainment; (3) use parents' life experiences as examples of pathways to follow or avoid; (4) provide extracurricular experiences with the dual goal of providing additional educational experiences and teaching time management skills; and (5) "threaten" involvement in a more intrusive manner if achievement declines. The strategies pertaining to communication and family discussions are consistent with the work presented by Jones and Schneider (Chapter 4, this volume) and reflect the academic socialization construct that often is missing from theories of involvement.

In contrast with the popular notion that adolescents wish that their parents would decrease or cease involvement in their education, all of the adolescents said that they wanted their parents to be involved in their education. Teens from all three ethnic groups indicated that they wanted their parents to assist them in managing their course schedule and selecting classes. While having this hope and expectation, Latino teens said that their parents often lacked the necessary information and language skills to provide this help. They desired it nevertheless. They also indicated that their parents and teachers should communicate. Reflecting their increasing autonomy and independence, teens wanted their parents to give them more responsibility, to show interest in the things that were of interest to the teens, and to discuss larger projects and assignments, each of which reflects academic socialization. Also, consistent with their increasing autonomy and independence, teens agreed that they did not want their parents to double check their homework, chaperone field trips, go through their bookbags, or lecture them about their future.

Common strategies across two ethnic groups: Latinos and African Americans. Whereas these groups are different culturally, they share the experiences of being an ethnic minority in the United States, being discriminated against, and being the target of negative stereotypes (Hill et al., 2005). Teens and parents from both ethnic groups, independently, agreed that parents should monitor friendships and peer interactions to ensure that teens did not get involved in the wrong crowd, and they agreed that parents should assist with planning for the future. Among parents, both African Americans and Latinos expressed the importance of providing or arranging for direct supervision before and after school. This was not mentioned by European American parents. Further, African American and Latino parents were concerned about their teens' experiences with discrimination and described the important role of helping them manage discrimination and stand up for injustices to themselves and their peers.

Latino and African American teens agreed that they wanted their parents to attend school events in which they participated (e.g., sports, theater, concerts, etc.), but not chaperone events. They also accepted the reality that their parents should attend parent–teacher conferences. Although they did not want their parents to micromanage their homework, they did want their parents to remind them of due dates for larger projects and other homework assignments. Finally, African American and Latino teens wanted their parents to share stories from their own life that would help them stay focused.

Common strategies across two ethnic groups: Latinos and European Americans. Both European American and Latino parents and teens mentioned that parents should attend the PTA meetings. Latino and European American parents discussed the importance of linking school success to future goals in order to help teens understand the purpose and utility of education. In addition, Latino and European American parents talked about how they needed to provide school supplies for their teens. However, they discussed this from somewhat different perspectives. European American parents wanted to make sure their teens had all of the needed materials to do their best work, beyond basic school supplies. Latino parents, on the other hand, discussed the unfortunate fact that Latino teens often were bullied and their school supplies taken, resulting in a regular need to provide basic school supplies. Among the strategies raised by teens, Latinos and European Americans indicated that parental discussions about current events were an important way to support their education.

Common strategies across two ethnic groups: European and African Americans. African American and European American parents and teens discussed the usefulness of emailing teachers as a form of communication. As mentioned in Chapter 8, the use of email, Web sites, and e-bulletin boards is an effective method for maintaining communication between parents and teachers without undermining adolescents' sense of autonomy and independence; it also circumvents many barriers, including conflicting schedules for parents and teachers. African American and European American parents also discussed the importance of family time and limiting television viewing as a means of supporting the educational outcomes of their teens, consistent with the findings in Chapter 4. African American and European American teens were resigned to the fact that, despite their desires against it, their parents likely would volunteer at school. In this context, they agreed that it was fine for their parents to volunteer, as long as they did not encounter their parents (e.g., volunteering in the main office or for a different grade). Further, these teens acknowledged their parents' expertise on some topics—largely related to parents' occupations and interests—and desired help from their parents in these areas.

Across these three research projects, it can be firmly concluded that parental involvement in education still matters for middle school students. Whereas parental involvement at school is less salient, communication between parents and teachers remains important. Further, involvement out of school broadens to take on a somewhat different form, which we have described as academic socialization. It builds on the parent–adolescent relationship, centers around socializing teens toward future goals, and proactively provides linkages between schoolwork and adolescents' own goals and interests. This form of involvement often is left out of theories of family–school relations and requires the most knowledge and information for parents to effectively support teens' achievement, which may explain differences in the effectiveness of involvement between parents with and without a college degree, as found in Hill and colleagues (2004). There were many points of convergence across parents and teens from different ethnic groups. However, ethnic minority families emphasized the need to carefully manage peer interactions and out-of-school time, based on concerns about the costs of teens' getting involved with deviant peers.

NEXT STEPS FOR RESEARCH

Although the body of research on parental involvement in education during adolescence is growing, it remains in need of a theory and framework that integrate existing knowledge about the structure and organization of middle schools, our understanding of adolescent development, and our understanding of the dynamics of the parent–adolescent relationship as it is renegotiated during early adolescence. Further, another key limitation is that the field lacks a valid measure of parental involvement in education and family–school relations that includes the uniquely effective strategies for middle school, such as academic socialization. Among the more than 70 empirical reports reviewed for possible inclusion in the meta-analysis, rarely was the same measure used across studies. The field needs a valid, reliable, and developmentally appropriate measure of parental involvement during middle school.

Although most educational policies, programs, and research focus on grades and test scores, they are not the only important outcomes (see Chapters 1, 4, and 5). Adolescents' sense of efficacy increases as they internalize their own goals and mature in their ability to make decisions and apply their knowledge. Parental involvement during adolescence may be better understood as equipping teens to engage in school, achieve academically, and develop into independently motivated lifelong learners.

POLICY AND PRACTICE RECOMMENDATIONS

Despite the need for more research, there are some consistent conclusions across studies that can inform policies and programs for parental involvement in middle school.

- Make the pathway from middle school courses to college transparent for families.
- Help teens identify goals and provide parents with information that will assist them in helping their teens understand the utility of education to reach their goals.
- Help parents understand how they can help their teens apply what they are learning in school to events in the real world.
- Affirm and support teens as they demonstrate increasing levels of responsibility and sound decisionmaking.
- Use parents' own mistakes and successes as examples for their teens to learn the benefits of education.

- Communicate expectations for educational attainment early and consistently.
- Discuss incidences of discrimination in school and possible solutions to or management of them. Doing so may decrease the development of an "oppositional identity" against school and education.

ACKNOWLEDGMENTS

The authors thank Dawn Whitherspoon, Ph.D., Megan Golonka, Andrea Malone, Claudia Ruiz, and Yeney Hernandez for their assistance with conducting the focus groups and transcribing the discussions. Portions of the research findings presented in this chapter were funded by an NICHD grant (1R03HD050297-02). Correspondence should be directed to Nancy E. Hill at nancy@duke.edu.

REFERENCES

Auerbach, S. (2006). "If the student is good, let him fly": Moral support for college among Latino immigrant parents. *Journal of Latinos and Education, 5*(4), 275–292.

Baker, D. P., & Stevenson, D. L. (1986). Mothers' strategies for children's school achievement: Managing the transition to high school. *Sociology of Education, 59*(3), 156–166.

Balli, S. J., Wedman, J. F., & Demo, D. H. (1997). Family involvement with middle-grades homework: Effects of differential prompting. *Journal of Experimental Education, 66*(1), 31–48.

Bandura, A., Barbaranelli, C., Caprara, G. V., & Pastorelli, C. (1996). Multifaceted impact of self-efficacy beliefs on academic functioning. *Child Development, 67*(3), 1206–1222.

Barber, B. K., & Olsen, J. A. (2004). Assessing the transitions to middle and high school. *Journal of Adolescent Research, 19*(1), 3–30.

Boykin, A. W., Tyler, K. M., Watkins-Lewis, K., & Kizzie, K. (2006). Culture in the sanctioned classroom practices of elementary school teachers serving low-income African American students. *Journal of Education for Students Placed at Risk, 11*(2), 161–173.

Bronstein, P., Ginsburg, G. S., & Herrera, I. S. (2005). Parental predictors of motivational orientation in early adolescence: A longitudinal study. *Journal of Youth and Adolescence, 34*(6), 559–575.

Catsambis, S. (2001). Expanding knowledge of parental involvement in children's secondary education: Connections with high school seniors' academic success. *Social Psychology of Education, 5*(2), 149–177.

Cooper, H. (1989). *Homework*. New York: Longman.

Cooper, H. (2007). *The battle over homework: Common ground for administrators, teachers, and parents.* Thousand Oaks, CA: Corwin.

Correa, V. I., & Tulbert, B. (1993). Collaboration between school personnel in special education and Hispanic families. *Journal of Educational & Psychological Consultation, 4*(3), 253–265.

Cross, W. E. (2003). Tracing the historical origins of youth delinquency & violence: Myths & realities about black culture. *Journal of Social Issues, 59*(1), 67–82.

Dika, S. L., & Singh, K. (2002). Applications of social capital in educational literature: A critical synthesis. *Review of Educational Research, 72*(1), 31–60.

Driessen, G., Smit, F., & Sleegers, P. (2005). Parental involvement and educational achievement. *British Educational Research Journal, 31*(4), 509–532.

Eccles, J. S., & Harold, R. D. (1996). Family involvement in children's and adolescents' schooling. In A. Booth & J. F. Dunn (Eds.), *Family–school links: How do they affect educational outcomes?* (pp. 3–34). Mahwah, NJ: Erlbaum.

Fan, X., & Chen, M. (2001). Parental involvement and students' academic achievement: A meta-analysis. *Educational Psychology Review, 13*(1), 1–22.

Ferguson, R. F. (1998). Teachers' perceptions and expectations and the black–white test score gap. In C. Jencks & M. Phillips (Eds.), *The black–white test score gap* (pp. 273–317). Washington, DC: Brookings Institution Press.

Goodnow, J. J. (2002). Parents' knowledge and expectations: Using what we know. In M. H. Bornstein (Ed.), *Handbook of parenting: Vol. 3. Being and becoming a parent* (2nd ed., pp. 439–460). Mahwah, NJ: Erlbaum.

Greico, E. M., & Cassidy, R. C. (2001). *Overview of race and Hispanic origin* (Census brief). Retrieved July, 2008, from www.census.gov/prod/2001pubs/czkbr01-1.pdf

Gutman, L. M., & Midgley, C. (2000). The role of protective factors in supporting the academic achievement of poor African American students during the middle school transition. *Journal of Youth and Adolescence, 29*(2), 223–248.

Hidalgo, N. M., Pedraza, P., & Rivera, M. (2005). Latino/a families' epistemology. In P. Pedraza & M. Rivera (Eds.), *Latino education: An agenda for community action research* (pp. 375–402). Mahwah, NJ: Erlbaum.

Hill, N. E. (in press). Culturally-based world views, family processes, and family school interactions. In S. L. Christenson & A. Reschly (Eds.), *The handbook on school–family partnerships for promoting student competence.* New York: Routledge.

Hill, N. E., Castellino, D. R., Lansford, J. E., Nowlin, P., Dodge, K. A., Bates, J. E., & Pettit, G. (2004). Parent academic involvement as related to school behavior, achievement, and aspirations: Demographic variations across adolescence. *Child Development, 75*(5), 1491–1509.

Hill, N. E., & Craft, S. A. (2003). Parent–school involvement and school performance: Mediated pathways among socioeconomically comparable African American and Euro-American families. *Journal of Educational Psychology, 95*(1), 74–83.

Hill, N. E., Murry, V. M., & Anderson, V. D. (2005). Sociocultural contexts of African American families. In V. C. McLoyd, N. E. Hill, & K. A. Dodge (Eds.), *African American family life: Ecological and cultural diversity* (pp. 21–44). New York: Guilford Press.

Hill, N. E., & Taylor, L. C. (2004). Parental school involvement and children's academic achievement: Pragmatics and issues. *Current Directions in Psychological Science, 13*(4), 161–164.

Hill, N. E., & Torres, K. (in press). Negotiating the American dream: The paradox of Latino students' goals and achievement and engagement between families and schools. *Journal of Social Issues.*

Hill, N. E., & Tyson, D. F. (2009). Parental involvement in middle school: A meta-analytic assessment of strategies that promote achievement. *Developmental Psychology, 45*(3), 740–763.

Hill, N. E., Tyson, D. F., Bromell, L., & Flint, R. C. (2008, March). *Translating parental goals into action: A multi-ethnic, qualitative study of parental involvement in middle school.* Paper presented at the biennial meeting of the Society for Research on Adolescence, Chicago.

Hill, S. A., & Sprague, J. (1999). Parenting in black and white families. *Gender and Society, 13*(4), 480–502.

Hughes, D., & DuMont, K. (1993). Using focus groups to facilitate culturally anchored research. *American Journal of Community Psychology, 21*(6), 775–806.

Hughes, D., Rodriguez, J., Smith, E. P., Johnson, D. J., Stevenson, H. C., & Spicer, P. (2006). Parents' ethnic-racial socialization practices: A review of the research and directions for future study. *Developmental Psychology, 42*(5), 747–770.

Jones, T. G. (2003). Contribution of Hispanic parents' perspectives to teacher preparation. *School Community Journal, 13*(2), 73–97.

Lareau, A. (1987). Social class differences in family–school relationships: The importance of cultural capital. *Sociology of Education, 60*(2), 73–85.

Lareau, A., & Horvat, E. M. (1999). Moments of social inclusion and exclusion: Race, class, and cultural capital in family–school relationships. *Sociology of Education, 72*(1), 37–53.

Linney, J. A., & Seidman, E. (1989). The future of schooling. *American Psychologist, 44*(2), 336–440.

Lynch, E. W., & Stein, R. C. (1987). Parent participation by ethnicity: A comparison of Hispanic, black, and Anglo families. *Exceptional Children, 54*(2), 105–111.

Mitchell, H. H. (1975). *Black belief: Folk beliefs in America and West Africa.* New York: Harper & Row.

Ogbu, J. U. (1978). *Minority education and caste: The American system in cross-cultural perspective.* New York: Academic Press.

Pollock, M. (2004). *Colormute.* Princeton, NJ: Princeton University.

Reese, L. (2002). Parental strategies in contrasting cultural settings: Families in Mexico and "El Norte." *Anthropology and Education Quarterly, 33*(1), 30–59.

Reynolds, A. J., & Gill, G. S. (1994). The role of parental perspectives in the school adjustment of inner-city black children. *Journal of Youth and Adolescence, 23*(6), 671–695.

Rodríguez, J. L. (2002). Family support for academic achievement among three generations of Mexican American high school students. *Applied Developmental Science, 6*(2), 88–94.

Sankofa, B. M., Hurley, E. A., Allen, B. A., & Boykin, A. W. (2005). Cultural expression and black students' attitudes toward high achievers. *The Journal of Psychology, 139*(3), 247–259.

Sigel, I. E., & McGillicuddy-DeLisi, A. V. (2002). Parent beliefs are cognitions: The dynamic belief systems model. In M. H. Bornstein (Ed.), *Handbook of parenting: Vol. 3. Being and becoming a parent* (2nd ed., pp. 485–508). Mahwah, NJ: Erlbaum.

Stanton-Salazar, R. D., & Dornbusch, S. M. (1995). Social capital and the reproduction of inequality: Information networks among Mexican-origin high school students. *Sociology of Education, 68*(2), 116–135.

Stevenson, H. C., Davis, G., & Abdul-Kabir, S. (2001). *Stickin' to, watchin' over, and gettin' with: An African American parent's guide to discipline.* San Francisco: Jossey-Bass.

Tenenbaum, H. R., & Ruck, M. D. (2007). Are teachers' expectations different for racial minority than for European American students? A meta-analysis. *Journal of Educational Psychology, 99*(2), 253–273.

Tyler, K. M., Boykin, A. W., Miller, O., & Hurley, E. A. (2006). Cultural values in the home and school experiences of low-income African American students. *Social Psychology of Education, 9*(4), 363–380.

U.S. Census Bureau. (2006). American community survey. Retrieved January 9, 2009, from http://www.census.gov/population/www/socdemo/hispanic/hispanic_pop_presentation.html

Vogt, D. S., King, D. W., & King, L. A. (2004). Focus groups in psychological assessment: Enhancing content validity by consulting members of target population. *Psychological Assessment, 16*(3), 231–243.

Wolf, R. M. (1979). Achievement in the United States. In H. J. Walberg (Ed.), *Educational environments and effects* (pp. 313–330). Berkeley, CA: McCutchan.

Yan, W., & Lin, Q. (2005). Parent involvement and mathematics achievement: Contrast across racial and ethnic groups. *Journal of Educational Research, 99*(2), 116–127.

4

Rethinking the Role of Parenting

Promoting Adolescent Academic Success and Emotional Well-Being

NATHAN JONES
BARBARA SCHNEIDER

A DOLESCENTS' STRATEGIES FOR OBTAINING educational advantages in high school are well defined: attend school regularly, perform well on tests, and receive good grades. The actions or behaviors parents should follow to provide educational advantages for their adolescents are less certain. Parental involvement in school-based activities is the primary strategy by which adults seek educational advantages for younger children, but many parents are unclear about the roles they should have in their adolescents' education. Parents often struggle to strike a balance between fostering independence and placing high academic demands and social responsibilities on their teenagers. New analyses of data from a study of 500 families in eight communities across the United States suggest that an alternative way of conceptualizing parental involvement in adolescents' lives may help to promote the academic success—and emotional well-being—of teenagers, in and outside of the classroom.

PARENTS AND SCHOOLS—
TRADITIONAL VIEWS OF PARENTAL INVOLVEMENT

Conventional measures of parental involvement for improving children's academic success primarily emphasize parents' interactions with schools (e.g., Baker & Stevenson, 1986; Eccles & Harold, 1993, 1996; Epstein &

Becker, 1982; Epstein & Dauber, 1991; Feuerstein, 2000; Hoover-Dempsey & Sandler, 1997; Hoover-Dempsey et al., 2005; Jeynes, 2005; Lee & Bowen, 2006). The goal of much of this research was to tease out specific parent practices that have a positive influence on student outcomes. For the parents of young children and children in middle school, a number of parental strategies (including participating in decisionmaking at school, having an active relationship with their children's teachers, and regularly participating in volunteer school events) are positively associated with student achievement (Baker & Stevenson, 1986; Eccles & Harold, 1993; Fan & Chen, 2001; Hill & Craft, 2003; Hoover-Dempsey & Sandler, 1997; Jeynes, 2005). Parental involvement also is linked to other forms of academic success, including positive attitudes about school, improved homework habits, reduced absenteeism, and lower dropout rates (Astone & McLanahan, 1991; Baker & Stevenson, 1986; Epstein, 1987; Miedal & Reynolds, 1999). In addition, there is some evidence that parental involvement may influence other subjective measures of student well-being that are likely to support academic achievement, such as children's sense of self-concept, self-regulation, and control over schooling outcomes (Fantuzzo, Davis, & Ginsburg, 1995; Grolnick, Ryan, & Deci, 1991; Grolnick & Slowiaczek, 1994).

Although there are clear and defined ways for parents of young children to participate in school-based activities, there are considerably fewer opportunities for parents of adolescents. Some school-based parental involvement activities for adolescents have been shown to be related to student achievement and college plans, including discussions about high school courses, college choices, and financial planning (Hill, 2008). Generally, however, school-based activities open to parents occur infrequently (e.g., occasional events such as back-to-school nights). Those that occur more regularly (such as sporting events or music recitals) are often less directly related to academic outcomes. It is perhaps not surprising, then, that the relevance and relationship of parental involvement in school to adolescents' educational expectations, grades, and well-being have been less explored.

Traditional measures of parental involvement in school seem particularly inappropriate when conceptualizing the role of the family in teenagers' schooling careers. For example, when teachers contact adolescents' parents, it is often to resolve issues related to misbehavior, tardiness, cutting classes, or poor grades. High school teachers sometimes instruct their students to rely on school resources rather than their parents for help with their homework. Such strategies can promote adolescent independence but perhaps at some cost, for example, introducing doubts about parents' substantive knowledge of school assignments, especially in subjects such as calculus, biology, or computer technology.

On balance, then, it seems desirable for both parents and researchers to reconceptualize parental involvement to promote academic success. In each case it seems beneficial to focus less directly on parental involvement in school, and more closely on the quality of interactions families have with their teenagers, including the time they spend together, the types of discussions they have about the future, the central messages parents communicate to their teenagers regarding the aspirations and educational expectations they have for them, and the characteristics of parental involvement with their adolescents at home. These activities are the focus of our research.

CHARACTERISTICS OF PARENTAL INVOLVEMENT IN THE HOME

Researchers who have studied the influence of the home environment on adolescents' school performance have examined aspects of the family experience, as well as adolescents' perceptions of this experience (Hektner & Asakawa, 2000). A common thread in these investigations is that family context plays a central role in school outcomes. Parents make choices about the types of activities they support at home, and many of these decisions relate both directly and indirectly to their adolescents' education. As Coleman (1988) articulated in his theory of social capital, such choices provide a means of conveying norms, standards, and expectations. In the family, social capital typically is seen as the quality of relationships that parents have with their children (Schneider & Coleman, 1993). We expand on Coleman's conceptualization by introducing other direct behavior mechanisms that parents employ to build social capital, such as boundary setting and monitoring of adolescent behaviors.

One element missing from Coleman's treatment of parent–child interactions is how social relationships beyond behaviors and expectations affect subjective well-being, specifically related to emotionality. In the psychological literature, research on parent–adolescent emotional interactions suggests that love and discipline are among the traditionally conceptualized parenting practices critical to an adolescent's social and academic development (Damon, 1983; Maccoby & Martin, 1983). Also pertinent is psychology's extensive consideration of parenting styles (see, e.g., Bornstein, 2002) and their relationships to discipline and emotional well-being.

In her classic work on parenting styles, Baumrind (1966, 1991) suggested that *authoritarian* parents—those who attempt to shape and control the attitudes and behaviors of their children by restricting their autonomy— are likely to promote in their adolescents lower levels of individualism, social consciousness, and autonomy. Alternatively, adolescents with *authoritative* parents (who try to strike a balance between being demanding and responsive) are likely to exhibit higher levels of these behaviors and a higher sense of well-being than those with authoritarian parents. Baumrind found that adolescents with authoritarian parents are more likely to have problem behaviors and perform poorly on verbal and math tests; adolescents with authoritative parents are more likely to achieve academically and exhibit psychosocial competence. These findings have been replicated in recent research by Aunola, Stattin, and Nurmi (2000); Glasgow, Dornbusch, Troyer, Steinberg, and Ritter (1997); and Steinberg (1996).

The issue of balance, particularly as it relates to support and challenge (which share similar characteristics to the ideas of responsiveness and demandingness) has been examined by Hauser (1991), who found that supportive (affective enabling) and challenging (cognitive enabling) "moves" in family conversations are related to better adolescent ego development. What these moves in conversation suggest is that through their choice of parenting practices, adults can provide particular expressions of challenge and emotional support to their children.

Exploring concepts of support and challenge beyond conversation, Rathunde, Carroll, and Huang (2000) show that parents whom adolescents describe as challenging express high expectations for them, encourage them to take on academic responsibilities, reinforce standards (e.g., always try to do one's best), manage time wisely, and assess their strengths. Teenagers whose parents engage with them in this way have higher grades and self-esteem than adolescents who report their parents doing less of these things. Rathunde and colleagues (2000) found that most adolescents feel their families are supportive. Adolescents who report high levels of support in their families indicate that their parents love and accept them, and describe their families as cooperative and willing to help one another. What is less likely is a balance between challenge and support. Adolescents in families where there is such a balance are more likely to plan strategically for their futures, achieve their goals, and feel good about themselves.

Schneider and Stevenson (1999) also looked at support and challenge, issues of time families spend together, and the frequency and content of communication regarding school and future plans. They found that adolescents with clear plans for their futures spend a significant amount of time with their parents discussing actions and strategies that can best help them achieve their educational and occupational goals. They do so in an environment that is also loving, caring, and supportive.

Our research suggests that there is value in considering not only the qualities of support, challenge, and monitoring, but also the actual time that parents spend with their teenagers in relation to ambition and well-being. Specifically, we reconceptualize parental involvement to encompass four qualities of parent–adolescent interactions in the home that affect academic achievement and emotional well-being: (1) the amount of time parents spend with their adolescents; (2) participation in shared activities; (3) strategic actions taken by parents (e.g., promoting self-regulation, time management, and autonomy of decisionmaking); and (4) parents' boundary-setting activities (e.g., presence of rules and educational supervisory activities enacted at home). Understanding these characteristics of the parent–adolescent relationship, we argue, provides a picture of adolescents' educational experiences within the home and the consequences they may have for students' future schooling careers.

Family Time

Quality family time occurs when parents and adolescents communicate with one another, discuss future goals, and reinforce values (Schneider & Stevenson, 1999; Schneider & Waite, 2005; Snyder, 2007). The adolescent literature suggests that teenagers are actively seeking an independent identity for themselves, sometimes placing them in conflict with their parents. Recent research shows, however, that most adolescents feel their parents are loving and accepting. What adolescents perceive as troubling are situations in which their parents do not intervene and offer assistance. Teenagers express a desire to interact with their parents and frequently talk about turning to them for advice on a number of issues. Unfortunately, today most parents work and adolescents spend large amounts of time alone, at a workplace, or with peers. Time spent as a family is seriously compromised not because adolescents do not want to spend time with their parents, but because the demands of parent work often collide with and overpower the needs of children (Schneider & Waite, 2005).

Parent–Adolescent Activities

Reading to children and engaging in school-related activities (such as visiting the library or museums) have been shown to improve young children's academic performance (Crosnoe & Trinitapoli, 2008; Kurdek & Sinclair, 1988; Sénéchal & LeFevre, 2002). Crosnoe and Trinitapoli (2008) found, for example, that "young people who spent more time with their parents in activities outside the home (e.g., recreational, cultural activities) when aged 7–9 showed more growth in math achievement up until they were aged 12–14 than their peers whose shared time with parents occurred in the home" (p. 44). They suggest that shared activities have developmental significance for young children, providing opportunities for parents to bond with them, develop specific skills and tasks, and expose them to novel experiences. Less explored is whether adolescents would see a similar developmental benefit to engaging in shared activities with their parents. We suspect the answer would be yes and that the primary benefits of such shared activities would be positive influences on adolescents' emotional well-being, although such activities likely hold promise for their school performance as well.

Research shows that when parents and children are together, even activities like family chores are not perceived as burdensome (Lee, 2005; Lee, Schneider, & Waite, 2003). Participating in household work may give adolescents the opportunity to develop a sense of responsibility and may enhance feelings of personal competence and self-esteem—as long as adolescents are engaged in activities that provide them with feelings of control, autonomy, and creativity (Csikszentmihalyi & Schneider, 2000; Goodnow, 1988; Rathunde, 2001). However, time spent on chores has been shown to have either no association (Hofferth & Sandberg, 2001) or a negative association (Elder & Conger, 2000) with adolescent academic achievement, suggesting that in cases where adolescents commit a significant portion of their time to doing housework, they may have less time for schoolwork. Thus, how parents structure teenagers' housework, both in terms of the amount and nature of this work, appears to have consequences for their academic and social development.

Strategizing

Parents often join their adolescents in strategizing on both academic and nonacademic plans for the future. For example, parents often discuss with their adolescents strategies for becoming self-regulated in their actions, which in turn promotes teenagers' abilities to make family, financial, and occupational plans that satisfy long-term goals (Schneider & Owens, 2005). Adolescents who are capable of self-regulation do not rely entirely on parents or others to achieve their goals, but instead develop a sense of agency whereby they can weigh alternatives and select options that are more closely aligned with their interests. Having chosen a flexible course of action, these adolescents are in a position to monitor and evaluate their actions to determine whether they are moving toward their goals.

Parents also can teach their adolescents strategies for making decisions semi-autonomously, by both modeling the practice of weighing options and engaging in conversations related to the positives and negatives associated with different choices (Hektner & Asakawa, 2000).

While families vary in the degree to which adolescents are given decisionmaking responsibility—and parents need to encourage adolescents to investigate different options before taking action—adolescents develop important skills through joint decisionmaking, whether related to school (e.g., what courses to take, what extracurricular activities to become involved in) or other activities (such as summer jobs, social outings, and dating).

Finally, parents strategize with their adolescents regarding how they spend their nonschool time. In the afternoon and evening, are teenagers and their parents strategic about choosing activities that are purposeful, such as school and homework activities? Or, do adolescents participate in activities that are nonproductive and do not promote positive development? Schneider (forthcoming) found that when engaged in activities perceived as relating to neither work nor play, young people were less likely to feel productive or happy. In addition, they felt less sociable, proud, and challenged, and the activities in which they were engaged were perceived as meaningless to them. When parents and adolescents approach time management strategically, it directly impacts adolescents' emotional well-being and has consequences for their ability to excel academically.

Boundary Setting

In addition to strategizing with their teenagers on ways to organize their lives, parents engage in a variety of practices that set boundaries for their adolescents. The purpose of these actions is not simply to control adolescent behavior, but to instill in their teenagers patterns that promote academic success and prepare them for adulthood. Patterson and Stouthamer-Loeber (1984) describe parents who engage in high levels of monitoring as having an awareness of their adolescents' companions and knowing where their adolescents are and what they are doing most of the time. Related to their teenagers' education, parents monitor whether they have completed their homework, regularly attend classes, and are fully committed to their education. In monitoring their adolescents' actions, parents often implement systems of incentives and sanctions, rewarding students for high grades and completing school assignments, while punishing students for performing poorly in school or for placing social priorities ahead of schoolwork. In creating such a system, parents express to their children their own values and norms, encouraging adolescents to develop priorities in line with parental expectations.

In monitoring their adolescents' behavior through sanctions and rewards, parents establish boundaries for their teenagers by structuring (as opposed to strategizing) how nonschool time is used. Increasingly, parents are filling their children's nonschool time with multiple activities; it is not unlikely that in a given week teenagers will work at a paid job and attend sports practices, religious services, and other structured activities scheduled by their parents. Parents often proactively manage the degree to which their adolescents are engaged or idle, with the belief that participation in structured activities promotes positive development, while spending time alone or in purposeless activities does not. Thus it is important to consider parents' boundary-setting behaviors— including sanctions/rewards and time management—in conceptualizing parental involvement that supports adolescent academic success and emotional well-being.

EXAMINING PARENT–ADOLESCENT RELATIONSHIPS

To investigate the correlation of each of these aspects of parent–adolescent relationships (family time, parent–adolescent activities, strategizing, and boundary setting) with teenagers' schooling outcomes (including grades), academic expectations, and emotional well-being, we employ data from the 500 Family Study of 500 middle-class, dual-earner families in eight communities across the United States.[1] Using a variety of methods, including interviews and surveys with parents and their adolescents, the 500 Family Study examines the complex dynamics of today's families and the strategies they use in coping with the demands of work and home life.[2] Many of the survey items have been used in other national studies, making it possible to compare the 500 families' responses with other populations. The 500 Family Study is well suited to an analysis of the relationship between parent actions and student outcomes because it allows the researcher to examine dimensions of work and family life from the perspectives of both parents and children.[3]

Our analysis draws on data from surveys of adolescents and their parents. The parent survey asked how frequently parents engaged in various activities with their adolescents, both in and out of the home, and included items related to conversations between parents and adolescents on time use, educational and career plans, and rules and decisionmaking. Parents also were asked how frequently they monitored their teenagers' activities, how they structured nonschool time, and the degree to which they allowed adolescents to make decisions on their own. The adolescent survey focused on many of the same issues, including family relationships and experiences, school experiences, psychological well-being, and schooling and career plans for the future.

Drawing on items from the parent survey, we considered four composite characteristics of parent behavior and attitudes: proportion of time spent with family, parent–adolescent activities, parent strategizing, and parent boundary setting. In defining the adolescent outcomes associated with parental involvement, we broadened our focus beyond academic achievement to incorporate measures of educational expectations and emotional well-being. A description of the variables and survey questions is provided in the appendix to this chapter.

In addition to completing surveys, parents and their children also participated in the experience sampling method (ESM), a unique approach for examining how individuals spend their time, whom they spend their time with, and what activities they are engaged in over the course of a typical week (Csikszentmihalyi & Larson, 1984; Prescott, Csikszentmihalyi, & Graef, 1981). Developed by Mihaly Csikszentmihalyi and his colleagues, the ESM is a week-long collection activity, in which participants respond to a signaling device (e.g., a pager or watch) preprogrammed to beep eight times each day, generating measures and data that previous research has shown to be reliable and valid compared with data collected through other methods (Csikszentmihalyi & Larson, 1987; Mulligan, Schneider, & Wolfe, 2000).

An additional advantage of the 500 Family Study is its focus on middle- and upper-middle class, dual-earner families, a population that often is underrepresented in studies of parental involvement (Schneider & Waite, 2005). Both the fathers and the mothers in the sample are more highly educated than the general population, with 70% of fathers and 55% of mothers holding master's degrees. Many of the parents in this sample are goal-directed, and we can anticipate that they hold these same expectations for their children. Even though the parents in this sample place a high value on education, their work demands limit the time they have available for their children. With their available family time curtailed, we suspect these parents would be particularly strategic in making the most of this time, engaging in a variety of behaviors that are likely to influence their adolescents' academic futures. The following section provides a summary of the findings from the 500-family study.

THE ASSOCIATION OF
PARENTING STRATEGIES AND STUDENT OUTCOMES

To estimate the association between parent actions and adolescent academic performance and well-being, we developed three models. Parent activities (including the amount of time that parents spend with their children, the frequency of shared experiences between parents and children, the degree to which parents set boundaries for their children, and the amount of strategizing parents do with their children) were examined to determine their association with adolescents' academic expectations, grades, and emotional well-being. With the exception of the measure of parent time spent with children, the parent-related measures of interest (parent–adolescent activities, strategizing, and boundary setting) were categorized in four groups to distinguish parents who often engaged in these activities from those who did so less often. Grouping parents in this manner allowed us to focus our analyses on those parents who strategized the least with their children or set boundaries most often. For each relationship of interest, individual models were estimated for mothers and fathers in order to determine whether differential patterns emerged between parents.[4]

We also considered the potential impacts of adolescent behavioral problems and perceived pressure from parents, as both are conventionally assumed to predict academic achievement and emotional well-being. For example, a teenager with multiple behavioral problems or a negative self-image is more likely to struggle in school than one who does not have these characteristics. Similarly, we also accounted for parental depressive symptoms, which we suspected would mediate the influence of parental actions on adolescent outcomes. If the four parental behaviors of interest were found to be positively significantly related to academic performance and well-being, even taking into account these adolescent- and parent-level differences, then we could have more confidence that parent activities at home are more likely to be associated with specific adolescent outcomes.

Academic Expectations

To investigate the relationships among our family variables and adolescent expectations, our first model tested the impact of the four parenting behaviors on academic expectations. We found a significant effect for strategizing for mothers who engaged in these behaviors frequently but not all the time. There was not a significant effect for fathers.

Related to participating in shared activities with adolescents, we saw that for the category of fathers who exhibited the second highest levels of shared activities, such participation was associated with higher educational expectations. For mothers and fathers, we did not find a significant effect for boundary setting or proportion of time spent discussing college expectations.[5] In none of these analyses could we see a relationship between adolescent problems or parental depressive symptoms and academic expectations.

Adolescent Grades

A second model was developed to explore the impact of parental actions on adolescents' grades. We found that adolescents whose mothers most frequently set boundaries for them were likely to have lower grades than adolescents whose mothers set the fewest boundaries. Specifically, teenagers whose mothers set high levels of boundaries for them were only about a fifth as likely to have high grades as those whose mothers set the fewest boundaries. In contrast, our findings indicate that when mothers chose to participate in some shared activities with their adolescents, their children were likely to have higher grades. For mothers and fathers, neither strategizing nor spending higher proportions of time with their adolescents had a significant impact on grades. As would be expected, there was a significant relationship between adolescent problems and grades; however, including parents' depressive symptoms did not change the results.

Emotional Well-Being

A third model explored the relationship between parent behaviors and adolescents' emotional well-being. Our results revealed that for mothers, only when they set the highest levels of boundaries did it have an adverse effect on their adolescents; the estimated effect was strong. The amount of strategizing that parents engaged in with their adolescents did not seem to influence emotional well-being. Similarly, there was not an effect for mothers or fathers who participated in activities with their adolescents. As for the proportion of time that parents spent with their adolescents, we saw no effects on emotional well-being for mothers or for fathers. For each of the parent behaviors, we saw a negative effect of adolescent problems and parent depressive symptoms on emotional well-being.

CONCLUSIONS AND POLICY IMPLICATIONS

When children are young, parental involvement in school-based activities is a logical and often successful strategy for promoting the educational attainment assumed necessary to meet parents' typically high ambitions and expectations for their offspring. As children mature, limiting conceptions of parental involvement to such school-based interactions risks underestimating the roles parents can play in equipping their adolescents with the ability to strategize and make educational decisions that are compatible with both their own and their adolescents' interests, expectations, and well-being. Reconceptualizing parental involvement in adolescence to incorporate relationships at home brings together multiple qualities of parent–adolescent interactions, including the qualities of strategizing, monitoring, and participating in shared time and activities. Based on our findings, it does not appear that the proportion of time parents spend with their children is related to academic and emotional outcomes. This has consequences for families in which the time parents can spend with their children is limited by their work. In such cases, parents can still take actions that support positive development in their teenagers. For example, when mothers engage in shared activities with their children (going to a museum, church, or a sporting event), there is a positive relationship with students' grades. Just as shared activities promote cognitive development and well-bring in young children, it appears that the same may be true for adolescents. If mothers take time to strategize with their teenagers about future schooling, career, and life opportunities, this, too, can lead to higher academic expectations. These findings are consistent with much of the work done on the impact of parenting on adolescent ambitions. Of course, it is also possible that strategic behaviors by parents may be reflected in the behaviors of adolescents; as parents strategize, so too do their children, and the two processes reinforce each other.

Even in the case of parents who are actively involved in the education of their children, strictly adhering to rules and regulations is not likely to promote positive outcomes. Instead, when parents regulate how their adolescents spend time and what activities they engage in, there are negative consequences for academic performance and emotional well-being. Given the age and developmental cycle of most adolescents, it would seem that teenagers need opportunities to exercise some degree of agency with respect to their future plans (Lerner & Steinberg, 2004). Our findings complement the work of Lareau (2003), which emphasizes how the differences in lower- and middle-class parenting strategies (with middle-class parents focusing on strategizing more than rule setting) are related to differences in educational outcomes. Our findings support this body of research, suggesting that by focusing on boundaries, parents may be less likely to engage in tasks that could be beneficial to their children's education, including strategizing and participating in activities with them.

As children grow older, the time they spend with their parents lessens, and the influence of their peers increases. Although adolescence is not necessarily the "storm and stress" that some have described, it is a period of some conflict during which teenagers are vulnerable as they develop their identities. Our analyses of the 500 Family Study data suggest that the ways in which mothers interact with their adolescents, when they do have time, can be critical for teenagers in their preparation for adulthood. Interaction helps teenagers develop skills and abilities that will benefit their education and also strengthens their family relationships, providing a source of social capital that the adolescents can draw upon in planning for the future. Prior research has shown how the strength of these familial ties leads to increased academic performance (Coleman & Hoffer, 1987; Stevenson & Baker, 1987). Both through active discussions on the subject of schooling and through time shared participating in mutually enjoyable activities, parents can play an active role in the development of their adolescents into adulthood.

Related to fathers, our results should be interpreted with caution because of random nonresponse. The overall message from these data is that fathers do not have the same positive impact as mothers on their adolescents' academic and emotional development. While this may be the case for our sample, it is likely that we have not sufficiently captured the actions that fathers can take to promote positive academic outcomes in their teenage children. At the very least, these findings suggest that our models provide more accurate estimates of beneficial actions of mothers than of fathers. Future studies should investigate further the ways in which fathers can influence the development of their adolescents.

For policymakers, we suggest that the goals of parental involvement programs should vary by level of schooling, taking into account the developmental differences between young children and adolescents, as well as the changes in the parent–child relationship as teenagers enter high school. Our results, like those of Lareau (2003) and others, indicate that many of the things that parents do to advantage their adolescents occur outside of schools. Middle- and upper-middle class parents are active in building social supports for their adolescents—by spending time with their children, engaging in shared activities, and actively strategizing about their futures—and these can be valuable experiences that may lead to distinct advantages in and outside of school (Lareau, 2003). Consequently, parental involvement programs at the high school level are more likely to be successful if they promote similar kinds of attitudes and behaviors for parents of adolescents from less advantaged backgrounds. Schools potentially can accomplish this goal when parents are unable to, by focusing on helping adolescents self-regulate their behaviors and supporting them in making schooling decisions and collaboratively strategizing for their futures.

APPENDIX: DESCRIPTIONS OF VARIABLES

Description

I. Dependent Variables	
Grades	Grades the student received on the last report card, as reported by parents, with scores ranging from 8 = mostly As to 1 = mostly Ds.
Academic Expectations	Measured by the question: "How far do you think you will go in school?" where responses range from 1 = less than college graduation to 3 = more than college.
Emotional Well-being	Composite measure taken from five survey items asking if the children feel good about who they are, if they feel appreciated, if they feel that they are just as good as others, if they feel on top of things, and if they feel in control of their lives. For every adolescent, mean scores are determined across the variables, which range from 0 = rarely to 3 = often.
II. Independent Variables	
Child's Perception of Self	Composite measure taken from nine items in student survey: it is difficult to be myself; others notice when I am down; I feel appreciated for who I am; if I have a problem, I get help; I do things I like to do, w/o embarrassment; I am only noticed when there is a problem; no matter what, I know I will be loved; I have lots of friends; I am popular. Scores range from 0 = never to 3 = often.
Child's Behavioral Problems	Composite measure taken from 25 questions in the student survey, including questions related to drugs, crime, school problems, and sexual activities. Scores range from 0 = never to 3 = often.
Parent Time w/Child	Measure of the proportion of parents' time that is spent with their adolescents. Using time use data, the measure is calculated by dividing the number of responses by the parent when with child over the total number of responses by the parent.
Interactions	Composite measure taken from 14 questions in the parent survey related to how often the parent and teenager do activities together (talk about news and everyday events, prepare meals, do household chores, watch TV, eat, shop, do sports, listen to music, do crafts, volunteer, attend religious ceremonies, and have shared hobbies). Scores range from 1 = rarely/never to 4 = everyday/almost daily.
Strategizing	Composite measure taken from 16 questions in the parent survey asking how often parents engage in conversations with their teenagers around the following topics: free time, school, college plans, career plans. Scores range from 0 = never to 3 = often.

	Description
Boundary Setting	Composite measure taken from 10 questions in the parent survey, including: how often do you (or your spouse) check the teen's homework, call to check on the teen, ask teen to check in, limit TV/video games, limit time going out with friends. Scores range from 0 = never to 3 = often.

NOTES

1. The 500 Family Study is archived at the Inter-university Consortium for Political and Social Research and is publicly accessible at http://dx.doi.org/10.3886/ICPSR04549

2. For a full description of the multiple data collections used in this study, see Schneider and Waite (2005).

3. Of the 512 families who participated in the study, 157 had young children but no adolescents; these families were excluded from this analysis (Schneider & Waite, 2005).

4. Father data are missing for several of the parenting measures (e.g., 105 of 327 fathers did not answer the questions on boundary setting). Consequently, our discussion relies primarily on our findings associated with mothers.

5. The direction of the relationship between boundary setting and expectations was in most cases negative.

REFERENCES

Astone, N. M., & McLanahan, S. S. (1991). Family structure, parental practices and high school completion. *American Sociological Review, 56*(3), 309–320.

Aunola, K., Stattin, H., & Nurmi, J. (2000). Parenting styles and adolescents' achievement strategies. *Journal of Adolescence, 23*(2), 205–222.

Baker, D. P., & Stevenson, D. L. (1986). Mothers' strategies for children's school achievement: Managing the transition to high school. *Sociology of Education, 59*(3), 156–166.

Baumrind, D. (1966). Effects of authoritative parental control on child's behavior. *Child Development, 37*(4), 887–907.

Baumrind, D. (1991). The influences of parenting style on adolescent competence and substance use. *Journal of Early Adolescence, 11*(1), 56–95.

Bornstein, M. H. (Ed.). (2002). *Handbook of parenting: Vol. 4. Social conditions and applied parenting.* Mahwah, NJ: Erlbaum.

Coleman, J. (1988). Social capital in the creation of human capital. *American Journal of Sociology, 94*(S1), S95–S120.

Coleman, J. S., & Hoffer, T. (1987). *Public and private high schools: The impact of communities.* New York: Basic Books.

Crosnoe, R., & Trinitapoli, J. (2008). Shared family activities and the transition from childhood into adolescence. *Journal of Research on Adolescence, 18*(1), 23–48.

Csikszentmihalyi, M., & Larson, R. (1984). *Being adolescent: Conflict and growth in the teenager years*. New York: Basic Books.

Csikszentmihalyi, M., & Larson, R. (1987). Validity and reliability of the experience-sampling method. *Journal of Nervous and Mental Disease, 175*(9), 526–536.

Csikszentmihalyi, M., & Schneider, B. (Eds.). (2000). *Becoming adult: How teenagers prepare for the world of work*. New York: Basic Books.

Damon, W. (1983). *Social and personality development*. New York: Norton.

Eccles, J. S., & Harold, R. D. (1993). Parent–school involvement during the early adolescent years. *Teachers College Record, 94*(3), 568–587.

Eccles, J. S., & Harold, R. D. (1996). Family involvement in children's and adolescents' schooling. In A. Booth & J. F. Dunn (Eds.), *Family–school links: How do they affect educational outcomes?* (pp. 3–34). Mahwah, NJ: Erlbaum.

Elder, G. H., & Conger, R. D. (2000). *Children of the land: Adversity and success in rural America*. Chicago: University of Chicago Press.

Epstein, J. L. (1987). Toward a theory of family–school connections: Teacher practices and parent involvement. In K. Hurrelmann, F. X. Kaufmann, & F. Losel (Eds.), *Social intervention: Potential and constraints* (pp. 121–136). Berlin, NY: de Gruyter.

Epstein, J. L., & Becker, H. J. (1982). Teachers' reported practices of parent involvement: Problems and possibilities. *The Elementary School Journal, 83*(2), 103–113.

Epstein, J. L., & Dauber, S. L. (1991). School programs and teacher practices of parent involvement in inner-city elementary and middle schools. *The Elementary School Journal, 91*(3), 289–305.

Fan, X., & Chen, M. (2001). Parental involvement and students' academic achievement: A meta-analysis. *Educational Psychology Review, 13*(1), 1–22.

Fantuzzo, J. W., Davis, G. Y., & Ginsburg, M. D. (1995). Effects of parent involvement in isolation on student self-concept and mathematics achievement. *Journal of Educational Psychology, 87*(2), 272–281.

Feuerstein, A. (2000). School characteristics and parent involvement: Influences on participation in children's schools. *The Journal of Educational Research, 94*(1), 29–39.

Glasgow, K. L., Dornbusch, S. M., Troyer, L., Steinberg, L., & Ritter, P. L. (1997). Parenting styles, adolescents' attributions, and educational outcomes in nine heterogeneous high schools. *Child Development, 68*(3), 507–529.

Goodnow, J. J. (1988). Children's household work: Its nature and functions. *Psychological Bulletin, 103*(1), 5–26.

Grolnick, W. S., Ryan, R. M., & Deci, E. L. (1991). Inner resources for school achievement: Motivational mediators of children's perceptions of their parents. *Journal of Educational Psychology, 87*(4), 508–517.

Grolnick, W. S., & Slowiaczek, M. L. (1994). Parents' involvement in children's schooling: A multidimensional conceptualization and motivational model. *Child Development, 65*(1), 237–252.

Hauser, S. (1991). *Adolescents and their families*. New York: Free Press.

Hektner, J., & Asakawa, K. (2000). Learning to like challenges. In M. Csikszentmihalyi & B. Schneider (Eds.), *Becoming adult: How teenagers prepare for the world of work* (pp. 95–112). New York: Basic Books.

Hill, L. D. (2008). School strategies and the "college-linking" process: Reconsidering the effects of high schools on college enrollment. *Sociology of Education, 81*(1), 53–76.

Hill, N. E., & Craft, S. A. (2003). Parent–school involvement and school performance: Mediated pathways among socioeconomically comparable African American and Euro-American families. *Journal of Educational Psychology, 95*(1), 74–83.

Hofferth, S. L., & Sandberg, J. F. (2001). How American children use their time. *Journal of Marriage and the Family, 63*(2), 295–308.

Hoover-Dempsey, K. V., & Sandler, H. M. (1997). Why do parents become involved in their children's education? *Review of Educational Research, 67*(1), 3–42.

Hoover-Dempsey, K. V., Walker, J. M. T., Sandler, H. M., Whetsel, D., Green, C. L., Wilkins, A. S., & Clossen, K. E. (2005). Why do parents become involved? Research findings and implications. *The Elementary School Journal, 106*(2), 105–130.

Jeynes, W. H. (2005). A meta-analysis of the relation of parent involvement to urban elementary school student academic achievement. *Urban Education, 40*(3), 237–269.

Kurdek, L. A., & Sinclair, R. J. (1988). Relation of eighth graders' family structure, gender, and family environment with academic performance and school behavior. *Journal of Educational Psychology, 80*(1), 90–94.

Lareau, A. (2003). *Unequal childhoods: Class, race, and family life.* Berkeley: University of California Press.

Lee, J. S., & Bowen, N. K. (2006). Parent involvement, cultural capital, and the achievement gap among elementary school children. *American Educational Research Journal, 43*(2), 193–218.

Lee, Y. S. (2005). Measuring the gender gap in household labor: Accurately estimating wives' and husbands' contributions. In B. Schneider & L. J. Waite (Eds.), *Being together, working apart: Dual-career families and the work-life balance* (pp. 229–247). New York: Cambridge University Press.

Lee, Y. S., Schneider, B., & Waite, L. J. (2003). Children and housework: Some unanswered questions. *Sociological Studies of Children and Youth, 9,* 105–125.

Lerner, R. M., & Steinberg, L. (2004). The scientific study of adolescent development: Past, present, and future. In R. M. Lerner & L. Steinberg (Eds.), *Handbook of adolescent psychology* (2nd ed., pp. 1–12). Hoboken, NJ: Wiley.

Maccoby, E. E., & Martin, J. (1983). Socialization in the context of the family: Parent–child interaction. In P. H. Mussen (Series Ed.) & E. M. Hetherington (Vol. Ed.), *Handbook of child psychology: Vol. 4. Socialization, personality, and social development* (4th ed., pp. 1–101). New York: Wiley.

Miedal, W. T., & Reynolds, A. J. (1999). Parent involvement in early intervention for disadvantaged children: Does it matter? *Journal of School Psychology, 37*(4), 379–402.

Mulligan, C., Schneider, B., & Wolfe, R. (2000). *Time use and population representation in the Sloan Study of Adolescents* (NBER Technical Working Paper #265).

Patterson, G. R., & Stouthamer-Loeber, M. (1984). The correlation of family management practices and delinquency. *Child Development, 55*(4), 1299–1307.

Prescott, S., Csikszentmihalyi, M., & Graef, R. (1981). Environmental effects on cognitive and affective states: The experiential time sampling approach. *Social Behavior and Personality, 9*(1), 23–32.

Rathunde, K. (2001). Family context and the development of undivided interest: A longitudinal study of family support and challenge and adolescents' quality of experience. *Applied Developmental Science, 5*(3), 158–171.

Rathunde, K., Carroll, M. E., & Huang, M. P. (2000). Families and the forming of children's occupational future. In M. Csikszentmihalyi & B. Schneider (Eds.), *Becoming adult: How teenagers prepare for the world of work* (pp. 113–139). New York: Basic Books.

Schneider, B. (forthcoming). Challenges of transitioning into adulthood. In I. Schoon & R. Silbereisen (Eds.), *Transitions from school to work.* Cambridge: Cambridge University Press.

Schneider, B., & Coleman, J. S. (Eds.). (1993). *Parents, their children, and schools.* Boulder, CO: Westview Press.

Schneider, B., & Owens, A. (2005). Self-regulation and the transition to adulthood. *Academic Exchange Quarterly, 9*(4), 62–66.

Schneider, B., & Stevenson, D. (1999). *The ambitious generation: American teenagers motivated but directionless.* New Haven, CT: Yale University Press.

Schneider, B., & Waite, L. J. (Eds.). (2005). *Being together, working apart: Dual-career families and the work-life balance.* New York: Cambridge University Press.

Sénéchal, M., & LeFevre, J. (2002). Parental involvement in the development of children's reading skill: A five-year longitudinal study. *Child Development, 73*(2), 445–460.

Snyder, K. A. (2007). A vocabulary of motives: Understanding how parents define quality time. *Journal of Marriage and Family, 69*(2), 320–340.

Steinberg, L. (with Brown, B. B., & Dornbusch, S. M.) (1996). *Beyond the classroom: Why school reform has failed and what parents need to do.* New York: Simon & Schuster.

Stevenson, D. L., & Baker, D. P. (1987). The family–school relation and the child's school performance. *Child Development, 58*(5), 1348–1357.

5

Parents Still Matter

Parental Links to the Behaviors and
Future Outlook of High School Seniors

BELKIS SUAZO deCASTRO
SOPHIA CATSAMBIS

THE INFLUENCE OF PARENTS DURING adolescent development is not without controversy. Many educational practitioners, scholars, and even the public at large share the belief that parental involvement diminishes in both intensity and importance during adolescence. Some commentators even doubt whether parents can have any influence at all on their teens' behavior (Harris, 1998). Research, however, shows that parents remain a pivotal force for adolescents' academic success and life planning (Hossler & Stage, 1992; Schneider & Stevenson, 1999). In fact, adolescents may need parental guidance and support more than ever before, as postsecondary choices have grown and the transition from high school to adult life has become increasingly complex. Parental guidance and support are important for making a successful transition from high school to postsecondary education (Plank & Jordan, 2001; Schneider & Stevenson, 1999).

To date, few studies have considered an all-encompassing framework that captures the multitude of parenting activities geared toward the education of children at each stage of schooling. In this chapter we report findings from a study that used data from the National Educational Longitudinal Study (NELS-88) to investigate the types of parental practices that are associated with high school students' intrinsic motivation for schoolwork, educational plans, and expectations for their future. We examined the link between different parental involvement practices and the above-mentioned adolescent attitudes and behaviors. These attitudes and behaviors represent some of the major developmental tasks that high school students face (i.e., independent decisionmaking and planning for the future). Our findings revealed that parental practices that focused more on supporting and guiding adolescents' decisionmaking skills, and less on disciplining and controlling their behavior, were effective for high school students

More specifically, our study showed that high school seniors whose parents actively participated in school activities, sought information about postsecondary education, and encouraged their teens to take the necessary steps for college attendance were more likely than others to believe that they would be successful in life and to make plans for attending college. These students also were motivated to work hard in school and to avoid disciplinary and attendance problems. The links between parental activities and student attitudes and behaviors were observed for students of all backgrounds. Where racial/ethnic differences did emerge, they showed European American parents contacting the school more often than minority parents about problems pertaining to their sons' or daughters' school attendance. In addition, the parental involvement activities of European American parents were more closely linked to their high school seniors' chances of pursuing a postsecondary education than were the activities of minority parents.

PARENTAL INVOLVEMENT
AND STUDENT OUTCOMES DURING HIGH SCHOOL

Evidence on the effectiveness of parental involvement at the secondary level is often inconsistent across studies, or even across various parental practices within the same study. Some researchers report positive effects of parental involvement on student achievement (Astone & McLanahan, 1991; Keith et al., 1993; Lee, 1994; Stevenson & Baker, 1987; Sui-Chu & Willms, 1996), others report negative effects for some parental activities (Milne, Myers, Rosenthal, & Ginsburg, 1986; Muller, 1995), and yet others report no effects (Keith, 1991; Lee, 1994). Such inconsistencies have led some scholars to conclude that not all family practices are effective for adolescents' educational success (Epstein, 2001; Lareau, 2000; Muller, 1995, 1998). However, we propose that limited measures of parental activities may underestimate the potential contributions of parental involvement to adolescent development. Students at certain developmental stages may need different kinds of involvement from their parents (Muller, 1995).

Evidence from national data on the effectiveness of parental practices by student grade level and educational outcomes reveals some general patterns that exist in the United States regarding types of parental involvement in adolescents' high school education. When adolescents reach high school, many parents become less concerned with the daily supervision of their teens and more concerned with their high school learning opportunities and their future (Catsambis & Garland, 1997). The shift in parental focus coincides with the "psychological distancing" that occurs between parents and teens due to the biological, cognitive, and psychological changes that occur during puberty. The developmental changes that teens experience bring about a greater desire for autonomy and independence and a need to spend more time with friends and peers (see the introduction for a review of family relations during adolescent development).

The organization of high schools, by providing opportunities for decisionmaking and life planning, also socializes adolescents to exercise greater autonomy and independence. High schools allow students to make curricular and coursework choices, offer courses that will help students meet the financial and social responsibilities of their adult life, and employ counselors for career and college advisement. It is likely that successful high school students in the United States are those whose parents' practices promote and support them in making decisions and developing plans for the future (Steinberg, 1998).

Despite shifts in parenting practices from a "hierarchical authority" to a "discussion-based decisionmaking style" (see introduction) and changes in adolescents' attitudes and behaviors that promote decisionmaking and future planning, much of the literature on parental involvement focuses on hierarchical parenting practices and their effects on academic outcomes, such as middle school and high school test scores, high school completion, and high school coursework (Catsambis, 2001; Muller, 1995, 1998). Using national data, Muller (1998) found that family practices that positively influence students' test scores in middle school and through 10th grade lose their explanatory power by the time adolescents reach their senior year. A second study using the same data also found that parenting activities that are effective in earlier years, such as behavioral supervision, have little influence on high school seniors. Other indicators of parental involvement, however, such as parental expectations and encouragement, still influence high school seniors' test scores and, especially, course credits completed (Catsambis, 2001).

The positive influence of parental educational aspirations on adolescents' academic success is by far the most important and consistent finding across all studies. High parental aspirations for their adolescents positively influence students' achievement at all levels of education and promote high educational and occupational aspirations for adolescents (Astone & McLanahan, 1991; Catsambis, 2001; Hossler & Stage, 1992; Schneider & Stevenson, 1999; Singh et al., 1995). More recent research, however, indicates that although high parental aspirations and support encourage students to have high occupational ambitions, it does not help them construct a clear life plan that will allow them to realize these ambitions. In order for adolescents to successfully manage their transition from high school to college and beyond, parents need to take an active role in channeling adolescents' ambitions and helping them manage and organize their lives around educational and occupational goals (Schneider & Stevenson, 1999). Early and sustained communication between parents and adolescents facilitates students' development of realistic life plans and helps them take the necessary steps for college attendance (i.e., planning and taking college entrance exams, completing college applications, visiting postsecondary institutions, and obtaining information about financial aid) (Plank & Jordan, 2001).

PARENTAL INVOLVEMENT VARIATIONS BY RACE/ETHNICITY

Overall, the evidence regarding race/ethnic variations in the levels of parental involvement has produced inconsistent results. Some findings show Hispanic and African American parents to be more involved in their adolescents' education compared with European Americans once other factors are controlled (Keith et al., 1993; Sui-Chu & Willms, 1996), while others show no such differences (Hill et al., 2004). Research is equally mixed on the effectiveness of parental involvement across social groups. Adolescents with affluent and college-educated parents have higher levels of school outcomes than their disadvantaged peers partly because advantaged parents are able to draw from their experience about how schools operate and their networks of other well-educated parents to advocate for their teens and engage in parenting practices that complement schools' efforts (Lareau, 2000, 2003; Lareau & Horvat, 1999). While these resources generally are not available to poor and less well-educated parents, evidence shows that when disadvantaged parents learn how to navigate American schools and engage in parenting practices that support schools' learning activities, their adolescents also experience academic and social success (Nicolau & Ramos, 1990). Thus, differences in research findings may be explained by limitations in existing theory and research that have not adequately considered cultural variations in parenting practices or school and community barriers to effective parental involvement (Hidalgo, Siu, Bright, Swap, & Epstein, 1995; Hoover-Dempsey & Sandler, 1997; Lareau, 2000; Stanton-Salazar & Dornbusch, 1995).

Language differences, perceptions of parent and teacher roles, and experiences with schools are examples of social and cultural factors that may influence racial/ethnic variations in parenting practices. For example, some parents may not feel that their English skills are good enough to discuss with teachers the educational opportunities of their teens or other issues pertaining to school governance that promote adolescent development. Other parents may hold culture-specific expectations regarding parent–school relationships. For example, because the responsibilities of parents and teachers are sharply divided in Spanish-speaking countries, some Hispanic parents may defer decisions about learning and postsecondary guidance to teachers and school administrators because these officials are seen as the experts of the American education system (Nicolau & Ramos, 1990). Unfortunately, some teachers may misinterpret the deference of Hispanic parents as disinterest and an inability to help with their adolescents' education. Some parents also may have done poorly in school or experienced negative teacher interactions. As a result, uneasiness with their own educational experience, and lack of understanding of how school structures and channels of communication operate, may give parents the sense that they are not welcome or needed in schools to support their adolescents' educational development (Cotton & Wikelund, 1989). Moreover, working long hours and living in neighborhoods threatened by violence and negative peer influences may challenge some parents' beliefs that their efforts can have a noticeable influence on the behaviors, plans, and expectations of their adolescents (Furstenberg, Cook, Eccles, Elder, & Sameroff, 1999). Racial and ethnic minority families are particularly vulnerable to these circumstances because they are more likely to be immigrants, poor, and residents of economically disadvantaged neighborhoods. Potential challenges emerge when schools do not understand parents' behaviors and thus do not reach out to parents to establish parent–school relationships that promote the educational development of adolescents.

In addition to differences in parents' social and cultural circumstances, group variations in parenting practices may depend in part on school climate. According to Moos (1979), a positive school climate is one in which families are able to develop relationships with teachers, other school personnel, teachers, and other families; share knowledge of adolescent social and educational development; and are encouraged to participate in decisionmaking processes that affect the quality of education. In many communities, parents and school are unable to work together because schools do not have regular structures such as progress reports, newsletters, conferences, or even personal notes from teachers to communicate educational matters. Often, parent–school communications occur primarily when adolescents are already experiencing academic and behavioral difficulties. Furthermore, many high schools are unable to fund staff training to improve working relations with parents, fund a parent liaison particularly for non-English speakers, or provide other opportunities for fostering close family–school partnerships with all of the ethnic and cultural groups they serve. Since the 1980s, several parent–school initiatives, most notably the James Comer School Development Program (Comer, 1988) and the National Network of Partnership Schools (Epstein & Sanders, 2002), have assisted parents and schools in creating successful collaborations that cultivate shared norms, values, and goals. Importantly, both of those programs help schools learn about students' cultural and socioeconomic backgrounds and how to communicate with families from diverse backgrounds. Parents also learn what to do at home to enhance the learning and social development promoted in schools (Epstein, 2001). Without parent–school collaboration, cultural differences between parents and schools may limit opportunities for strengthening adolescents' educational development.

INVESTIGATING THE RELATIONSHIPS BETWEEN PARENTAL INVOLVEMENT AND ADOLESCENT MOTIVATION, FUTURE PLANS, AND EXPECTATIONS

We used data from the National Educational Longitudinal Study of 1988, a nationally representative survey sponsored by the U.S. Department of Education, National Center for Education Statistics. NELS88 is based on a representative sample of the nation's eighth graders in 1988 who were followed through their transition into high school and 8 years after their scheduled high school completion (Ingles, Thalji, Pulliman, Bartot, & Frankel, 1994). NELS88 is one of the few national data sources that contain both student and parent surveys at more than one point in time. We considered a subsample of 13,580 students who were surveyed in 8th grade in 1988 and again in 12th grade in 1992 and whose parents also were interviewed in both years.

We used Epstein's (2001) framework of parental involvement as a heuristic device to identify parenting practices that emanated from existing connections between families, communities, and schools (Furstenberg et al., 1999; Hoover-Dempsey & Sandler, 1997; Schneider & Coleman, 1993). We identified 15 different practices of parental involvement relevant for the education of high school seniors and explored the degree to which they mattered for students' school-related motivation, future plans, and expectations. Our findings revealed that five different parenting practices were associated with the above student outcomes. These were practices that focused on establishing common parent–teen activities and parent–school communication about student behaviors, encouraging college attendance, learning about postsecondary opportunities, and supporting high schools by volunteering and participating in school events. These five indicators represent four parenting areas in Epstein's (2001) typology (parent obligations to provide safety and health, school obligation to communicate with families, parental involvement in school, and parental involvement in learning activities at home).

PARENTAL INVOLVEMENT AND ADOLESCENTS' SCHOOL-RELATED MOTIVATION

Our research investigated whether the above-mentioned parenting practices during students' senior year in high school were associated with seniors' intrinsic motivation for schoolwork, even when we compared students of similar demographic, academic, family, and school characteristics. Using multivariate statistical techniques, we compared students with similar demographic and academic characteristics and found that during 12th grade, parent–school contacts about students' behaviors were associated with problematic student behaviors, while parents' encouragement for postsecondary education, common parent–teen activities, and support of school were associated with positive student behaviors.

Students' level of daily preparation for school (school preparedness) was positively related to parents' active encouragement for postsecondary education and negatively related to parent–school contacts. Students who tended to come prepared to school had parents who actively encouraged them to attend college. Their parents did not contact the school as often as parents whose adolescents faced behavioral problems at school.

Parents tended to contact the school frequently when their teens had disciplinary problems during high school. Social background variables were weakly related to both school preparedness and incidence of disciplinary problems, while the negative association between achievement and disciplinary problems was reduced by about one-third when we introduced the parental involvement variables. This indicates that responsive involvement in parent–teen activities and encouraging college attendance lowered the incidence of disciplinary problems at school for all students, even those with low levels of achievement.

Problems with students' school attendance were somewhat fewer in families with active parental encouragement for postsecondary attendance and parental involvement in school activities. However, high school seniors' attendance problems were very strongly related to parent–school contacts about students' behavior. In fact, the association between parent–school contacts and student behaviors was the strongest observed in this analysis. This association suggests that parents contacted school when their teens experienced attendance problems.

A number of other studies that use NELS88 data have reported a relationship between parent–school contacts and problematic student behaviors or low achievement (Ho & Willms, 1996; Lee, 1994; Muller, 1998). Explaining these associations empirically has proved to be difficult. Most researchers do not believe that parent–school contacts "cause" problematic student behaviors (Muller, 1998). Rather, they are considered as evidence of parent and school efforts to deal with existing problems in student behavior or achievement. Our analyses confirmed this interpretation because our indicator of parent–school contacts was specific to students' current attendance or behavior problems. These parent–school contacts were higher for students with a high incidence of attendance or disciplinary problems in 12th grade. Our findings also showed that the potential influence of parent–school contacts may vary by race/ethnicity. The positive association between this type of parental involvement and problematic behavior was somewhat lower for Asian and African American students, indicating that when some members of these two groups contacted the school about their teen behavior, the misbehavior decreased.

Our analyses also showed that adolescent males were less likely to be ready for academic work (with completed homework, books, and pencils at hand) and more likely to experience disciplinary problems than their female counterparts, even among students with comparable levels of parental involvement. This pattern confirms a growing national trend showing that male students are falling behind their female peers in many different areas of schooling (Kleinfeld, 1998; NCES, 2000; Riegle-Crumb, 2007; Sommers, 2000).

PARENTAL INVOLVEMENT AND ADOLESCENTS' FUTURE PLANS AND EXPECTATIONS

Beliefs About Chances for Future Success

Comparisons of students with similar demographic, academic, family, and school characteristics supported our expectation that parents also can have an impact on high school seniors' beliefs and plans about their future. Specifically, we found that during students' senior year in high school, parents' active encouragement for college attendance (having high educational expectations for teens and frequently discussing with them taking the SAT/ACT or applying to colleges) was related to their teens' beliefs about their chances of future success. Parental college encouragement reduced the influence that student background had on students' beliefs about their chances of success in the future. This finding suggests that students with low academic achievement or limited financial resources can maintain positive beliefs about their future when their parents actively encourage them to pursue postsecondary education. Parents' active participation in activities that supported school and their increased knowledge about postsecondary education also were positively linked to high school seniors' positive outlook toward their future. The links of parental involvement activities with adolescents' future outlook tended to be uniform across racial and ethnic groups.

Plans for Attending College

Our research findings also revealed associations between parental activities and the postsecondary plans of adolescents. Students whose parents actively encouraged them to take the necessary steps for college attendance were more likely to plan postsecondary attendance and especially attendance at a 4-year college. These students were three times more likely to plan enrollment in a 4-year college right after high school than other students with comparable demographic characteristics and achievement levels. Students whose parents were involved in activities supporting school or sought to increase their knowledge about postsecondary opportunities also were more likely to plan to enroll in a 4-year college, and to a lesser extent in a 2-year college, than comparable students whose parents were less involved in these activities. Parental involvement practices related to participating in school activities or to encouraging students to attend college were much more important for the college plans of White than minority students. They also were especially important for male students, whose college plans tend to lag behind those of their female classmates. Our findings indicate that although parent activities supporting the norms and goals of high schools and the pursuit of a postsecondary education are important for the college transition of all students, they may be particularly important for males.

UNDERSTANDING THE LINKS BETWEEN PARENTAL INVOLVEMENT AND ADOLESCENTS' EDUCATIONAL SUCCESS

In our research we addressed the commonly held belief that parental involvement in adolescents' education declines as adolescents enter high school. We did so by taking into consideration that parenting practices have a multidimensional nature defined by the interrelationships between family, community, and school (Epstein, 2001). This perspective predicts that parental practices associated with adolescents' academic success change as students move through the different stages of schooling and may differ for students of different racial and ethnic backgrounds. At each stage of schooling, academic success will be associated with social and cultural conditions that allow families and schools to share common goals and tailor their practices to meet these goals. We expected that activities that provided guidance and support to adolescents would influence educational outcomes that are most closely related to the developmental tasks of adolescents, such as intrinsic motivation for schoolwork, life planning, and independent decisionmaking.

We identified five types of parental involvement in teens' education that are associated with high school seniors' school-related motivation, expectations about the future, and postsecondary plans. All are types of parental activities that seek to support school goals and guide adolescents in their quest for autonomy and preparation for the future (i.e., common parent–teen activities, active encouragement for college attendance, volunteering and participating in school events, parent–school contacts about student behavior, and parent willingness to learn about postsecondary opportunities). Our reported results were not affected by parents' level of involvement in these practices in prior grades (specifically, during 8th grade). Thus, our research indicates that it is never too late for parents to get involved in children's education. Their involvement, even during the last years of high school, can shape the behavior and postsecondary trajectory of adolescents.

Specifically, our analyses showed that parents who take an active part in their teens' preparation for college (i.e., communicating their aspirations to their teens, encouraging them to prepare for the SAT, and holding frequent discussions with them about taking the SAT/ACT and about applying to colleges) have teens who are motivated to do well in school and thus have few incidents of attendance and disciplinary problems during their senior year in high school. These adolescents are optimistic about their future success and plan to attend a 4-year college upon high school graduation. Continuing parental encouragement up to 12th grade seems to be very important, as it is highly predictive of high school seniors' college plans and their outlook about their future. Parents' efforts to participate in school activities and to learn about postsecondary education also are linked to seniors' motivation to learn as well as to their future outlook and college attendance plans. During the developmental phase in which adolescents begin to enjoy adult privileges but still lack full maturity, parents may be most effective by serving as a source of information and by guiding their teens while respecting their ability to make choices. It is perhaps for these reasons that students whose parents actively participate in school activities, seek information about postsecondary education, and encourage them to take the necessary steps for college attendance are more likely than others to believe that they will be successful in life and to make plans to attend college. Setting the goal of a college education may affect current behaviors by motivating adolescents to work hard in school and to avoid disciplinary and attendance problems. Parental encouragement is powerful even for some adolescents who do not have the financial resources or academic credentials to pursue a college education; students in these disadvantaged circumstances may plan to pursue postsecondary education if their parents take actions that encourage college attendance.

Unfortunately, our findings reveal that college encouragement and parent participation in activities that support school have less influence among racial and ethnic minority groups when compared with European American students. Minority students' future outlook and college plans are not as strongly related to such parental actions as are those of their White counterparts with similar social and academic background. The reasons behind the weaker links between parental practices that take place at the school and students' outcomes for minority students may be explained by the sociocultural and/or linguistic barriers discussed above and also in Chapter 6 and the conclusion. Perhaps, financial barriers to college attendance, family obligations, or limited knowledge about postsecondary educational pathways may affect minority students' future plans and aspirations disproportionately.

During high school, parent–teen social and recreational activities are associated with somewhat higher levels of school preparedness and lower incidence of disciplinary problems. Parent–teen activities may provide a forum for parents to teach acceptable social skills without undermining teens' power to decide appropriate social behaviors for themselves. These practices therefore may offer developmentally appropriate opportunities for parental guidance since, according to Steinberg (1998), adolescents develop norms and values not by adopting those handed down by their parents but rather by sorting through diverse ideas and experiences.

Parent–school contact is the only type of parental involvement that has an inverse relationship to school behaviors. These contacts involve communication between schools and parents about seniors' behavior and attendance problems. We reasonably conclude that these parent–school contacts represent attempts of both parties to deal with serious student behavioral problems. Our analyses show, however, that some minority parents, especially African Americans, may use contacts with school as a proactive form of involvement, since the association between parent–

school contacts and attendance problems is slightly weaker for them than for any other racial/ethnic group. It is interesting to note that parents' attempts to supervise and restrict teens' activities are not related to the incidence of problematic school behaviors. These data indicate that parental actions based on discipline and supervision lose their effectiveness during adolescence and that parents and schools contact each other in an effort to find alternative ways of coping with the problematic behavior of some adolescents.

Parent–school contacts as well as parental encouragement for postsecondary education tend to be important aspects of adolescents' family life. The results of our analyses support our expectation that parental involvement influences the attitudes and behaviors of students up to their senior year of high school.

Despite the positive effects of parental involvement activities (i.e., parent–teen activities, parent–school contacts, parent support of school, parent college encouragement) on student behaviors, the male disadvantage in these outcomes remained even after the parental involvement indicators were considered. By contrast, the introduction of parental activities (i.e., college encouragement, parent support of school, and parent knowledge of postsecondary opportunities) did reduce the male disadvantage in plans to attend a 2-year or 4-year college. Taken together, these findings suggest that to reduce school disengagement among male students, parents and schools must work together to create greater connections between high school experiences and future postsecondary trajectories. Research on postsecondary attendance consistently shows that when students are provided with relevant information about the college process, they are more likely to be proactive in their pursuit of a college education and consequently remain more engaged in their education than students without similar orientation (McDonough, 1997). By making transparent the strong link between high school experiences and postsecondary education, schools may be transformed into less alienating learning environments with clear connections to postsecondary success. This would be a benefit to all students but especially to males, who have fallen behind their female counterparts in academic performance and college attendance (NCES, 2000).

RECOMMENDATIONS TO
INCREASE PARENTAL INVOLVEMENT IN HIGH SCHOOLS

Based on our investigation, we provide the following recommendations for practice, which we present according to Epstein's typology of parental involvement. Individual parents and high schools can implement these recommendations as stand-alone programs or part of a district- or state-wide parental involvement initiative.

1. *Basic parental obligations to provide for the safety and health of their adolescents.* Both parents and schools share the same desire to provide safe learning environments for adolescents. High schools can assist parents in this process by offering seminars and forums that enhance parental knowledge of skills, activities, and strategies that help adolescents crystallize their future careers and education. High schools also should work with their school districts to provide after-school space for students and their parents to participate in extracurricular activities, educational and career conferences, or study hall. Unfortunately, many adolescents do not have a quiet and safe environment in which to do their homework and study with their peers. Since adolescent well-being is a concern shared by both parents and schools, high schools also could sponsor health forums to teach both students and their parents about health risks such as diabetes, obesity, teen pregnancy, and sexually transmitted diseases, as well as safety measures to guard against crime and Internet predators.

2. *Parent–school communication.* Our findings show that when parents contact schools about behavioral matters, it is an indication that their teens are experiencing disciplinary problems. Schools and families need to work together to increase their contacts about positive issues in order to reduce disciplinary problems. One way in which schools can promote learning and excellence is to assign an advisor (a teacher) to each student. Through the advisor, schools can communicate important information to parents and encourage regular contacts between parents and teachers before disciplinary problems emerge. This recommendation would be especially beneficial for minority parents since our analysis shows that increased contact with schools reduces minority students' disciplinary and attendance problems.

3. *Parental involvement at school.* Our findings show that parental support of school increases teens' chances of planning to attend a 4-year college and be successful in life, while at the same time reducing teens' disciplinary and attendance problems. It is likely that participating in school activities and volunteering provide parents with access to more knowledge about how their teens are doing as well as information about opportunities

to enhance their adolescents' educational experience. When parents spend time in their teens' school, teens are more likely to focus on their academics and avoid behavioral problems. To ensure the success of parental involvement programs, schools should conduct a needs assessment of concerns and issues, establish a parent–teacher liaison at the school, and develop a long-range parental involvement plan (Comprehensive School Reform Quality Center, 2005). Such a framework will support the creation of innovative programs such as college and career expositions to encourage parent participation by volunteering, attending events, and serving as speakers (Eccles & Harold, 1993). A well-developed parental involvement plan increases the likelihood that parental involvement in schools is improved and maintained.

4. *Parental involvement in learning activities.* Relevant learning activities for parents could include attending programs on postsecondary education and employment opportunities for adolescents. Schools should assist in this learning process by sending parents information about postsecondary opportunities. High schools also can institute academic contracts that teachers, parents, and students sign that specify appropriate behaviors and steps for high school completion and postsecondary educational endeavors. Such a contract would make transparent the expectations and requirements for a successful high school career. In addition, high schools should create an information center that provides parents, particularly minority families who may have limited financial resources or exposure to postsecondary opportunities, with information about their teens' high school, the college application process, college financial aid, and other postsecondary opportunities that are likely to assist teens with academic matters and future planning. This resource would be particularly beneficial to parents of male students. Our findings show that males' disadvantage in college attendance can be overcome by parental involvement related to support of school and postsecondary education.

THE ROLE OF LOCAL, STATE, AND FEDERAL GOVERNMENTS

Although parental involvement is not a new strategy for promoting the educational success of American adolescents, its effectiveness has been questioned in recent years, particularly during adolescents' high school years. Our work was built on current scholarship suggesting that success-ful types of family practices are those that operate in synergy with school practices and goals in order to support the developmental tasks, skills, and behaviors that adolescents must master during their transition to adulthood (Eccles et al., 1993; Epstein, 2001). We conclude that the impor-tance of parental practices does not decline during students' high school years and that parents still matter. Parental practices that are likely to be effective are those that allow parents to remain the "primary resource" of information for prosocial behaviors without undermining adolescents' de-veloping autonomy and independence. While our research demonstrates that parental involvement is significant, its effectiveness may be limited without the commitment of policymakers and legislators to fund efforts that create and sustain high school–family partnerships.

The present empirical study suggests that parental involvement is a resource for encouraging students to attend high school ready to learn, reducing disciplinary problems, directing students toward postsecond-ary education, and engendering positive attitudes about the chances of career success and prosperity, despite the challenge of having greater in-dependence and increased risks for disengaging from school. The study found parenting activities that support adolescents' autonomy and inde-pendence, while providing guidance for prosocial and educational behav-iors, to be effective in students' final year of high school, even after taking into consideration parental involvement in earlier grades. Through these attitudinal and behavioral outcomes, parental involvement has the poten-tial to influence academic outcomes. The benefits of parental involvement are aligned with the federal government's goals of improving student achievement and high school completion as indicated by the No Child Left Behind legislation.

Given all these positive outcomes, how can the federal, state, and local governments encourage parental involvement in American high schools? To strengthen the recommendations suggested above, govern-mental policies are needed to support school–family programs at the high school level. High schools need financial and technical support from their school district, the state, and the federal government to im-plement innovative parental involvement programs, create greater col-laborations across other youth programs (e.g., youth employment and internships), and evaluate progress made by parental involvement ef-forts (also see the conclusion). Although these policy recommendations are also the main features of NCLB, no funding has been provided to states and school districts to support such programs. Furthermore, as Hill and Chao indicate (in the introduction), there are no status updates on the effectiveness of parental involvement programs throughout the country in annual follow-ups on the progress of NCLB. Without strong federal commitment in the form of funding and technical assistance, high schools are unable to start or fully launch school–family programs that promote adolescents' academic success in high school and upward mobility in their postsecondary destination.

State and local governments also can support school–family partnerships by establishing a parental involvement office in their departments of education. The office may be strengthened by establishing a parent liaison who maintains regular communications with the parent–teacher contacts in high schools. An office and a liaison are first steps toward securing funding and establishing policies with clear goals and objectives. Such policies should support long-range planning, data collection, and program evaluation. Policies specific to program design and implementation are important components because most parental involvement initiatives do not have specific guidelines for middle schools and high schools, and consequently fail to address the needs of students based on their developmental stage. High schools also should be allocated resources to facilitate meetings that are held off school grounds to accommodate parents with demanding work schedules and responsibilities. Similarly, provisions should be made to designate a physical space where parents can meet and receive information on educational and career opportunities relevant to both students and parents. Local school districts also should train teachers and parents on effective strategies for developing and managing school–family partnerships. To ensure program success and relevancy, teachers, principals, and superintendents should be evaluated on whether their school–family efforts promote progress in parental involvement and, in turn, whether such progress is related to educational outcomes.

Parental involvement has the potential to strengthen both schools and families. On the school side, parental involvement can help schools keep students academically engaged and focused on high school completion and postsecondary attendance. On the family side, parental involvement can deepen the bond between parents and their adolescents and thus facilitate greater adult guidance during a period when adolescents tend to spend less time with their parents and more time with friends and peers. As increasing numbers of high schools across the United States attempt to forge closer connections with students' families and communities, research in this area is needed to guide their partnership efforts and promote adolescents' success in high school and in adult life. Future research must consider the interaction between parents' efforts, school goals and programs, and adolescents' developmental needs at each stage of schooling.

ACKNOWLEDGMENTS

This research was supported by funds from the U. S. Department of Education, Office of Educational Research and Improvement (OERI) to the Center for Research on the Education of Students Placed at Risk (CRESPAR) at Johns Hopkins University; from the American Educational Research Association (AERA) and the U.S. Department of Education, Institute of Education Sciences (IES) to the Community College Research Center at Teachers College; and from the PSC-CUNY Research Award Program. The opinions expressed are the authors' and do not represent the position or policy of OERI, AERA-IES, or PSC-CUNY. The authors wish to thank Joyce Epstein for her most helpful comments and suggestions. Please send correspondence to: Belkis Suazo deCastro, Community College Research Center, Teachers College, Columbia University, 525 West 120th Street, New York, NY 10027. Email: belkisdeCastro@gmail.com

REFERENCES

Astone, N. M., & McLanahan, S. S. (1991). Family structure, parental practices and high school completion. *American Sociological Review, 56*(3), 309–320.

Catsambis, S. (2001). Expanding knowledge of parental involvement in children's secondary education: Connections with high school seniors' academic success. *Social Psychology of Education, 5*(2), 149–177.

Catsambis, S., & Garland, J. E. (1997). *Parental involvement in students' education: Changes from middle grades to high school* (Rep. No. 18). Center for the Education of Students Placed at Risk, Johns Hopkins University, Baltimore.

Comer, J. P. (1988). Educating poor minority children. *Scientific American, 259*(5), 42–48.

Comprehensive School Reform Quality Center. (2005). *Works in progress: A report on middle and high school improvement programs.* Washington, DC: Author.

Cotton, K., & Wikelund, K. R. (1989). Parent involvement in education. Retrieved January 3, 2009, from the Northwest Regional Educational Laboratory Web site: http://www.nwrel.org/scpd/sirs/3/cu6.html

Eccles, J. S., & Harold, R. D. (1993). Parent–school involvement during the early adolescent years. *Teachers College Record, 94*(3), 568–587.

Eccles, J. S., Midgley, C., Wigfield, A., Buchanan, C. M., Reuman, D., Flanagan, C., & MacIver, D. (1993). Development during adolescence: The impact of stage-environment fit on young adolescents' experiences in schools and families. *American Psychologist, 48*(2), 90–101.

Epstein, J. L. (2001). *School, family and community partnerships: Preparing educators and improving schools.* Boulder, CO: Westview Press.

Epstein, J. L., & Sanders, M. G. (2002). Family, school, and community partnerships. In M. H. Bornstein (Ed.), *Handbook of parenting: Vol. 5. Practical issues in parenting* (2nd ed., pp. 407–437). Mahwah, NJ: Erlbaum.

Furstenberg, F. F., Jr., Cook, T. D., Eccles, J., Elder, G. H., Jr., & Sameroff, A. (1999). *Managing to make it: Urban families and adolescent success.* Chicago: University of Chicago Press.

Harris, J. R. (1998). *The nurture assumption.* New York: Free Press.

Hidalgo, N. M., Siu, S., Bright, J. A., Swap, S. M., & Epstein, J. L. (1995). Research on families, schools and communities: A multicultural perspective. In J. A. Banks (Ed.), *Handbook on research on multicultural education* (pp. 498–524). New York: Macmillan.

Hill, N. E., Castellino, D. R., Lansford, J. E., Nowlin, P., Dodge, K. A., Bates, J., & Pettit, G. (2004). Parent-academic involvement as related to school behavior, achievement, and aspirations: Demographic variations across adolescence. *Child Development, 75*(4), 1491–1509.

Ho, E. S. C., & Willms, J. D. (1996). The effects of parental involvement on eighth grade achievement. *Sociology of Education, 69*, 126–141.

Hoover-Dempsey, K. V., & Sandler, H. M. (1997). Why do parents become involved in their children's education? *Review of Educational Research, 67*(1), 3–42.

Hossler, D., & Stage, F. K. (1992). Family and high school experience influences on the postsecondary educational plans of ninth-graders. *American Educational Research Journal, 29*(2), 425–451.

Ingels, S. J., Thalji, L., Pulliman, P., Bartot, V. H., & Frankel, M. R. (1994). *National educational longitudinal study of 1988. Second follow-up: Student component data file user's manual.* Washington, DC: OERI, U.S. Department of Education.

Keith, R. Z. (1991). Parental involvement and achievement in high school. In S. B. Silvern (Ed.), Advances in reading/language research: A research annual (Vol. 5: Literacy through family, community, and school interaction) (pp. 125–141). Greenwich, CT: Elsevier Science/JAI.

Keith, T. Z., Keith, P. B., Troutman, G. C., Bickley, P. G., Trivette, P. S., & Singh, K. (1993). Does parental involvement affect eighth-grade student achievement? Structural analysis of national data. *School Psychology Review, 22*(3), 474–496.

Kleinfeld, J. S. (1998). *The myth that schools shortchange girls: Social science in the service of deception.* Fairbanks, AK: Author.

Lareau, A. (2000). *Home advantage: Social class and parental intervention in elementary education* (2nd ed.). Lanham, MD: Rowman & Littlefield.

Lareau, A. (2003). *Unequal childhoods: Class, race and family life.* Berkeley: University of California.

Lareau, A., & Horvat, E. M. (1999). Moments of social inclusion and exclusion: Race, class, and cultural capital in family–school relationships. *Sociology of Education, 72*, 37–53.

Lee, S. (1994). *Family–school connections and students' education: Continuity and change of family involvement from the middle grades to high school.* Unpublished doctoral dissertation, Johns Hopkins University, Baltimore.

McDonough, P. M. (1997). *Choosing colleges: How social class and schools structure opportunity.* Albany: State University of New York Press.

Milne, A. M., Myers, D. E., Rosenthal, A. S., & Ginsburg, A. S. (1986). Single parents, working mothers, and the educational achievement of school children. *Sociology of Education, 59*(3), 125–139.

Moos, R. H. (1979). *Evaluating educational environments: Procedures, measures, findings, and policy implications.* San Francisco: Jossey-Bass.

Muller, C. (1995). Maternal employment, parent involvement, and mathematics achievement among adolescents. *Journal of Marriage and the Family, 57*(2), 85–100.

Muller, C. (1998). Gender differences in parental involvement and adolescents' mathematics achievement. *Sociology of Education, 71*(4), 336–356.

National Center for Education Statistics. (2000). *Trends in educational equity of girls & women* (NCES 2000-030). Washington, DC: U.S. Government Printing Office.

Nicolau, S., & Ramos, C. L. (1990). *Together is better: Building strong relationships between schools and Hispanic parents.* Washington, DC: Hispanic Policy Development Project.

Plank, S. B., & Jordan, W. J. (2001). Effects of information, guidance, and actions on postsecondary destinations: A study of talent loss. *American Educational Research Journal, 38*(4), 947–979.

Riegle-Crumb, C. (2007). *More girls go to college: Academic and social factors behind the female postsecondary advantage.* Retrieved October 9, 2008, from the Texas Higher Education Opportunity Project Web site: http://www.texastop10.princeton.edu/workingpapers.html

Schneider, B., & Coleman, J. (Eds.). (1993). *Parents, their children, and schools.* Boulder, CO: Westview.

Schneider, B., & Stevenson, D. (1999). *The ambitious generation: America's teenagers, motivated but directionless.* New Haven, CT: Yale University Press.

Singh, K., Bickley, P. G., Trivette, P. S., Keith, T. Z., Keith, P. B., & Anderson, E. (1995). The effects of four components of parental involvement on eighth grade student achievement: Structural analysis of NELS88 data. *School Psychology Review, 24,* 299–317.

Sommers, C. H. (2000). *The war against boys: How misguided feminism is harming our young men.* New York: Simon & Schuster.

Stanton-Salazar, R. D., & Dornbusch, S. M. (1995). Social capital and the reproduction of inequality: Information networks among Mexican-origin high school students. *Sociology of Education, 68*(2), 116–135.

Steinberg, L. (1998). *Adolescence.* New York: McGraw-Hill.

Stevenson, D. L., & Baker, D. P. (1987). The family–school relation and the child's school performance. *Child Development, 58*(5), 1348–1357.

Sui-Chu, E. H., & Willms, J. D. (1996). Effects of parental involvement on eighth-grade achievement. *Sociology of Education, 69*(2), 126–141.

6

Diversities in Meaning and Practice

The Parental Involvement of Asian Immigrants

RUTH K. CHAO
AKIRA KANATSU, NICOLE STANOFF
INNA PADMAWIDJAJA, CHRISTINE AQUE

I N REVIEWS EXAMINING HOW PARENTS' involvement in school (for children 5 to 17 years of age) changes throughout their children's schooling, researchers generally have reported that parents are less involved with older than with younger children. However, as there have been so few studies focusing on parental involvement during middle and high school, it is not clear whether such declines depend on the type of involvement. In a summary of the literature by Keith and colleagues (1993) focusing on involvement during high school, four general types were identified: (1) parents' expectations for children's school achievement; (2) participation in school activities and programs (e.g., involvement in PTA); (3) discussions between parents and children about school; and (4) a home structure that supports learning (e.g., family rules about homework). Stevenson and Baker (1987) specifically found that parents' *participation in school* (i.e., involvement at the school) declined during middle and high school. However, there may be some types of involvement that actually increase, particularly during high school, when more emphasis is placed on grades for entrance into college. Consequently, parents may become more involved during these years in ways that increase adolescents' chances of getting into college.

However, not only are there variations in the type of support parents provide their children in middle and high school, but there are also ethnic differences in the type of support provided, particularly between recent immigrants and European Americans (who predominantly have been in this country for more than three generations). Chao (2000a) has distinguished between types of involvement labeled as "managerial" in contrast to the more "structural" support provided by Asian immigrant parents. Because many Asian immigrant parents believe that their children should already know how to manage their schoolwork, studying, and time, this managerial type of involvement may decline, while the structural type of support increases for Asian immigrants. Both types of involvement in high school depend partly on factors related to socioeconomic and also immigrant status. These factors contribute to linguistic and cultural barriers to parents' managing and helping with their children's schoolwork. However, these barriers imply that immigrant parents are less involved in their adolescents' schooling and schoolwork than nonimmigrant parents and, in particular, European Americans. This may not be the case with many Asian immigrant groups due to the cultural emphasis placed on schooling. In fact, good parenting for Asian immigrants is reflected in how well their children do in school (Chao, 1994). This chapter focuses on cultural explanations for the parental involvement of Asian immigrant and European American parents of high school students, after accounting for socioeconomic and immigrant status. Additionally, although much of the research on Asian Americans has tended to treat them as a monolithic group, this chapter will explore variation among them in terms of both ethnicity and immigrant status or generation.

PARENTAL INVOLVEMENT
IN SCHOOL FOR ASIAN AMERICAN STUDENTS

Studies that include Asian American students, particularly recent immigrants, indicate very different findings from those for European Americans, even when student age is considered. In four studies involving eighth-grade students from the National Educational Longitudinal Study (1988) data, Asian Americans generally scored lower than European Americans on some measures of parental involvement, including discussions about school, helping with homework, and participating in school (Ho & Willms, 1996; Kao, 1995; Mau, 1997; Peng & Wright, 1994). In these same studies, Asian Americans scored higher than European Americans on home structure, preparing for ACT/SAT tests, planning for college, and providing resources such as a place to study, a personal computer, and savings for college. Thus, Asian immigrant parents offered more indirect types of support in terms of structuring the home to support learning, in addition to high expectations for school success. On the other hand, European American parents tended to offer more direct types of involvement, such as participating at the school, discussing courses or coursework, and helping with homework. Thus, even when Asian immigrant parents have the linguistic and socioeconomic resources to manage the schooling of their adolescents, they may feel this is mostly the responsibility of the adolescent.

These ethnic differences in parents' managerial and structural support become most apparent when their children are in high school. Many Asian American parents do not get as involved with the schoolwork of older children or adolescents (Chao & Sue, 1996; Choi, Bempechat, & Ginsburg, 1994). Asian American parents most often begin fostering school skills in their children very early on so that by the time they reach high school, they already have the necessary skills to study well and succeed in school. Studies have shown that East Asian parents, in particular, exert the most intensive educational socialization in the early years of their children's schooling, with this socialization decreasing as children become older (Chao, 2000a; Schneider & Lee, 1990).

CULTURAL EXPLANATIONS FOR THE PARENTAL INVOLVEMENT OF ASIAN IMMIGRANTS

Such emphasis on fostering school skills early on is rooted in cultural ethno-theories about children's development and parents' role in that development (Chao, 2000b). Chao has discussed specifically the importance of the cultivation metaphor in Confucian thinking about parents' role in their children's development. In Japanese, the character for cultivating a plant is the same as that for cultivating a person. This metaphor emphasizes the importance of early educational intervention, but only when children are ready. That is, in the shaping and framing of a plant's growth, the gardener is careful to allow the particular inner tendencies of the plant to first show in order to foster its full potential. In terms of the child's schooling, parents must begin as early as possible to provide the support necessary for the flourishing of the child's own abilities. Thus, the managerial types of involvement, focusing on fostering school skills for perseverance, focus, and studying, begin even before children enter school. When children reach high school, they should already know how to study and manage their time.

Thus, during high school Asian immigrant parents may not help their adolescents with their homework, or be directly involved in or participate at the teen's school. Rather, they may become increasingly focused on their adolescents' eventual entrance into college and the particular college and major they would like for their teens. As high school is typically the last step in the pipeline to college, the stakes become much higher. Additionally, although these parents may not help their children with homework by the time they are in high school, they may provide extra resources for them, such as purchasing extra textbooks or other study materials; assigning extra work from these books, when needed, in addition to securing a tutor for them; and helping them prepare for the SAT. Not only do we know little about what parents actually are providing their children during high school, we know even less about how this support or involvement may vary across ethnic groups according to socioeconomic and immigrant status, in addition to cultural factors.

DIFFERENCES AMONG ASIAN AMERICANS

There also may be important differences among Asian Americans due to ethnicity or nationality. For example, East Asian immigrants, including Chinese, often are distinguished from Filipino immigrants in terms of their (1) sociocultural ideologies, (2) country of origin's economic and political relationship to the United States, and (3) fluency in English and other sociodemographic factors. Family relationships for Chinese, and other East Asians (Koreans and Japanese), have tended to emphasize fairly unifying "Confucian-based" principles of filial piety, age stratification, and the veneration of age (Chao, 1994, 1995). Such unifying cultural principles may be more difficult to define among Filipinos in light of the effects of prior U.S. and Spanish colonization on Filipino society and of island differences in dialects, subsistence economies, and sociocultural ideologies (Bacho, 1997; Blair & Qian, 1998; Espiritu, 1995; Kitano & Daniels, 1995). However, Catholicism often has been recognized as a unifying foundation for defining Filipino family relationships, due to former Spanish rule of the Philippines. Blair and Qian (1998) have found that Catholicism also may be important in the educational success of Filipino Americans in that it was positively associated with adolescents' school performance, while no association was found for Chinese adolescents. Thus, neither Confucian nor Western ideologies may adequately explain the parental practices of Filipino Americans.

Subsequent U.S. colonization imposed on the Philippines an English-medium educational system. Thus, Filipino immigrants also tend to be more fluent English speakers than other Asian immigrants, including Chinese and Koreans, and next to Asian Indians, have the highest rates of high school and college completion, with females actually surpassing males. However, these completion rates are somewhat lower among native-born than foreign-born Filipinos, and some researchers have argued that Filipino Americans are more economically disadvantaged than other Asian American groups (Agbayani-Siewert & Revilla, 1995; Barringer, Gardner, & Levin, 1993; Kitano & Daniels, 1995; Zhou, 1999). Thus, even though this study often uses the broader ethnic category of "Asian Americans," a central goal of the study is to recognize that "pan-ethnic" groupings may be problematic for understanding parental involvement practices for adolescents.

CHANGES ACROSS TIME
IN PARENTAL INVOLVEMENT IN SCHOOL

Although deCastro and Catsambis (Chapter 5, this volume) provided a summary of studies that examined the effects of parental involvement on adolescents' school achievement, these studies did not include examinations of whether parental involvement is related to later school performance or to changes over time. Longitudinal studies that have been conducted primarily used data from the National Educational Longitudinal Study (Catsambis, 2001; Fan, 2001; Hong & Ho, 2005; Keith et al., 1993; Reyes, Gillock, Kobus, & Sanchez, 2000), and findings from these studies reflect those summarized in Chapter 5 involving primarily one time point only. Although these studies often assessed the multidimensionality of parental involvement based on established frameworks (see Chapters 1 and 5), the studies found that many aspects of parental involvement, with the exception of parental expectations and aspirations, often have no effects or negative effects on achievement in high school. However, although aspirations may be one strategy for how parents can be involved, they reflect more of a belief or attitude than a practice. Additionally, in the latter set of studies, a few differences have been reported for Asian Americans and European Americans, but the specific types of parental involvement in school that are related to academic growth are not consistent across studies. For instance, the study by Hong and Ho (2005) found that both parental aspirations and participation in school were related to initial achievement levels, and communication and participation were related to growth in achievement. On the other hand, Keith and colleagues (1993), also using NELS data, examined one latent factor for parental involvement consisting of parental aspirations and communication, using both parent and adolescent reports.

Moreover, one of the greatest limitations of the longitudinal studies relying on NELS data is that parental involvement itself was assessed only at the initial time point at 8th grade and at 12th grade, whereas school performance was captured at a number of points. Thus, when changes in levels are reported, the focus has been on school performance rather than parental involvement.

Further understanding is needed of how parental involvement changes during high school and whether these changes differ for Asian immigrants compared with European Americans. However, rather than examining Asian immigrants together, or as a whole, two generations (first and second) of three ethnic groups (Chinese, Korean, and Filipino) each will be compared with European Americans. Additionally, we examined differences between European Americans and each of the Asian immigrant groups in their levels and rates of change in school performance based on report card data.

We expected that both European American and Asian immigrant parents may be providing more support during the first year or two of high school, and then may taper off in subsequent years. However, this may be the case only for the managerial types of involvement, particularly participating in school and helping with homework. That is, as students mature or become more responsible for their schooling and homework over time, parental involvement in these areas becomes less crucial. On the other hand, structural involvement may be more crucial over time, with parents either maintaining or even increasing this type of involvement as youth progress through high school. Because structural involvement entails the provision of important resources for youth, it may be necessary for improving adolescents' grades and ultimately their chances of entering college.

There also may be important differences in both levels and changes in involvement across time between Asian immigrant and European American parents. European American parents are expected to be higher on managerial involvement at all three time points, although they will show declines across time similar to those of Asian immigrant parents. On the other hand, with structural involvement, Asian immigrant parents will be higher than European Americans at all three time points. In addition, although there may be increases across time in structural involvement for Asian immigrant parents, particularly in planning for college, these increases may be less apparent for them than for European Americans. As discussed above, Asian immigrant parents believe that planning for college is crucial early on in high school. Thus, for Asian immigrants, the levels of structural involvement may be higher than those of European Americans, whereas their growth or increase over the ensuing years of high school will not be as pronounced as for European Americans.

MULTICULTURAL FAMILIES AND ADOLESCENTS STUDY

Based on survey data from the Multicultural Families and Adolescents Study (MFAS) of youths' reports of parental practices, we assessed a range of different types of both managerial and structural involvement. Managerial involvement included (1) participates in school (e.g., "attends PTO/PTA meetings" and "volunteers at my school"), (2) helps with homework, and (3) checks homework, whereas structural involvement consisted of (1) plans for college (e.g., "has talked to me about what college I should attend" and "has talked to me about what my college major should be"), (2) provides/purchases extra materials, and (3) provides after-school study groups/classes. MFAS involved a sample of 2,111 9th-grade students from eight different high schools in the greater Los Angeles area who were followed up into 10th and 11th grades. The sample comprised 595 Chinese American (198 first- and 397 second-generation), 567 Korean American (174 first- and 393 second-generation), 342 Filipino American (117 first- and 225 second-generation), and 607 European American students. Each ethnic group consisted of similar proportions of males and females. Among the first-generation youth, the average age of immigration was 7.45 years (7.64 years for Chinese, 8.90 for Koreans, and 7.41 for Filipinos).

Comparisons across the ethnic/generational groups (first- and second-generation Chinese, Koreans, and Filipinos, as well as European Americans) in the levels of parental involvement are based on means computed for each group at each grade level. In addition, we compared these ethnic/generational groups in how much their mean levels of parental involvement actually changed between or across grade levels (i.e., between 9th and 10th, and between 10th and 11th grades) by computing the difference in their means between these grade levels. All comparisons controlled or accounted for potential differences in students' gender, school, cohort (i.e., year in which they began 9th grade), and socioeconomic status (i.e., their parents' educational levels, whether parents owned their homes, and whether adolescents resided with a single parent).

Managerial Involvement

Participates in school and helps with homework. Similar patterns of ethnic group differences/similarities were found for both participates in school and helps with homework, with mean levels of participates in school displayed by grade for each ethnic group in Figure 6.1. At baseline or 9th

Figure 6.1. Participates in School and Helps with Homework by School Grade

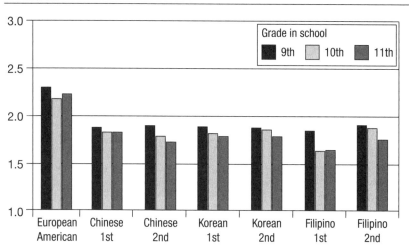

grade, European American students reported significantly higher levels of these types of managerial involvement for their parents than all of the Asian groups. Additionally, there were significant declines from 9th to 10th grade for European American parents, but these declines were not significantly different from the rates of the Asian American groups. By 11th grade, European American parents still had significantly higher levels of participation than all the Asian American groups.

Checks homework. Unlike the pattern of findings for participation in school and helping with homework, all groups were similarly high on checks homework at ninth grade. Declines from 9th to 10th as well as 10th to 11th grade were found for European Americans. The Asian groups reported similar rates of decline as the European Americans, with the following exceptions: Compared with European American youth, less decline was reported by first-generation Filipino youth from 9th to 10th grade, whereas from 10th to 11th grade *greater* declines were reported by first-generation Chinese and second-generation Koreans. Thus, as displayed in Figure 6.2, checking homework is a parental strategy that is used a great deal in all groups. However, greater declines in this strategy are reported for some generations of Chinese and Koreans than for European Americans, and less decline is reported by Filipinos, specifically first-generation immigrants.

Figure 6.2. Checks Homework by School Grade

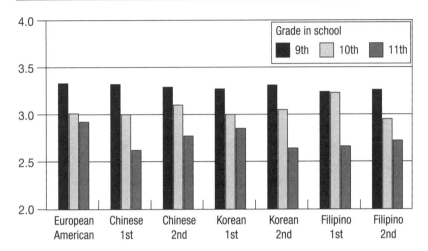

In summary, as expected, although European Americans were higher on two out of the three types of managerial involvement, their rates of decline were similar to those of the Asian American groups. However, contrary to expectations, similar levels of one aspect of managerial involvement—checking homework—were reported by European Americans and Asian Americans. The lack of ethnic differences in the checking of homework may be because teachers, in an effort to increase parental involvement, may either require parents to sign off on homework or assign homework that requires parental input. On the other hand, consistent with expectations, similar rates of decline in checking homework were reported by some of the Asian American groups relative to the European Americans.

Structural Involvement

Plans for college. All the Asian ethnic/generational groups reported significantly higher levels of plans for college than European Americans at baseline, with the exception of first-generation Filipinos. Mean levels are displayed by grade level for each ethnic group in Figure 6.3. There were significant increases for European Americans at both time intervals. However, *across* groups, first-generation Filipinos reported greater increases from 9th to 10th grade than European Americans, but between 10th and 11th grade European Americans reported greater increases than both generations of Filipino Americans. Likewise, significantly greater increases were found for European Americans compared with second-generation Koreans. By 11th grade, both generations of the East Asian groups were still significantly higher than European Americans, but the Filipinos were not.

Provides extra materials. At baseline or ninth grade, although in Figure 6.4 it appears that the East Asian groups were only somewhat higher than European Americans, based on tests of mean levels, second-generation Koreans were *significantly* higher than European Americans, and first- and second-generation Filipinos were significantly lower. Unlike the increases across time that were found with plans for college, for European Americans there were no changes across time in providing extra materials. Also, their rates of change did not differ from the Asian American groups, with one exception: First-generation Filipino youth reported greater increases between 9th and 10th grade than European American youth. See Figure 6.4 for the levels of this involvement. Thus, with both plans for college and providing extra materials, first-generation Filipino youth reported greater increases between 9th and 10th grade than European Americans.

Provides after-school study groups and classes. Similar to the findings for plans for college, at baseline both generations of the East Asian groups reported higher levels than European Americans. Although there were no significant changes across time/grade level for European Americans, similar to plans for college, greater increases were reported for European Americans than for second-generation Koreans from 9th to 10th grade and than for second-generation Chinese from 10th to 11th grade. That is,

Figure 6.3. Plans for College by School Grade

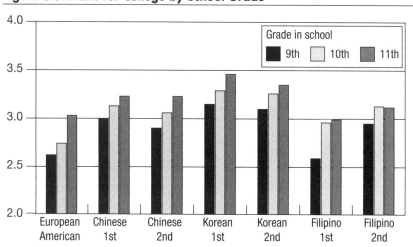

Figure 6.4. Provides Extra Materials by School Grade

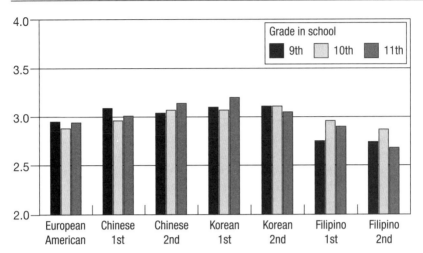

providing after-school study groups/classes actually declined for these latter two groups. However, by 11th grade, the East Asian groups were still higher than European Americans, with the exception of first-generation Chinese. See Figure 6.5 for the levels of this involvement.

Figure 6.5. Provides After-School Study Groups/Classes

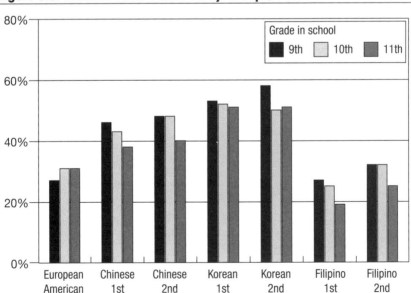

In summary, for *structural* involvement, as expected, the East Asian youth reported higher initial levels than did European American youth. However, contrary to expectations, only second-generation Koreans were higher than European Americans on providing extra materials, and Filipinos, in fact, were substantially lower. In rates of change, as expected, substantially greater increases were reported in both planning for college and providing after-school study groups/classes for European Americans than for second-generation Chinese, Koreans, and Filipino Americans. Also as expected, the rates of change for first-generation Filipinos were different from those of European Americans, but contrary to expectations these rates *increased* more for the former than for the latter group. Thus, expectations for group differences were supported somewhat for Chinese and Korean Americans, but more so for the second generation than the first, and were not supported for first-generation Filipinos.

Grade Point Averages

Additionally, displayed in Figure 6.6 are the GPAs for each ethnic group. At 9th grade, all the East Asian groups had significantly higher GPAs than European Americans. Significant declines in GPA were found between 10th and 11th grade, and first-generation Chinese and Koreans, and also second-generation Koreans, had even greater declines than European Americans. These greater declines for Chinese and Korean American youth are consistent with what has been found with college grades in that these groups

Figure 6.6. Grade Point Average by School Grade

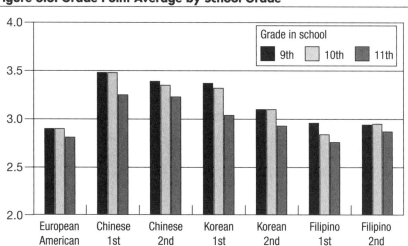

show greater rates of decline than European Americans in their freshman year (see review provided by Tseng, Chao, & Padmawidjaja, 2007). However, even with these greater declines, GPAs by 11th grade were still significantly higher for the East Asian groups than the European Americans.

CONCLUSIONS AND POLICY IMPLICATIONS

Much of our current understanding of parental involvement during high school reflects not only the features of European American parenting, but also features that are most salient during the elementary school years. Some parents may feel that because of the high stakes, grades count or matter during high school and they need to make sure that their children apply themselves in school and study. However, others may feel that such demands on children should be made much earlier, and that by high school it is too late. In attempting to learn about how parents support their children during middle and high school, we have to consider not only the developmental context of this period, but also the sociocultural context of immigrant families.

Although policies such as the No Child Left Behind Act include the importance of parental involvement throughout students' schooling, NCLB makes no mention of whether this involvement must change in accordance with the developmental changes in students. Policy and program recommendations recognize that involvement and family–school linkages must begin early in the transition to school. However, they often do not recognize that high school students need additional types of support that are different from those in elementary school.

One promising aspect of NCLB is its inclusion of parents with limited English proficiency by requiring schools to provide "information and school reports . . . in a format and, to the extent practicable, in a language such parents understand." This is a particularly lofty goal given the number of different ethnic groups or nationalities of Asian immigrants and their various languages even within a single ethnic group. With federal funding in education decreasing overall, it is imperative that schools begin to assess and tap into other types of resources or assets they do have, one of them being the parents themselves. This requires schools to make an even greater effort to contact, and even specifically survey, the parents or family members of their student body. These efforts are necessary in order to ascertain whether they have immigrant parents who are fluent in English and knowledgeable about the school system, so that they can provide the language support needed by other immigrant parents who have limited English proficiency.

Even those Asian immigrants who are already fluent in English upon their arrival in the United States, such as those from the Philippines, nonetheless may not be familiar with the U.S. school system generally and more specifically with state and local requirements. On the other hand, many of the more affluent Chinese immigrants from Taiwan may have limited English fluency, but some knowledge of the school system. Studies have found that even before immigrating to the United States, many affluent immigrants from Taiwan actually selected the neighborhoods where they wanted to settle or buy real estate based on the quality of the schools (Chao, 2000a; Chao & Tseng, 2002). Often information on the quality of specific schools was provided to them by other immigrants already living in the United States. Their own informal social networks provided them with the knowledge that the quality of U.S. schools varied greatly, and that educational success in the United States depended on the type of school their children attended. Schools or school staff may be completely unaware of the potential knowledge and resources that some more acculturated and/or affluent Asian immigrants may possess. These parents may already be providing knowledge or resources informally to other immigrant parents through their social networks that could be utilized more formally by the schools. In addition to the language and other support suggested above for Asian immigrant parents, schools also must be prepared to suggest specific strategies used by Asian immigrant parents, including (1) monitoring and checking homework, (2) providing guidance in planning for the next steps beyond high school, and (3) providing resources such as extra textbooks, study guides, and tutors.

ACKNOWLEDGMENTS

The research presented in this chapter for the Multicultural Families and Adolescents Study was supported by a grant from the National Institutes of Health (NIH/NICHD) awarded to Ruth K. Chao.

REFERENCES

Agbayani-Siewert, P., & Revilla, L. (1995). Filipino Americans. In P. G. Min (Ed.), *Asian Americans: Contemporary trends and issues* (pp. 134–168). Thousand Oaks, CA: Sage.

Bacho, P. (1997). The tragic sense of Filipino history. In M. P. Root (Ed.), *Filipino Americans: Transformation and identity* (pp. 1–10). Thousand Oaks, CA: Sage.

Barringer, H., Gardner, R. W., & Levin, M. J. (1993). Asian and Pacific Islanders in the United States. In *The population of the United States in the 1980s: A census monograph series*. New York: Russell Sage Foundation.

Blair, S. L., & Qian, Z. (1998). Family and Asian students' educational performance. *Journal of Family Issues, 19*(4), 355–374.

Catsambis, S. (2001). Expanding knowledge of parental involvement in children's secondary education: Connections with high school seniors' academic success. *Social Psychology of Education, 5*(2), 149–177.

Chao, R. K. (1994). Beyond parental control and authoritarian parenting style: Understanding: Chinese parenting through the cultural notion of training. *Child Development, 65*(4), 1111–1120.

Chao, R. K. (1995). Chinese and European-American cultural models of the self reflected in mothers' child rearing beliefs. *Ethos, 23,* 328–354.

Chao, R. K. (2000a). Cultural explanations for the role of parenting in the school success of Asian American children. In R. W. Taylor & M. C. Wang (Eds.), *Resilience across contexts: Family, work, culture, and community* (pp. 333–363). Mahwah, NJ: Erlbaum.

Chao, R. K. (2000b). The parenting of immigrant Chinese and European American mothers: Relations between parenting styles, socialization goals, and parental practices. *Journal of Applied Developmental Psychology, 21*(2), 233–248.

Chao, R. K., & Sue, S. (1996). Chinese parental influences and their children's school success: A paradox in the literature on parenting styles. In S. Lau (Ed.), *Growing up the Chinese way: Chinese child and adolescent development* (pp. 93–120). Hong Kong: Chinese University Press.

Chao, R., & Tseng, V. (2002). Parenting of Asians. In M. H. Bornstein (Ed.), *Handbook of parenting: Vol. 4. Social conditions and applied parenting* (2nd ed., pp. 59–93). Mahwah, NJ: Erlbaum.

Choi, E., Bempechat, J., & Ginsburg, H. (1994). Educational socialization in Korean American children: A longitudinal study. *Journal of Applied Developmental Psychology, 15*(3), 313–318.

Espiritu, Y. L. (1995). Introduction: Filipino settlements in the United States. In Y. L. Espiritu (Ed.), *Filipino American lives* (pp. 1–36). Philadelphia: Temple University Press.

Fan, X. (2001). Parental involvement and students' academic achievement: A growth modeling analysis. *Journal of Experimental Education, 70*(1), 27–61.

Ho, E. S. C., & Willms, J. D. (1996). The effects of parental involvement on eighth grade achievement. *Sociology of Education, 69,* 126–141.

Hong, S., & Ho, H. Z. (2005). Direct and indirect effects of parental involvement on student achievement: Second-order latent growth modeling across ethnic groups. *Journal of Educational Psychology, 97*(1), 32–42.

Kao, G. (1995). Asian Americans as model minorities? A look at their academic performance. *American Journal of Education, 103*(2), 121–159.

Keith, T. Z., Keith, P. B., Troutman, G. C., Bickley, P. G., Trivette, P. S., & Singh, K. (1993). Does parental involvement affect eighth-grade student achievement? Structural analysis of national data. *School Psychology Review, 22*(3), 474–496.

Kitano, H. H. L., & Daniels, R. (1995). *Asian Americans: Emerging minorities* (2nd ed.). Englewood Cliffs, NJ: Prentice Hall.

Mau, W. C. (1997). Parental influences on the high school students' academic achievement: A comparison of Asian immigrants, Asian Americans, and White Americans. *Psychology in the Schools, 34*(3), 267–277.

Peng, S. S., & Wright, D. (1994). Explanation of academic achievement of Asian American students. *Journal of Educational Research, 87*(6), 346–352.

Reyes, O., Gillock, K. L., Kobus, K., & Sanchez, B. (2000). A longitudinal examination of the transition into senior high school for adolescents from urban, low-income status, and predominantly minority backgrounds. *American Journal of Community Psychology, 28*(4), 519–544.

Schneider, B., & Lee, Y. (1990). A model of academic success: The school and home environment of East Asian students. *Anthropology and Education Quarterly, 21*(4), 358–377.

Stevenson, D. L., & Baker, D. P. (1987). The family–school relation and the child's school performance. *Child Development, 58*(5), 1348–1357.

Tseng, V., Chao, R. K., & Padmawidjaja, I. (2007). Asian Americans' educational experiences. In F. Leong, A. Inman, A. Ebreo, L. Yang, L. Kinoshita, & M. Fu (Eds.), *Handbook of Asian American psychology* (2nd ed., pp. 102–123). Thousand Oaks, CA: Sage.

Zhou, M. (1999). Coming of age: The current situation of Asian American children. [Special issue: Second generation Asian Americans' ethnic identity.] *Amerasia Journal, 25*(1), 1–28.

PART II

Facing the Challenges

Feasibility of Parental Involvement During Adolescence

7

Reaching Out to All Families

Developing Parental Involvement
Workshops for African American
Parents of Middle School Students

JELANI MANDARA

T HE ACADEMIC PROBLEMS OF African American middle school
students have been well documented (Perie, Moran, & Lutkus,
2005). Studies show that the transition from elementary to middle
school is associated with significant decreases in academic performance
and increases in adjustment problems for most students, but especially
for African American students (Estell et al., 2007; Graham, Bellmore, &
Mize, 2006). Early adolescence represents a critical time of development
when youth have to cope with precipitous changes in cognitive development, hormonal fluctuations and physical maturation, and different
peer networks (Brinthaupt & Lipka, 2002; Burchinal, Roberts, Zeisel, &
Rowley, 2008). African American early adolescents seem to be especially
vulnerable to academic adjustment problems during this time because of
the plethora of added social pressures and stressors they must navigate
(Burchinal et al., 2008). For instance, African American middle school students experience much lower academic expectations from teachers and
peers compared with most other groups of students (McKown & Weinstein, 2008; Walters & Bowen, 1997). For many African American students,
the transition to middle school is also their first exposure to racially diverse environments. This may be compounded by the fact that it is also
a time when their transition into formal operational stages of cognitive
development allows them greater awareness of societal stereotypes and
the social ramifications of race.

The empirical evidence clearly shows that academically oriented
parenting practices are among the best predictors of achievement and

protective factors during the middle school years (Burchinal et al., 2008; Mandara & Murray, 2007). Unfortunately, there have been relatively few attempts to translate this wealth of knowledge into empirically sound parental involvement prevention interventions. A recent review found only 24 randomized parental training prevention interventions between 1980 and 2003 that focused primarily on academic achievement (Fishel & Ramirez, 2005). One of the underlying reasons for this dearth of parental involvement interventions may be that most of us who trained to conduct basic research are not clear about the process of translating research into practical prevention interventions. Many authoritative sources clearly explain the process for implementing (Stormshak, Dishion, Light, & Yasui, 2005) and evaluating (Shadish, Cook, & Campbell, 2002) parental training interventions, but few offer suggestions for designing and developing such programs. This is particularly true for programs focused on academic achievement. This chapter, therefore, illustrates the steps in translating empirically sound research into culturally sensitive parental involvement workshops for groups of parents. Given the importance of contextual factors to the design of the workshops, this chapter also discusses specific issues workshop developers must consider when attempting to create such programs for African American parents of middle school students.

GENERAL OVERVIEW

The development of parental involvement workshops should begin with empirically sound process theories. One such example is presented in Figure 7.1 and described below. A detailed curriculum, describing the major parenting factors, subfactors, and/or specific behaviors parents should use with their early adolescents, then needs to be developed (Brody et al., 2004). An illustrative outline is presented in Figure 7.2, which also will be discussed in more detail below. Iteratively with the development of the curriculum, workshop developers must decide on the format in which the material will be delivered. A variety of workshop formats have been used in family-based prevention intervention research, but there is little empirical evidence regarding which are the most effective. This chapter discusses the pros and cons of several decisions that must be made, and offers suggestions for working with African American parents of middle-school-aged students at each phase of the process. Finally, workshop developers must write a detailed manual describing the curriculum and delivery format.

Figure 7.1. Example of a Culturally Based Conceptual Model Guiding Workshop Development

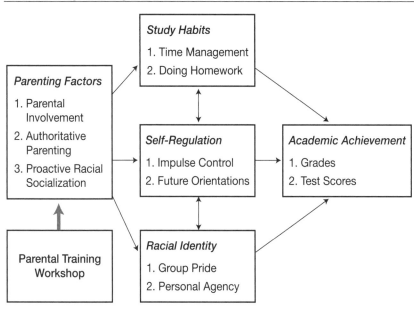

Conceptual Model of
Parental Involvement for African American Adolescents

For the sake of illustration, the conceptual model illustrated in Figure 7.1 describes the mechanisms by which participation in a hypothetical program is expected to increase academic achievement among African American middle school students. The model hypothesizes that there are three main psychosocial factors that protect students from academic adjustment problems during this critical period. First, based on social identity theory (Tajfel & Turner, 1986) and theories of racial identity (Mandara, 2006), many African American early adolescents identify with social stereotypes of African Americans as less academically oriented. Like early adolescents in general, they tend to think and behave according to social stereotypes of their group, while downplaying the importance of the stereotypes associated with other groups. Thus, the model predicts that those early adolescents who have a proactive racial identity, exhibited by a secure sense of self, comfort with and feelings of pride for the larger African American community, and a sense of personal and collective agency over their

Figure 7.2. Example of a Partial Outline of Parental Involvement Workshop Factors, Subfactors, and Specific Behaviors

General Factors ➜ Subfactors ➜ Specific Behaviors

I. Parental Involvement

    A. At-Home Involvement

        1. Cognitive Stimulation

            a. Have plenty of books freely available for youth to read.

            b. Have adolescents learn to play cognitively stimulating games such as chess, Scrabble, or dominoes.

            c. Take youth on learning field trips to museums, libraries, and other cognitively stimulating places.

            d. Keep television, video game, radio, and phone time to a minimum.

        2. Home Organization

            a. Keep noise level and chaos to a minimum.

            b. Keep adequate lighting and house uncluttered.

            c. Do not overburden youth with too many household chores.

            d. Make sure adolescents go to bed on time. Make sleeping as comfortable as possible.

            e. Make sure youth eat before school.

        3. Monitoring Schoolwork

            a. Make time for homework everyday.

            b. Monitor homework, exams, and other assignments.

            c. Have youth use some down time to get ahead in courses.

            d. If possible, have desk in quiet location where youth can study.

            e. Have youth do a few hours of math and reading each day during summer months.

    B. Parent–School Communication

destiny (Mandara, 2006), will have higher academic achievement because they are less likely to internalize negative stereotypes of African Americans. The second major protective factor for African American early adolescents is the development of strong self-regulatory skills. Self-regulation refers to the ability to resist temptations that may have immediate gratification but long-term negative consequences. Because of the enormous social pressures from negative peer groups (Walters & Bowen, 1997), negative media exposure (Ward, 2004), and low expectations from teachers (McKown & Weinstein, 2008), African American adolescents must have strong self-regulatory skills to resist engaging in anti-academic behaviors and stay focused on their long-term academic goals. The model further suggests that like all students, African American middle school students who have good study habits will perform better in school.

The conceptual model also implies that caregivers have the capacity to foster proactive racial identity, strong self-regulatory skills, and good study habits in African American early adolescents by utilizing various socialization strategies that empirical research suggests will develop these important traits. Thus, the hypothetical prevention intervention will teach parents various techniques for improving parental involvement, such as helping with homework when needed, creating a cognitively stimulating home environment, and communicating effectively with teachers about the parents' goals and expectations for their children's academic success. The intervention program also will teach parents fundamental behaviors of authoritative parenting, such as how to be highly responsive to early adolescents while still maintaining appropriate behavioral control. The hypothetical prevention intervention also will teach parents how to promote proactive racial identity by understanding their early adolescents' changing awareness of racial stereotypes and how to utilize racial socialization messages that facilitate pride and a sense of agency during this period.

Important Contextual Issues When Working with African American Parents of Middle School Students

Having a sound theory of the process by which the workshop is expected to impact middle school students' achievement is important, but not sufficient for developing culturally sensitive parenting workshops. Developers also must be familiar with the norms and customs of the group, which can facilitate or hinder program efficacy. There are many such sociocultural issues workshop developers must be aware of that inhibit African American parental involvement during this time. They include issues of cultural mismatch between parents and teachers (Delpit, 1995), parents' lack of confidence in their ability to help their children (McCarthey, 2000), and parents' beliefs about their role in the educational process more generally (Hoover-Dempsey & Sandler, 1997). These should be among the primary foci of the workshop. However, there are a few other fundamental issues that are very difficult to address, but that can derail any intervention effort if ignored.

One of the most well-studied difficulties of conducting medical research or interventions with African Americans is the degree of mistrust they have for health professionals (Moseley, Freed, Bullard, & Goold, 2007). For many justifiable reasons (Washington, 2006), the average

African American is leery of the intentions of most health professionals. Mistrust is also a strong negative predictor of participation in programs and adherence to treatment for African Americans (O'Malley, Sheppard, Schwartz, & Mandelblatt, 2004). For better or for worse, this mistrust of mainstream institutions does not end with healthcare settings. Many African American parents have misgivings about the education system and its surrogate programs, such as parenting workshops implemented through the school. This may be especially the case for African American parents of middle school students because this is usually the first time their children are faced with often-severe, race-based academic tracking (Oakes & Lipton, 1999). This mistrust is one of the main predictors of African American parents' lower rates of at-school involvement (Oakes & Lipton, 1999). Whether workshop developers are aware of it or not, they are surrogates of mainstream institutions (e.g., universities, middle schools, hospitals), and as such they assume the legacy of those institutions in African American communities.

There is no easy remedy for this problem. It takes time to build up relationships, and workshop developers should plan on a long development period. The main factor inhibiting trust seems to be the fear that those implementing the program only want to take information and other resources from the community without giving much in return. The promise of helping their children perform better in school is by far the best selling point, but it is not enough. Having relationships with key community members and having African American staff members also will help, but can take the program only so far. Ultimately, the community must have trust in the main people behind the workshop, whether they are African American or not. Thus, a fundamental feature of the workshop design has to include methods for developing rapport with parents and sharing resources among participants. This will help increase recruitment and adherence, and reduce attrition.

A related but slightly different issue that workshop developers must be aware of when working with African American parents is their assumption that the parenting practices that are effective for European American children may not be effective for their children. For instance, most African American parents are aware of the many unique social pressures their adolescents will face during middle school. Thus, one of the greatest challenges when working with African American parents is getting them to accept what they may perceive as mainstream ideas about parenting. Probably the most promising method for getting African American parents to believe in and utilize the methods taught in the workshop is to show them evidence of the effectiveness of the methods with African American youth similar to theirs. Evidence from prior efficacious prevention programs obviously would be best. Even if such evidence is not available, facilitators can show them clear and concise graphs illustrating the correlations between the parenting factors identified in the workshop and the academic success of African American youth.

Finally, workshop developers must address many logistic concerns. Although the purpose of this chapter is to illustrate the process of designing and developing parental involvement workshops, it is difficult to do this without some understanding of the real-world complications that may occur when trying to implement the workshops. When working with African American parents of middle-school-aged teens in particular, workshop developers have to be cognizant of the fact that over half of the participants will be single working mothers by the time their children are in the early adolescent years. Many will have younger children to care for as well. Workshop developers also must account for the fact that the literacy levels of many poor African American parents can be surprisingly low. Furthermore, unlike many elementary schools, middle schools often are further from their homes and in racially homogeneous communities that African American parents are not always comfortable entering. Thus, workshop developers must address potential scheduling conflicts, time constraints, transportation needs, childcare requirements, and traditional social climates. They also must know whether the workshop will be delivered at community sites easily accessible to program participants.

If funding allows, the community liaison model used by Brody and colleagues (2004) in their prevention interventions with rural African American families may be the most successful method for addressing the many logistic, recruitment, and engagement issues workshop developers may encounter. They describe community liaisons as respected residents of the communities that will be served. The liaisons help to develop rapport and address many of the concerns of participants. The liaisons may be responsible for a variety of duties, especially developing relationships with families, contacting parents regularly, explaining materials and exercises to parents, picking up and dropping off those parents who are without transportation, helping the facilitator with the sessions, and providing daycare services during the workshop.

WORKSHOP DESIGN AND DEVELOPMENT

Once the theoretical model and larger macro issues have been addressed, this information must be translated into a functional curriculum. Workshop developers must define what they wish parents to learn and how they expect them to learn it. More specifically, during this stage, workshop developers must develop the content and delivery format, and decide on exercises to help parents learn the content. Each topic should be developed by following several systematic and iterative steps. These are discussed in more detail below.

Workshop Content Development

The content development stage is probably the most esoteric step in the process. The long history of curriculum development and research on survey instrument development, as well as workshop developers' expert knowledge of the topic, should be brought to bear at this stage. Probably the best place to begin is by outlining the parenting topics to be covered in the workshop across at least three levels of generality. For instance, using the conceptual model in Figure 7.1 as a guide, the curriculum could be divided into three major parenting factors: (1) parental involvement, (2) authoritative parenting, and (3) proactive racial socialization. Then, each major factor could be divided into subfactors. Each subfactor could be further divided into smaller components, depending on the complexity of the constructs. Finally, each subfactor should be divided into the specific parenting behaviors that relate to that subfactor. Figure 7.2 illustrates an outline for the parental involvement factor. The outline would need to be replicated for the authoritative parenting and racial socialization factors.

To generate the outline and specific parenting behaviors, it is wise for researchers to collaborate and brainstorm about ideas. Moreover, empirical descriptions of the major parenting factors should guide the development of an initial outline of the general parenting factors that will be the focus of the workshop (see Baumrind, 1971, and Barber, Stolz, & Olsen, 2005, for examples). Items from well-established survey and observational instruments are also excellent sources of ideas for the specific parenting behaviors to include in the workshop. Conducting interviews or focus groups with parents, especially parents of high-achieving youth, is another method for generating specific parenting behaviors that promote adolescents' school success. The behaviors in Figure 7.2 were derived partially from these sources.

Once the preliminary outline has been generated, it is important to get feedback on the parenting behaviors from experts in the field. Experts rate the parenting behaviors as if they were items from a survey. Similar to Likert's (1932) scaling method, experts can rate the degree to which the parenting behaviors are reflective of the factor they were assigned to. This may be important when decisions about which factors or subfactors to include must be made. It also will be important when attempting to evaluate the program and assess the mediators. Furthermore, because the amount of time per session may be limited, there may be situations in which only the most important behaviors can be discussed with parents. In that case, experts also should rate the degree of importance of each behavior. Each of these matrices of expert ratings will allow the researcher to make a more informed decision about the factors, subfactors, and specific parenting behaviors that should be the focus of the workshop.

During the content development stage, workshop developers must be concerned with the scope, or the breadth and depth, of the curricular content that can be covered. The realities of the context in which the program will be delivered should guide each decision. Parenting behaviors do not exist in a vacuum, and many behaviors have meaning only in the context of other behaviors. For instance, research shows that parental behavioral control and support each have very different meanings depending on the level of the other (Mandara, 2006). Teaching parents to be supportive without also teaching them effective methods of behavioral control may not produce the intended results because both are needed in order to be effective. Given this, the most detailed and comprehensive programs will likely be the most efficacious. Unfortunately, such programs rarely are feasible in most community settings. In most situations, parents will have limits on the number of sessions they can attend, as well as the time they can spend at each session. Given the logistic issues discussed above, this is especially the case when working with poor and working-class African American parents of middle school students.

As discussed above, there are other practical issues, such as costs for facilitators, facilities, parking, and childcare providers, that must be considered as well. I suggest beginning with a very comprehensive and detailed workshop. Once decisions about the number of sessions parents will be exposed to and the time of each workshop have been made, the least important factors, subfactors, and specific behaviors can be eliminated. This again is why ratings of degree of importance from experts can be so valuable in designing a workshop.

Workshop Format Development

After the general scope of the workshop content has been decided, the format in which the material will be delivered must be determined. The most important goals at this stage are to design a delivery format that maximizes the learning and utilization of the material. To achieve these goals in the specific context in which the workshop will be delivered, workshop developers must consider the degree to which the material will be integrated, the sequence in which it will be presented, and the degree of interaction between the facilitators and parents. These are discussed in more detail below.

Degree of integration. One of the primary decisions to be made concerns the degree to which the content will be integrated versus independent across the curriculum. Integrated workshops are those in which each of the major factors is discussed in every session. Independent workshops are those in which only one major factor is discussed in each session. There are pros and cons at both extremes.

The fully integrated approach allows the facilitator to discuss parenting behaviors in the context of other behaviors, which is how they exist in the real world. Parents taking their middle school student to purchase personal reading material do not ignore their racial socialization or behavioral control duties during that time. Rather, the factors occur simultaneously. Integrated workshops can teach parents how these factors can be merged into a cohesive parenting style or pattern. Given that humans learn best when material is presented in the context of other related concepts (Murphy & Medin, 1985), integrated workshops will likely facilitate learning.

However, there are also practical advantages to an independent format. For one, the integrated approach requires that parents attend all the sessions to have a full understanding of each major topic. One missed session can have important implications for successfully learning each factor in the integrated format, whereas with the independent format a missed session means that parents will miss learning about one topic. In the real world in which the workshops will be delivered, most parents will miss at least one session. With the integrated format, an absence increases the chances they will have more difficulty catching up in future sessions. The logic of the independent format is that most sessions do not depend on the others. Thus, an absence will not have the same impact.

Another advantage of the independent session format is that workshops can be modified easily to fit different contexts. For instance, facilitators may be able to conduct five or six sessions with parents at the local middle school, while they may be able to conduct only three workshops with parents in a drug rehabilitation facility. That requires only dropping the least important topics. Such flexibility is not possible with the fully integrated format.

The flexibility of the independent format also has advantages for the evaluation of workshops. This format allows the effects of each major factor to be assessed easily, since some sessions can be given to some parents and not to others. The independent format also allows for an easy assessment of dosage effects, or the degree to which a parent is exposed to the workshop. For example, an evaluation of dosage may show that the effects of the workshop do not increase after the average parent attends the four most important sessions. Knowing these features of the workshop obviously has very important programmatic implications, but it is not as easily assessed in a fully integrated format.

Therefore, optimal learning will be facilitated in the fully integrated format, but the realities of the context, or the competing demands of parents, may make that format impractical. The fully integrated approach is best in situations where absences will be few, such as court-mandated parenting programs. Although learning will not be optimized, the independent session format will likely be more practical in most real-world contexts. This is particularly the case given the concerns of African American parents of middle school students discussed previously. One possibility is to combine the two formats. The first session, which is rarely missed by parents, can be designed to be more integrative and can discuss the general theoretical model, the psychosocial factors the workshop is attempting to modify in their children, and then each of the major socialization factors in an integrative fashion. The remaining sessions can be focused on individual factors.

Sequence of material. Regardless of the degree of integration or independence, one of the most important considerations is the order or sequence in which the sessions will be offered, as well as the order in which content material within each session will be presented. As with any course, the content can be presented from the top-down or from the bottom-up. Top-down formats are those in which the presentation begins with the most general concepts (e.g., parental involvement) and progresses through the subfactors (e.g., at-home involvement) down to the specific behaviors (e.g., reading a book together). The bottom-up format is one in which the specific behaviors are the primary focus of the workshops. The sessions usually begin with a list of the specific behaviors parents should perform. The facilitators eventually may explain the larger context of the behaviors, but usually not. As with other workshop aspects, depending on the context, there are pros and cons to top-down and bottom-up formats.

The intention of top-down formats is to give the specific parenting behaviors more background to aid in understanding them. This format helps to connect the specific behaviors to the larger hierarchy of socialization strategies and goals. Research suggests that the top-down method aids in learning novel concepts because the method facilitates more contextual knowledge (Pazzani, 1991). Giving parents more perspective also may help them to understand and remember to use the behaviors taught. Another advantage of the top-down approach is that it facilitates parents' "buy-in" of the material. Once they begin to understand the logic of the parenting practices taught in the workshops, they are more likely to believe in the method and take it up in their daily activities. As discussed above, this is an important concern when working with African American parents.

There are also some disadvantages to the top-down approach. The main disadvantages are due to the limitations of the real-world situations in which the workshops will be delivered. For instance, the time it takes to get to the specific behaviors can be a major limitation of the top-down format. When the number of sessions and especially the time of each session are limited, it may be difficult to explain the larger theoretical issues and still have time for the specific behaviors. Even when time is available, many parents with the time constraints described earlier really just want to know what they can do that day. They are understandably most concerned with pragmatic issues in their day-to-day life. Often they just want the facilitator to give them a list of behaviors, and then they will pick and choose the behaviors they think are appropriate for their children.

Thus, when deciding on the sequence, workshop developers must take into consideration the difficulty of the content, the amount of time available with the parents, and the degree to which the parents have bought into the ideas. The top-down approach will facilitate learning and uptake of the material, but it takes longer and may not be feasible when the number of sessions or time of each session is limited. The bottom-up approach is usually more feasible and desired by parents, but they also are less likely to use the behaviors in their day-to-day activities. Given the problem of buy-in discussed above, when working with African American parents it may be best to spend the time necessary to explain the larger theoretical factors before getting to the specific behaviors. If the parents do not practice the strategies taught in the workshop, then the efficacy of the workshop obviously will be limited. It will help to remind parents that the specific day-to-day behaviors of interest will be discussed eventually, but doing that will not completely solve the motivation and engagement issues at this stage.

Degree of interaction. Another very important set of decisions workshop developers must make when designing the format of the workshop concerns the degree to which the sessions will be interactive versus scripted. Interactive workshops are those in which parents are actively involved through questioning, feedback, and participating in various exercises. The facilitator may ask the parents for their understanding of the material and their thoughts and suggestions about various topics. Also, the parents may be divided into smaller groups and work on projects such as role playing or writing down their short-term and long-term goals for their children. In the alternative format, sessions are presented by the facilitator or even by video following a set script. Whereas the interactive workshops are like labs in science classes, the scripted workshops are more like structured lectures. Like the other format options, each choice has pros and cons to consider.

Although the empirical evidence is limited, most programs are developed under the assumption that prevention interventions that use interactive formats are more efficacious than those using scripted formats (Kumpfer & Alvarado, 2003). This is because interactive methods are most strongly associated with participant engagement, and engagement facilitates learning the material presented in the workshops. Another important advantage of interactive methods is that they can help parents question the logic of their parenting practices. As discussed above, most parenting practices are based on parents' cultural world view. Parents rarely think about why they parent the way they do. However, many traditional culturally based practices may not be optimal in modern environments. The old philosophy that "children should be seen and not heard," is one glaring example of an archaic parenting idea that hinders cognitive development. Exercises that promote self-reflection and questioning of parents' own motives can do a lot to change minds about less than optimal parenting practices. Such exercises are conducive to more interactive formats.

Although the interactive format presents many opportunities for parent engagement, learning, and buy-in, there are also significant obstacles to using the format effectively. The exercises and questions take time. For instance, many highly interactive family-based prevention interventions require a minimum of 12 sessions plus follow-ups. Many require up to 20 two-hour sessions. Given the time limitations that workshop developers will have to deal with, reflection, feedback, and small-group exercises may not be feasible.

The main potential problems of the interactive format are related to lack of fidelity. Although fidelity is a multidimensional concept, it primarily refers to the degree to which the workshop is implemented in a way consistent with the underlying conceptual model and manual (Hogue, Liddle, Singer, & Leckrone, 2005). Research shows that prevention interventions with greater fidelity are much more likely to achieve their intended outcomes than those programs that are lower in fidelity (Hogue et al., 2005). The open-ended nature of the interactive format often can reduce workshop fidelity because it leaves open the possibility that the group will stay focused on one topic longer than expected, which can limit their time on other equally important topics. It is also very common for the exercises to take the parents down an unintended road. This can greatly impact the degree to which the program is administered in the way it was intended. Similarly, adapting an interactive workshop to different contexts can be difficult without jeopardizing fidelity. The scripted format has fewer of these concerns.

Thus, this is another difficult decision workshop developers must make depending on the cultural context and logistic limitations. When working with African American parents, workshop developers must be careful not to overgeneralize or reinforce stereotypes about cultural norms. However, it is likely that many African American parents will be more comfortable with interactive workshops because of their experiences with the African American church. That does not mean African American parents cannot adapt to different situations, but I think it does mean that the completely scripted video-based format may not work as well with them. Thus, some combination of script and facilitator interaction may be the best option in most community settings with African American parents.

Preparation of a Manual for the Workshop and Conducting Practice Sessions

Once the preliminary decisions at each stage of development have been made, it is advisable to go about the tedious process of writing a preliminary manual describing the workshop, as well as conducting several practice sessions before administering the workshop to larger groups of parents. Not only will this help maintain the fidelity of the workshop, but, considering these parents' degree of uncertainty about the benefits of the program, an organized workshop also will help allay their doubts. A manual also can address concerns that program staff will only take resources without giving anything in return, because it makes schools or local communities less dependent on the workshop developers for future workshops.

The manual should be as detailed as possible and include information about the workshop content and delivery format. The manual should begin with a table of contents dividing the workshop into sessions, and each session should be divided into subsections. The manual should state exactly what the facilitator ought to say, depending on the degree of interaction designed. When possible, the manual also should include the goals, exercises, needed materials, information about the structure of groups, and approximate minutes to complete each subsection.

Designing the workshop and even writing the preliminary manual are relatively difficult and tedious, but actually conducting an organized and professional workshop for parents in the real world may be even more so. Parents will have varying levels of education and motivation, different time constraints, and varying degrees of willingness to share their thoughts and offer advice. To be able to efficiently handle these issues, practice sessions are virtually mandatory before attempting to conduct the workshop with larger groups of parents. Practice sessions also will help refine the content, delivery format, and manual. Conducting practice sessions with colleagues who will provide honest feedback is a good first step. Sessions with small groups of African American parents could then be conducted and videotaped. After each practice session, parents could rate the workshop on several dimensions, especially the effectiveness of delivery, feasibility of the strategies discussed, and degree to which the workshop will likely motivate other parents. Workshop developers could ask colleagues and experts to rate the videos along the same dimensions, as well as parents' responsiveness and engagement. These dimensions predict treatment outcomes in large-scale parenting prevention interventions (Brody et al., 2004). All the feedback should be used to continually refine the workshop and manual.

CONCLUSION AND POLICY RECOMMENDATIONS

Research has demonstrated that African American middle school students are at particular risk for achievement problems, but a long history of research also indicates that the use of particular parenting practices is conducive to achievement and helps protect youth from such social setbacks. Unfortunately, relatively few empirically sound parental involvement prevention interventions have been developed. This chapter outlined the major steps involved in developing a community-oriented parental involvement workshop. The focus was on African American parents of middle school students, but the information applies regardless of the specific targets of the workshop. I described the importance of understanding the sociocultural context in which the program will be delivered, and offered suggestions for working with African American parents of middle school students. In particular, I described methods that may help workshop developers gain the trust of community members and deal with logistic concerns such as parental time constraints. Important steps in the development of the workshop curriculum and format were discussed, such as how to derive the topics to be covered in the workshop from a process theory and deciding on the breadth and depth of the curricular content. The pros and cons workshop developers must consider when deciding on the degree to which the workshop format will be integrated, the sequence in which the material will be presented, and the degree of interaction between the facilitators and parents also were described. I asserted that methods that maximize learning and uptake may not be feasible in most community settings because of constraints on the number of sessions and time of each session, and the possibility of low attendance rates. The best choices always depend on the context in which the workshop will be delivered. Finally, I described the importance of writing and the contents of a detailed manual for the workshop.

The development of a sound workshop is not a trivial endeavor and may require significantly more time and financial resources than most people realize. Fortunately, parental involvement policies are abundant, but virtually all of the funds coming from such policies are given directly to public schools. Furthermore, most parental involvement policies have vague mandates that more often than not manifest as a mishmash of haphazard programs with questionable success. To help remedy this issue, the public schools should be given more-specific instructions for how to develop and/or implement parental involvement programs. Furthermore, a greater share of the funding should be directed to granting agencies for the support of empirically grounded parental training prevention interventions focused specifically on increasing academic achievement. Although such interventions may be relatively difficult and expensive, their potential importance to people's lives cannot be understated.

REFERENCES

Barber, B. K., Stolz, H. E., & Olsen, J. A. (2005). Parental support, psychological control, and behavioral control: Assessing relevance across time, culture, and method. *Monographs of the Society for Research in Child Development, 70*(4), 1–137.

Baumrind, D. (1971). Current patterns of parental authority. *Developmental Psychology Monographs, 4*(1), 1–103.

Brinthaupt, T. M., & Lipka, R. P. (2002). *Understanding early adolescent self and identity: Applications and interventions.* Albany: State University of New York Press.

Brody, G. H., Murry, V. M., Gerrard, M., Gibbons, F. X., Molgaard, V., McNair, L., et al. (2004). The Strong African American Families Program: Translating research into prevention programming. *Child Development, 75*(3), 900–917.

Burchinal, M. R., Roberts, J. E., Zeisel, S. A., & Rowley, S. J. (2008). Social risk and protective factors for African American children's academic achievement and adjustment during the transition to middle school. *Developmental Psychology, 44*(1), 286–292.

Delpit, L. (1995). *Other people's children: Cultural conflict in the classroom.* New York: New Press.

Estell, D. B., Farmer, T. W., Irvin, M. J., Thompson, J. H., Hutchins, B. C., & McDonough, E. M. (2007). Patterns of middle school adjustment and ninth grade adaptation of rural African American youth: Grades and substance use. *Journal of Youth and Adolescence, 36*(4), 477–487.

Fishel, M., & Ramirez, L. (2005). Evidence-based parent involvement interventions with school-aged children. *School Psychology Quarterly, 20*(4), 371–402.

Graham, S., Bellmore, A. D., & Mize, J. (2006). Peer victimization, aggression, and their co-occurrence in middle school: Pathways to adjustment problems. *Journal of Abnormal Child Psychology, 34*(3), 363–378.

Hogue, A., Liddle, H. A., Singer, A., & Leckrone, J. (2005). Intervention fidelity in family-based prevention counseling for adolescent problem behaviors. *Journal of Community Psychology, 33*(2), 191–211.

Hoover-Dempsey, K. V., & Sandler, H. M. (1997). Why do parents become involved in their children's education. *Review of Educational Research, 67*(1), 3–42.

Kumpfer, K. L., & Alvarado, R. (2003). Family-strengthening approaches for the prevention of youth problem behaviors. *American Psychologist, 58*(6–7), 457–465.

Likert, R. (1932). A technique for the measurement of attitudes. *Archives of Psychology, 140*(1), 1–55.

Mandara, J. (2006). The impact of family functioning on African American males' academic achievement: A review and clarification of the empirical literature. *Teachers College Record, 108*(2), 206–223.

Mandara, J., & Murray, C. B. (2007). How African American families can facilitate the academic achievement of their children: Implications for family-based interventions. In J. Jackson (Ed.), *Strengthening the educational pipeline for African Americans: Informing policy and practice* (pp. 165–186). New York: State University of New York Press.

McCarthey, S. (2000). Home-school connections: A review of the literature. *The Journal of Educational Research, 93*(3), 145–153.

McKown, C., & Weinstein, R. S. (2008). Teacher expectations, classroom context, and the achievement gap. *Journal of School Psychology, 46*(3), 235–261.

Moseley, K. L., Freed, G. L., Bullard, C. M., & Goold, S. D. (2007). Measuring African-American parents' cultural mistrust while in a healthcare setting: A pilot study. *Journal of the National Medical Association, 99*(1), 15–21.

Murphy, G. L., & Medin, D. L. (1985). The role of theories in conceptual coherence. *Psychological Review, 92*(3), 289–316.

Oakes, J., & Lipton, M. (1999). *Teaching to change the world.* Boston: McGraw-Hill.

O'Malley, A. S., Sheppard, V. B., Schwartz, M., & Mandelblatt, J. (2004). The role of trust in use of preventive services among low-income African-American women. *Preventive Medicine: An International Journal Devoted to Practice and Theory, 38*(6), 777–785.

Pazzani, M. (1991). The influence of prior knowledge on concept acquisition: Experimental and computational results. *Journal of Experimental Psychology: Learning, Memory and Cognition, 17*(3), 416–432.

Perie, M., Moran, R., & Lutkus, A. D. (2005). *NAEP 2004 trends in academic progress: Three decades of student performance in reading and mathematics* (NCES 2005-464). Washington, DC: U.S. Government Printing Office.

Shadish, W. R., Cook, T. D., & Campbell, D. T. (2002). *Experimental and quasi-experimental designs for generalized causal inference.* Boston: Houghton Mifflin.

Stormshak, E. A., Dishion, T. J., Light, J., & Yasui, M. (2005). Implementing family-centered interventions within the public middle school: Linking service delivery to change in student problem behavior. *Journal of Abnormal Child Psychology, 33*(6), 723–733.

Tajfel, H., & Turner, J. C. (1986). The social identity theory of inter-group behavior. In S. Worchel & L. W. Austin (Eds.), *Psychology of intergroup relations* (pp. 2–24). Chicago: Nelson-Hall.

Walters, K., & Bowen, G. L. (1997). Peer group acceptance and academic performance among adolescents participating in a dropout prevention program. *Child and Adolescent Social Work Journal, 14*(6), 413–426.

Ward, L. M. (2004). Wading through the stereotypes: Positive and negative associations between media use and black adolescents' conceptions of self. *Developmental Psychology, 40*(2), 284–294.

Washington, H. A. (2006). *Medical apartheid: The dark history of medical experimentation on black Americans from colonial times to the present.* New York: Doubleday.

8

Tapping Into Technology

*Using the Internet to Promote
Family–School Communication*

SUZANNE M. BOUFFARD

C OMMUNICATION IS AT THE HEART OF family–school relationships and effective family involvement. However, family–
school communication can be challenging for logistic, emotional,
and cultural reasons (Lightfoot, 2003). Educators often ask: How can we
promote more frequent and meaningful communication with families?
In today's information age, Internet technology, including email, Web
sites, and social networking technologies such as blogs, represents an
opportunity for increasing communication between families and schools.
These methods present a range of benefits, but they also pose challenges
for schools and families.

This chapter examines the growing trend of Internet-based family–
school communication, focusing on middle and high school students, their
families, and schools. At a time when many forms of family involvement
decline, the Internet presents the opportunity to facilitate family–school
communication in ways that are less threatening to adolescent autonomy than traditional methods. The chapter describes the rationale for and
prevalence of Internet-based family–school communication, opportunities
and challenges, and academic outcomes for adolescents. It concludes with
implications and considerations for educational practice and policy.

FAMILY–SCHOOL COMMUNICATION IN ADOLESCENCE

Across the developmental span, ongoing, bidirectional communication allows families and schools to share information about a range of topics—
including student progress, areas and strategies for improvement, and

opportunities for family participation at school—that can lead to more family involvement both at home and at school (Lunts, 2003). Although many forms of family involvement tend to decline as children enter adolescence (Eccles & Harold, 1993), family–school communication remains associated with a range of benefits. These positive outcomes include achievement (Grolnick & Slowiaczek, 1994), educational expectations and aspirations (Trusty, 1999), and course completion, high school graduation, and postsecondary enrollment (Anguiano, 2004; Catsambis, 2001; Eccles & Harold, 1993). Although some studies have found neutral or negative effects on these outcomes (Catsambis, 2001; Desimone, 1999; Sui-Chu & Willms, 1996), in most cases these relationships diminished or disappeared after controlling for prior achievement and students' behavioral and learning problems.

Research also has found that positive student outcomes are associated with other forms of family involvement that are incumbent upon communication, such as parental knowledge of school practices and coursework (Catsambis, 2001), helping students to enroll in college preparatory courses (Catsambis, 2001), and the quality of the parent–teacher relationship (Hill, 2001). Underscoring these findings, over 70% of high school dropouts surveyed in a recent study reported that more communication between their parents and schools might have prevented them from dropping out (Bridgeland, DiIulio, & Morrison, 2006).

Although offering clear benefits, establishing family–school communication can be challenging for a variety of reasons, including time constraints, conflicting schedules of families and teachers, and linguistic and cultural differences between families and teachers (Lightfoot, 2003). Furthermore, the outcomes of family–school communication depend on content, tone, and context. Due to time pressures and competing demands, families and schools often communicate only in the face of problems. As a result, teachers are more likely to communicate with the parents of children who experience more problems, get into more trouble, or require additional help (Dornbusch & Glasgow, 1996; Epstein, 1996; Henderson & Mapp, 2002; Lightfoot, 1978), a trend that may help to explain why teachers of lower-ability-track classes have more contact with parents than teachers of higher ability tracks (Dornbusch & Glasgow, 1996). This pattern can establish a cycle of negative interactions between parents and schools (Epstein, 1996) and a pattern of disagreements rooted in tension and distrust that Lightfoot (1978) termed "negative dissonance." Such patterns are particularly likely to occur when families and educators come from different backgrounds and social classes (Lightfoot, 1978). In addition to these challenges, which occur at all grade levels, middle and high school students have many teachers and also a need for more autonomy from parents, which may lead them to discourage family–school contact. For all of these reasons, families and teachers of adolescents need efficient and effective ways to communicate that reduce or eliminate common barriers.

PREVALENCE OF
INTERNET-BASED FAMILY–SCHOOL COMMUNICATION

Internet technology represents an opportunity for overcoming these barriers and increasing communication between families and schools. Internet platforms such as email, Web sites, electronic discussion boards, and blogs build on the success of home–school voicemail programs, which emerged in the 1980s and demonstrated increases in family–school communication and other forms of family involvement (Bauch, 1989). The broad range of technologies available today presents new opportunities. School Web sites can provide a wealth of general and specific information, including school policies, events and activities, student assignments and progress, and opportunities for family involvement. Email between parents, teachers, and other school staff can facilitate two-way communication about individual students, including course choices and future plans, academic progress, and strategies for promoting learning at home. A growing number of commercial products allows teachers to create their own Web sites and maintain online "student information systems" where parents can check grades. Many of these platforms rely on families having existing access to computers and the Internet, but others operate on school-loaned computers, game consoles, and Web TV (Chaboudy & Jameson, 2001; Penuel et al., 2002).

Building on anecdotal reports from educators (e.g., Farmer, 2000; Hernandez & Leung, 2004; Tobolka, 2006; Wilcox, 2006), recent studies have suggested that Internet-based family–school communication is fairly common. My analysis of a nationally representative sample of over 14,000 high school students and their parents and teachers found that more than one-third of families had used the Internet to communicate with schools (Bouffard, 2007). Similarly, another nationally representative survey of 754 middle and high school youth and their parents found that 28% of parents had emailed a teacher (Lenhart, Simon, & Graziano, 2001).

However, the potential of the Internet appears to be untapped for many families and schools. My analyses found that approximately half of the national sample had access to a computer but did not use it to communicate with schools, while approximately 10% had no access in any setting and the frequency of use was only once or twice a year. Furthermore, findings from a study conducted by the National School Boards

Association (2000) suggested that higher percentages of parents were interested in using Internet-based communication than currently were using it: 64% were interested in emailing school staff, 55% in communicating with the local school board via the Internet, and 56% in viewing their children's schoolwork online.

Teachers also appear to view the Internet as an opportunity: In a nationally representative survey, 68% of teachers reported that the most essential type of technology for teaching is a "teacher's computer station with access to electronic mail," rating this item more highly than telephones, classroom Internet access for students, and reference materials (Lanahan & Boysen, 2005). Although anecdotal reports suggest that some school administrators also are using Internet-based communication with families and the public (Wilcox, 2006), my analyses found that school administrators underestimated teachers' use of such communication. One potential reason for this finding is that teachers may be using technology to communicate with families outside of structured programs, for example, by using personal email accounts.

OPPORTUNITIES AND CHALLENGES OF INTERNET-BASED COMMUNICATION

Internet platforms offer both new opportunities and new challenges. Of particular concern, many of the challenges disproportionately affect families with lower incomes and less education. Taken together, these benefits and challenges suggest that Internet-based communication may best be viewed as one component of a larger communication strategy.

Potential Benefits

One benefit is that Internet-based communication can reduce some barriers to traditional forms of communication, particularly those that are related to time and scheduling. Internet-based communication is quick, efficient, unconstrained by mismatched parent and teacher work schedules, and part of the existing regular daily routine of many families, both at home and in the workplace (Abdal-Haqq, 2002). Internet-based communication also may allow parents of adolescents to obtain information without entering the school building or relying on fliers delivered by students, which adolescents may perceive as threats to their autonomy. Accessing information through Web sites also may circumvent the intimidation that some parents feel about talking with school personnel or entering the school building.

Internet-based communication can be archived and accessed easily, providing a written record of communication that can be stored and tracked over time (Guidry, 2004), and Web sites offer unlimited space to organize information and showcase student work (Miller, Adsit, & Miller, 2005). Web sites also can provide links to other information, particularly when they are part of a multilevel structure that includes classroom, school, and district pages (Lunts, 2003; Scaringello, 2002). In addition to these information-sharing functions, Web sites increasingly serve a public relations and marketing function. Some school districts and superintendents use Web sites and blogs to share information about their policies and practices so that their decisions will be more open and transparent to the public (Swann, 2006; Wilcox, 2006). Private, magnet, and charter schools use Web sites for marketing (Lunts, 2003), as do many public schools, which face declining enrollment (Padgett, 2007) and are mandated by the No Child Left Behind Act to communicate with parents about options for supplemental education services and school choice if the primary school is identified as underperforming (Mendez, 2004).

The Challenge of Access

However, the Internet also poses some significant challenges. Of greatest concern are issues of access and equity. Again using national data, I explored the likelihood of Internet-based family–school communication across a range of family background characteristics (Bouffard, 2007). Families with higher incomes and more education not only were more likely to have access to the Internet, but also were more likely to use it to communicate with schools when they did have access. Hispanic families were less likely to have access and less likely to use it to communicate with schools when they did. Contrary to hypotheses, parents' occupational types did not predict access or usage, although families with at least one full-time working parent were more likely to have access. Income was a stronger predictor of access for African Americans than for other families.

These findings about access are consistent with national statistics about Internet use and the "digital divide" more broadly. Although inequity in Internet access has been decreasing since the beginning of this decade (U.S. Department of Commerce, 2002), Americans of higher socioeconomic status are more likely to have access in their homes, workplaces, schools, and communities and through multiple technologies, including computers, cell phones, and wireless devices (DeBell & Chapman, 2006; Magill, 2007; U.S. Department of Commerce, n. d.). They also are more likely to have more efficient, high-speed Internet connections (Horrigan, 2008). According to the U.S. Census Current Population Survey, in 2007 92% of households earning $100,000 or more annually had Internet access compared with 51% of families earning less than $35,000 per year and 26% of those earning less than $15,000 per year (U.S. Department of Commerce, n. d.). Income and education have independent effects on access (U.S. Department of Commerce, 2002), and the digital divide is similar for education levels (U.S. Department of Commerce, n. d.). Findings about workplace access and usage mirror those for home usage, and few families rely on community centers for technology access (U.S. Department of Commerce, 2002). Members of different ethnic groups also have differential access to the Internet: Asian Americans are most likely to have Internet access at home, followed by (in decreasing order) Whites, African Americans, Latinos, and Native Americans (U.S. Department of Commerce, n. d.). There is some reason to be optimistic, however: The rate of broadband access is growing fastest among African American households and those with lower education levels (U.S. Department of Commerce, n. d.).

However, the findings from my study suggested that the story of differential use is more complicated than access alone. Families with lower incomes, less education, and Hispanic backgrounds were less likely to use the Internet to communicate with schools even when they did have access. Although statistics are not widely available, there may be group differences in experience, facility, and comfort with Internet technology. For example, Robinson, DiMaggio, and Hargittai (2003) found that individuals with more education were more likely to use the Internet for topics related to work, education, and political engagement, while those with less education were more likely to use it for social and entertainment purposes. Access and usage also may interact, so that families who have less access to or less experience with the Internet have less opportunity to become facile and comfortable with it (Horrigan, 2007; Penuel et al., 2002). Among those who have access, low levels of literacy and English skills also may serve as barriers. Even among those who speak and read English fluently, some may feel nervous or intimidated about possible mistakes in their spelling or grammar.

Relational and Logistic Challenges

Internet media also may change the nature of family–school communication. For example, email messages lack visual and nonverbal cues such as tone of voice and body language, which could lead to miscommunications and misunderstandings (Lunts, 2003). To date, research on the nature of and outcomes associated with Internet-based communication has been mixed. Some studies have found that Internet users reveal personal information more quickly (Tidwell & Walther, 2002) and are more likely to express traits they value but do not display during in-person interactions (Bargh, McKenna, & Fitzsimons, 2002), perhaps because of the need to compensate for the lack of visual cues and a sense of anonymity and safety. However, other studies have found that the lack of visual cues leads to depersonalization and reliance on preconceptions about the other party's social and demographic groups (Spears, Postmes, Lea, & Wolbert, 2002). Such a trend could be particularly problematic in family–school relationships, because teachers tend to see ethnic minority parents and White parents differently (Kohl, Lengua, & McMahon, 2000) and because parents may base their impressions of teachers on their own previous negative experiences with schools (see Chapter 3, this volume). This depersonalization also could result in more conflict; for example, a Florida superintendent discontinued his blog after numerous incendiary posts (which were more confrontational than other communications he received) (Wilcox, 2006).

Internet-based family–school communication poses logistic challenges, including failure to receive messages due to a change in service providers, computer problems, infrequent checking of email, a full mailbox that cannot accept more messages, and difficulty finding email addresses for teachers due to a lack of centralized email directories (Lunts, 2003). Furthermore, some families may have unrealistic expectations of an immediate email response (Abdal-Haqq, 2002), while teachers and administrators may be bombarded with a large volume of communication. This may be a problem particularly for middle and high school teachers, who have multiple classes. Maintaining and updating Web sites also can pose significant time and capacity challenges for schools (Hotz & Bailey, 2002). These challenges, along with concerns about privacy and security, may account for findings from several studies that most school Web sites do not follow best practices, are not conducive to family involvement, and are static, out of date, and lacking in interactive capacity (Lunts, 2003; Miller et al., 2005; Scaringello, 2002; Swann, 2006). Similarly, a small-scale evaluation of a program to help teachers use classroom Web sites found that two thirds of the teachers did not utilize the Web sites regularly, despite plans to do so and a belief that the training was useful (Friedman, 2006).

Determining the Appropriate
Uses for Internet-Based Communication

For all of these reasons, Internet-based communication may be more appropriate for some situations than for others. For example, conversations about sensitive topics and student problems may be best accomplished through face-to-face or phone contact, which allow for more nonverbal cues, opportunities for clarification, and immediate response. Similarly, topics that require an immediate response may be best served by real-time communication rather than Internet-based communication. To date, few data are available about when and why parents and schools use the Internet to communicate, or about how Internet-based communication can be incorporated into an overall communication strategy that works to build positive and trusting relationships.

OUTCOMES ASSOCIATED WITH INTERNET-BASED FAMILY–SCHOOL COMMUNICATION

All of these challenges and opportunities are likely to impact whether students benefit from Internet-based family–school communication. Based on previous literature, I developed a theoretical model of the process and potential outcomes of Internet-based family–school communication during adolescence (see Figure 8.1).

The left side of the model proposes that Internet-based communication leads to increased information sharing between parents and teachers. The hypothesis is that the Internet reduces barriers to family–school communication and leads to increased efficiency. Efficiency is one of two primary purposes of technology, the other being innovation (Coffman, 2004), and is the major reason for most technology use to date (Brynin & Kraut, 2006). It is then proposed that this increased efficiency promotes the use of the Internet for information sharing, consistent with previous research on the Internet's effect on communication and social interactions (Kraut et al., 2002; Wellman, Quan Haase, Witte, & Hampton, 2001). The next step of the model proposes that information sharing increases family involvement behaviors by helping parents to understand why and how to help students at home and enhances opportunities to participate in school events (Abdal-Haqq, 2002). Marshall and Rossett (1997) propose that this process can occur through multiple pathways, including providing

Figure 8.1. Theoretical Model of the Process of Internet-Based Family–School Communication

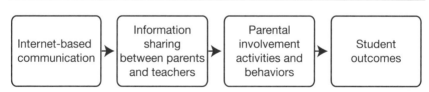

general school information, specific suggestions to promote learning at home, and feedback about individual students. In the final stage of the theoretical model, increased family involvement activities and behaviors lead to more positive student academic outcomes.

Outcomes Among High School Students: Achievement, Expectations, and Graduation

I tested portions of the model among high school students, their families, and teachers (Bouffard, 2007). Using nationally representative data from the National Center for Education Statistics, this study examined the following hypothesis: Internet-based family–school communication leads to two forms of developmentally appropriate family involvement (parent–student discussion about education and parental involvement in homework), which in turn lead to positive student academic outcomes (higher achievement test scores and educational expectations and lower likelihood of school dropout). For this study, parent–student discussion included measures of how often parents communicated with their teenagers about report cards, course selection, college preparation, and college applications. Parental involvement in homework included helping with and checking completion of homework.[1]

This study also explored an alternative hypothesis: that Internet-based communication would, on the contrary, reduce other family involvement behaviors, by replacing more traditional practices such as parent–teacher conferences and visits to the school. Such an outcome might result in less effective family–school relationships, given the importance of face-to-face contact for building trust and positive relationships between teachers and families (Mapp, 2004).

I examined the process of Internet-based communication over a 2-year period, from the time students entered 10th grade to the time most were in 12th grade. Results suggested that Internet-based communication was associated with benefits for students. High school students whose parents engaged in Internet-based communication with schools demonstrated higher achievement and educational expectations 2 years later, even when controlling for more traditional methods of family–school communication and previous achievement. These students also were significantly less likely to drop out of school, although the magnitude of this relationship was small. Furthermore, these results were consistent for students from all socioeconomic and ethnic groups, as well as for both males and females. Although families of lower socioeconomic status were less likely to have access to and engage in Internet-based communication with schools, their adolescents benefited as much as their middle-class peers when families did use the Internet. These findings suggest that the Internet may represent untapped potential, and that efforts to address gaps in Internet access and usage may be warranted.

However, the middle portion of the model was not supported, leaving unanswered questions about how and why Internet-based communication predicted academic outcomes. Although Internet-based family–school communication predicted parent–student discussion about education 2 years later, parent–student discussion did not explain the primary relationship. Parental involvement in homework did not explain the relationship either. In fact, parental involvement in homework was negatively associated with student outcomes, even when controlling for previous achievement in order to account for the possibility that parents became involved in homework because their children were struggling academically. These findings may have been due to the unmeasured factor of how parents were involved in homework, because previous research has suggested that outcomes vary according to the affective nature of homework involvement (Pomerantz, Wang, & Ng, 2005).

Next Steps: How and Why
Internet-Based Communication Benefits Students

These findings underscore the need for future research that examines how and why Internet-based family–school communication has benefits for students. In addition to exploring the context in which the communication occurs, research should examine other forms of family involvement that may explain the relationship between such communication and student outcomes. For example, Internet-based communication may be more likely to increase parents' monitoring of student progress and assignments, visiting colleges, and participating in school events.

In addition, it is likely that the processes and outcomes of Internet-based family–school communication vary according to the content, emotionality, and initiator of the communication. The tenor and tone of email conversations vary widely. Internet-based communication may prove more appropriate and beneficial for some topics than others. In this study, exploratory post hoc analyses suggested that families and schools used the Internet for communicating about positive or neutral topics, but used other methods for communicating when students had academic problems. Given the potential barriers and disadvantages cited above, such situations may prompt parents and teachers to communicate in person or via phone. If this is the case, the Internet may represent one tool in a larger toolbox for family educational involvement, one that is best used for general information sharing and facilitating other forms of involvement.

IMPLICATIONS FOR POLICY AND PRACTICE

Given the increasing role of the Internet in all aspects of life, it is likely that the use of Internet-based methods for family–school communication will grow. Gaps in access are decreasing, as has happened when other new technologies, such as telephones and cable television, reached a saturation point (Shields & Behrman, 2000). The prevalence of Internet-based family–school communication also is likely to increase in future generations, when children who grew up using the Internet become parents and educators. These trends have important implications for educational practice and policy.

Although decreasing, the persistent digital divide raises concerns that technology could exacerbate existing educational inequity, particularly because the lower socioeconomic status families who are least likely to have access are also least likely to be involved with schools in other ways. As Shields and Behrman (2000) have noted, market forces alone are not likely to close access gaps, prompting a role for the federal government, private philanthropy, and businesses. Many families also need training, to build technological knowledge, skills, and comfort. Investments should include demonstration programs that provide both access and training—along with evaluations to study feasibility, scale, and outcomes—and subsidy or tax incentive programs. In the meantime, educators should pay close attention to issues of access and usage, examining their assumptions about families' communication or lack thereof and providing multiple communication options.

Educators also should pay close attention to how and when they utilize the Internet to communicate with families. Critical questions to ask include: Are Internet-based methods the most appropriate and helpful way to communicate about this particular topic? Am I clear about the meaning or request of this email, or do I need to pick up the phone to get more clarification? Before I press the send or publish button, are there any statements that may be misinterpreted? As with all communications, it is essential for teachers and administrators to examine their own assumptions, world views, and potential biases, which may be exacerbated by a lack of visual cues and the abbreviated nature of Internet-based conversations.

Schools and educators also should establish policies and guidelines for Internet-based communication, including appropriate language and standard clauses encouraging families to call or visit if they have concerns or questions. Because of the potential for information overload, and because families and schools may have different expectations, educators may choose to share these policies with families and create family–school compacts outlining responsibilities and expectations. Even without formal policies, teachers can tell parents how they plan to handle electronic communication and establish realistic ground rules.

The design of school Web sites and other Internet platforms also warrants careful attention. Confusing, outdated, or otherwise poorly designed and maintained platforms—which research suggests are the norm—may alienate families and undermine efforts to build positive family–school relationships. Information about best practices for designing school Web sites and other platforms is widely available in practitioner journals (e.g., Swann, 2006).

Internet-based family–school communication opens many exciting avenues for family–school relationships. Emerging research suggests benefits of such communication during adolescence—when many other forms of family involvement decline—and for students from all backgrounds. Moving forward, it is critical to learn how to bring these methods to scale. The combined efforts of policymakers, researchers, businesses, and schools have the potential to leverage the Internet to realize the potential of family-school relationships for all students.

NOTE

1. Recent research suggests that the outcomes associated with parental involvement in homework vary according to how parents are involved and how students experience that involvement. For example, homework involvement is negatively associated with student outcomes when students feel that their parents' involvement is controlling or suggestive of low competence. This study did not make it possible to examine the context of homework involvement.

REFERENCES

Abdal-Haqq, I. (2002). Engaging families and communities in the work of schools: Issues and technology-based tools. In I. Abdal-Haqq (Ed.), *Connecting schools and communities through technology* (pp. 1–21). Washington, DC: National School Boards Association.

Anguiano, R. P. V. (2004). Families and schools: The effect of parental involvement on high school completion. *Journal of Family Issues, 25*(1), 61–85.

Bargh, J. A., McKenna, K. Y. A., & Fitzsimons, G. M. (2002). Can you see the real me? Activation and expression of the "true self" on the Internet. *Journal of Social Issues, 58*(1), 33–48.

Bauch, J. P. (1989). The transparent school model: New technology for parent involvement. *Educational Leadership, 47*(2), 32–34.

Bouffard, S. M. (2007). "Virtual" parental involvement: The role of the Internet in parent–school communication. *Dissertation Abstracts International, 68*(5B), 3421. (UMI No. AAI 3265263)

Bridgeland, J. M., DiIulio, J. J., & Morrison, K. B. (2006). *The silent epidemic: Perspectives of high school dropouts.* Washington, DC: Civic Enterprises.

Brynin, M., & Kraut, R. E. (2006). Social studies of domestic information and communication technologies. In R. Kraut, M. Brynin, & S. Kiesler (Eds.), *Computers, phones, and the Internet: Domesticating information technology* (pp. 3–20). Oxford: Oxford University Press. Retrieved March 6, 2006, from http://www.cs.cmu.edu/~kraut/RKraut.site.files/articles/Byrnin04-SocialStudiesOfICT.pdf

Catsambis, S. (2001). Expanding knowledge of parental involvement in children's secondary education: Connections with high school seniors' academic success. *Social Psychology of Education, 5*(2), 149–177.

Chaboudy, R., & Jameson, P. (2001). Connecting families and schools through technology. *The Book Report, 20*(2), 52–57.

Coffman, J. A (2004). A conversation with Jonny Morrell. *Evaluation Exchange, 10*(3), 12–13.

DeBell, M., & Chapman, C. (2006). *Computer and Internet use by students in 2003: Statistical analysis report* (NCES 2006–065). Washington, DC: U.S. Government Printing Office.

Desimone, L. (1999). Linking parent involvement with student achievement: Do race and income matter? *The Journal of Educational Research, 93*(1), 11–30.

Dornbusch, S. M., & Glasgow, K. L. (1996). The structural context of family–school relations. In A. Booth & J. F. Dunn (Eds.), *Family–school links: How do they affect educational outcomes?* Mahwah, NJ: Erlbaum.

Eccles, J. S., & Harold, R. D. (1993). Parent–school involvement during the early adolescent years. *Teachers College Record, 94*(3), 568–587.

Epstein, J. L. (1996). Perspectives and previews on research and policy for school, family, and community partnerships. In A. Booth & J. F. Dunn (Eds.), *Family–school links: How do they affect educational outcomes?* Mahwah, NJ: Erlbaum.

Farmer, L. (2000). Parent-friendly web pages. *Library Talk, 13*(1), 10–12.

Friedman, A. (2006). K–12 teachers' use of course websites. *Journal of Technology and Teacher Education, 14*(4), 795–815.

Grolnick, W. S., & Slowiaczek, M. L. (1994). Parents' involvement in children's schooling: A multidimensional conceptualization and motivational model. *Child Development, 65*(1), 237–252.

Guidry, K. R. (2004). Instant messaging: Its impact on and recommendations for student affairs. *Student Affairs Online, 5*(4). Retrieved March 6, 2006, from http://www.studentaffairs.com/ejournal/Fall_2004/InstantMessaging.htm

Henderson, A., & Mapp, K. (2002). *A new wave of evidence: The impact of school, family, and community connections on student achievement.* Austin, TX: Southwest Educational Development Laboratory.

Hernandez, S., & Leung, B. P. (2004). Using the Internet to boost parent–teacher relationships. *Kappa Delta Pi Record, 40*(1), 136–138.

Hill, N. E. (2001). Parenting and academic socialization as they relate to school readiness: The roles of ethnicity and family income. *Journal of Educational Psychology, 93*(4), 686–697.

Horrigan, J. B. (2007). *Don't blame me: It's the phone's fault!* Retrieved July 27, 2008, from the Pew Internet & American Life Project Web site: http://www.pewinternet.org/pdfs/Typology.ObDeck.Final.pdf

Horrigan, J. B. (2008). *Home broadband adoption 2008.* Retrieved July 27, 2008, from the Pew Internet & American Life Project Web site: http://www.pewinternet. org/pdfs/PIP_Broadband_2008.pdf

Hotz, C. M., & Bailey, G. D. (2002). Electronic communities: Supporting public engagement. In I. Abdal-Haqq (Ed.), *Connecting schools and communities through technology* (pp. 41–50). Washington, DC: National School Boards Association.

Kohl, G. O., Lengua, L. J., & McMahon, R. J. (2000). Parent involvement in school: Conceptualizing multiple dimensions and their relations with family and demographic risk factors. *Journal of School Psychology, 38*(6), 501–523.

Kraut, R., Kiesler, S., Boneva, B., Cummings, J., Helgeson, V., & Crawford, A. (2002). The Internet paradox revisited. *Journal of Social Issues, 58,* 49–74.

Lanahan, L., & Boysen, J. (2005). *Computer technology in the public school classroom: Teacher perspectives* (NCES 2005-083). Washington, DC: U.S. Government Printing Office.

Lenhart, A., Simon, M., & Graziano, M. (2001). *The Internet and education: Findings from the Pew Internet and American Life Project.* Retrieved June 15, 2008, from Pew Internet & American Life Project Web site: http://www.pewinternet.org/ pdfs/PIP_Schools_Report.pdf

Lightfoot, S. L. (1978). *Worlds apart: Relationships between families and schools.* New York: Basic Books.

Lightfoot, S. L. (2003). *The essential conversation: What parents and teachers can learn from each other.* New York: Random House.

Lunts, E. (2003). Parental involvement in children's education: Connecting family and school by using telecommunication technologies. *Meridian: A Middle School Computer Technologies Journal.* Retrieved June 22, 2004, from http://www.ncsu. edu/meridian/win2003/involvement/index.html

Magill, A. R. (2007). Parent and teenager Internet use. Retrieved January 7, 2009, from the Pew Internet & American Life Project Web site: http://www. pewinternet.org/pdfs/PIP_Teen_Parents_data_memo_Oct2007.pdf

Mapp, K. (2004, December). *Supporting student achievement: Family and community connections with schools.* Paper presented at the Family, School, and Community Connections Symposium: New Directions for Research, Practice, and Evaluation, Cambridge, MA.

Marshall, J., & Rossett, A. (1997). How technology can forge links between school and home. *Electronic School Online.* Retrieved June 10, 2004, from http://www. electronic-school.com/0197f3.html

Mendez, T. (2004, June 1). We are the parents. Is anyone listening? *Christian Science Monitor.* Retrieved June 4, 2004, from http://www.csmonitor.com/2004/0601/ p11s02-legn.htm

Miller, S., Adsit, K. I., & Miller, T. (2005). Frequency of appearance and stakeholders' judged value. *TechTrends: Linking Research and Practice to Improve Learning, 49*(6), 34–40.

National School Boards Association. (2000). *Safe and smart: Research and guidelines for children's use of the Internet.* Washington, DC: Author.

Padgett, R. (2007). Marketing schools for survival. *Education Digest: Essential Readings Condensed for Quick Review, 72*(9), 37–38.

Penuel, W. R., Kim, D. Y., Michalchik, V., Lewis, S., Means, B., Murphy, R., et al. (2002). *Using technology to enhance connections between home and school: A research synthesis.* Washington, DC: Planning and Evaluation Service, U.S. Department of Education.

Pomerantz, E. M., Wang, Q., & Ng, F. (2005). Mothers' affect in the homework context: The importance of staying positive. *Developmental Psychology, 41*(2), 414–427.

Robinson, J. P., DiMaggio, P., & Hargittai, E. (2003). New social survey perspectives on the digital divide. *IT & Society, 1*(5), 1–22.

Scaringello, F. (2002). Creating computerized communication linkages with parents: The future is now. In G. McAuliffe (Ed.), *Working with troubled youth in schools: A guide for all school staff* (pp. 125–131). Westport, CT: Bergin & Garvey.

Shields, M. K., & Behrman, R. E. (2000). Children and computer technology: Analysis and recommendations. *The Future of Children, 10*(2), 4–30.

Spears, R., Postmes, T., Lea, M., & Wolbert, A. (2002). When are net effects gross products? *Journal of Social Issues, 58*(1), 91–107.

Sui-Chu, E. H., & Willms, J. D. (1996). Effects of parental involvement on eighth-grade achievement. *Sociology of Education, 69*(2), 126–141.

Swann, P. A. (2006). Got web? Investing in a district website. *School Administrator, 63*(5), 24–29.

Tidwell, L. C., & Walther, J. B. (2002). Computer-mediated communication effects on disclosure, impressions, and interpersonal evaluations: Getting to know one another a bit at a time. *Human Communication Research, 28*(3), 317–348.

Tobolka, D. (2006). Connecting teachers and parents through the Internet. *Tech-Directions, 66*(5), 24–26.

Trusty, J. (1999). Effects of eighth grade parental involvement on late adolescents' educational expectations. *Journal of Research & Development in Education, 32*(4), 224–233.

U.S. Department of Commerce (2002). *A nation online: How Americans are expanding their use of the internet.* Washington, DC: Economics and Statistical Administration, National Telecommunications and Information Administration.

U.S. Department of Commerce, Economics and Statistics Administration, National Telecommunications and Information Administration. (n.d.). *Households using the Internet in and outside the home, by selected characteristics: Total, urban, rural, principal city, October 2007.* Washington, DC: Author. Retrieved January 7, 2009, from http://www.ntia.doc.gov/reports/2008/Table_HouseholdInternet2007.pdf

Wellman, B., Quan Haase, A., Witte, J., & Hampton, K. (2001). Does the Internet increase, decrease, or supplement social capital? Social networks, participation, and community commitment. *The American Behavioral Scientist, 45*, 436–455.

Wilcox, C. (2006). Blogging with the doors open. *School Administrator, 63*(5), 14–17.

9

Policy Levers and Entry Opportunities for Family–School Partnerships

ROBERT CROSNOE

T HAT STRONG CONNECTIONS BETWEEN families and schools are an educational resource and a social good is a widespread senti- ment in the American public that is reflected in many educational interventions and policies (Thurston, 2005). Yet, the tendency in the public and the policy world is to view such family–school partnerships—to use an increasingly popular term—in highly simplistic ways, with one-size-fits-all strategies and vague mandates that often distill the very concept into little more than a catchphrase. Section 1118 of No Child Left Behind is perhaps the culmination of this trend. Mandating that families and schools come together to create "compacts," this piece of the NCLB legis- lation is well intentioned. Yet, because inadequate recognition is given to critically important issues of timing, context, and process, it provides little in the way of actual direction (Epstein, 2005; Gamoran, 2007). As a result, we need to know more about how the *general* potential of family–school partnerships can translate into *specific* actions.

In this chapter, I discuss ways in which family–school partnerships can be viewed as one piece of a step-by-step process of addressing challenges facing the American education system, such as lagging performance rates and demographic disparities in such rates. My purpose is to support the exchange between educational research and educational practice, so that practice is guided by research evidence, and research is crafted to inform practice. I do so by posing three questions that can be asked about major educational issues: (1) where is action likely to make a difference, (2) when are the critical points of intervention, and (3) how can family–school part- nerships serve as a lever of action in such intervention?

To illustrate this framework, I first discuss the motivation behind and possible answers to these questions in general. Next, I apply this framework to a specific educational issue that, in addition to being quite timely, I also have studied extensively. This issue concerns the growing representation of Latino/a youth in the American student population and both the challenges and opportunities this demographic trend presents to schools.

BREAKING DOWN AN EDUCATIONAL ISSUE IN ORDER TO ACT

The education system is a massive operation and, as such, it has vulnerabilities and inefficiencies. Most efforts to intervene in the system, however, center on two problems. The first concerns obstacles to the general mission of the system, which is to produce a population of educated, informed, and involved individuals. The second concerns threats to a widely supported yet unofficial mission of the system, which is to facilitate societal equality (Arum, 2000; Labaree, 1997). With these two problems in mind, we can think about where, when, and how. Each of these questions comes with a seemingly endless number of answers, and the answer to any one question is dependent on the answers to the other two. The point, therefore, is not to come up with the right answer overall but instead to develop a logical, well-considered plan of action from a variety of alternatives.

Searching for Entry Points

The questions of where? and when? both concern the need to identify points of entry, which is the first step when facing large, seemingly intractable problems such as lagging performance and persistent performance disparities. Choosing a starting point is important.

Where in the system will an intervention yield significant change? A good place to look is the math/science pipeline, which consists of sequences of math and science coursework (Lee, Smith, & Croninger, 1997). The value of focusing on this domain of education is rooted in the sweeping economic restructuring of recent decades. In the modern global economy, technology, science, engineering, and business have become the high-growth, high-value sectors of the labor market. This trend, in turn, has increased the long-term returns for college degrees in general and higher education in these specialized fields in particular (Bernhardt, Morris, Handcock, & Scott., 2001; Fischer & Hout, 2006; Xie & Shauman, 2003). Not surprisingly, the math/science pipeline in secondary school is the primary channel into these specialized fields of study. Moreover, persistence in the pipeline is a strong predictor of matriculation in and completion of college regardless of field of study. Importantly, economic restructuring has had an especially pronounced impact on youth from historically disadvantaged segments of the population (e.g., the poor, racial/ethnic minorities, immigrants). The decline in the manufacturing sector of the economy is closing off what was long their primary route toward social mobility absent higher education. At the same time, they also face many institutional, organizational, and other obstacles—such as school segregation, limited funding, and teacher turnover—that have reduced their persistence in the math/science pipeline (Adelman, 1999; Schneider, 2007; Shettle et al., 2007).

Focusing on the math/science pipeline, therefore, allows insights into risks to and opportunities for using the education system to increase the number of educated individuals with high-level skills available for the more desirable and relevant jobs. It also offers a window into mechanisms of and remedies for the intergenerational transmission of inequality. In this way, the pipeline is a potential point of entry when targeting performance rates and disparities.

When in the system will an intervention produce significant returns? The importance of this question lies in the structure of the educational career, which consists of students' upward progress through a series of linked grades and stages (Dornbusch, Glasgow, & Lin, 1996). Failure to tailor action to specific periods will undermine the effectiveness of that action. The focus on the math/science pipeline highlights transitions between school levels (Barber & Olsen, 2004; Eccles, 2004). When moving up a stage of schooling (e.g., elementary to middle school), students have brief windows to redirect pathways. These transitions also represent the starting points of each new level. In this way, bad transitions can make for bad experiences, good transitions for good experiences. This quality of school transitions is especially relevant to demographic disparities in education. Transitions are the points at which disparities compound but also where they are most vulnerable to breaking down (Crosnoe, 2006).

Because the sequential, subject-specific nature of coursework characteristic of the math/science pipeline begins in secondary school, the transition between middle school and high school takes on added importance. It is a point at which slippage can occur between middle school status and high school coursework (e.g., high school coursework levels that are lower than what middle school achievement and classes would suggest), especially for students from historically disadvantaged groups (Crosnoe & Huston, 2007; Schiller, 1999). Thus, elucidating the role of the middle school to high school transition in the math/science pipeline can empower policy efforts, such as NCLB or curricular reforms, to raise the overall performance level of schools and/or reduce often-discussed achievement "gaps."

Searching for the Levers for Change

How can change be produced in the education system in feasible ways? This question concerns the need to identify policy levers. In general terms, a lever is a compelling force to induce or produce action. In policy terms, a lever is a social, institutional, or personal factor that, when activated, can effect change in a desired outcome. Thus, a lever must influence an outcome *and* be amenable to outside intervention. At issue is the balance between power and doability. A factor—let's say, peer influence—may have great impact on educational processes but be less valuable from a policy standpoint if it cannot be externally manipulated. In that event, it is not a good lever and must give way to less powerful but more workable factors.

In general, family dynamics are not considered subject to alteration through public policy even if they are undeniably important to student outcomes (Coleman, 1990; Huston, 2005). Parent–child attachment, for example, is important to how young people do in school, but intervening to change attachment patterns in families would be difficult and far from politically expedient. One family dynamic that is considered both important and policy amenable is parental involvement in education, a parenting behavior that makes up one half of the concept of family–school partnerships. Indeed, parental involvement is arguably the family dynamic most often viewed as a lever in large-scale educational policy, including NCLB. It has a documented impact on performance and can be actively cultivated by schools. The family–school partnership concept, as embodied in theory and policy, simply recognizes that the meaning, effectiveness, and experience of parental involvement depend on whether it has been encouraged and is positively received by the school (Epstein, 2005; Epstein et al., 2002).

Family–school partnerships may be a viable answer to the question of how? in general, but they should take a specific form when focusing on the math/science pipeline during the transition from middle to high school. At this point, communication between home and school about coursework is crucial to boosting persistence in the pipeline and reducing disparities in such persistence. Thus, family–school communication is a potential lever for producing change in the math/science pipeline during the middle to high school transition. If communication patterns can be established or improved, then increased math/science coursework levels and decreased disparities in such coursework may result.

Such communication could take the form of written reports sent from school to home, parent orientation and information sessions at school, or easy-to-access Web sites and other forms of electronic communication (see Chapter 8). Whatever the actual form of communication, three issues should be prioritized (Schneider, 2007).

- The structure of high school math/science coursework (e.g., what courses are available, how they are officially or typically sequenced)
- The long-term consequences of short-term decisions about coursework (e.g., how reaching certain coursework thresholds can influence college admission)
- The typical match between students' skills and the school's course offerings (e.g., what middle school curricula students should be exposed to and what skills they should master before entering a certain course in high school)

Given the nature of the transition between middle school and high school, three-way communication—linking family to middle school to high school—would be the effective policy lever for producing change in the math/science pipeline. Ideally, each actor in this triangle would talk to the other two. For example, middle school counselors and teachers would consult their high school counterparts and the parents of their eighth-grade students about coursework requirements and enrollments for ninth grade, and high school personnel would close the triangle by inviting the parents of their future students into the high school. Less ideal but still potentially valuable would be one of these actors bridging the other two; for example, parents consulting middle school and high school personnel even if the latter two do not consult each other. Most problematic would be no communication at all in this triangle.

Figure 9.1 gives an idea of how prevalent these different forms of family–school partnerships are. The data come from the National Educational Longitudinal Study (NELS88), a nationally representative study following over time more than 24,000 American eighth graders in over 1,000 schools in 1988 (see http://nces.ed.gov/surveys/NELS88). Parents reported whether they had been contacted by personnel at their eighth graders' middle schools about course selection and academic programs at the students' future high schools. Administrators at the receiving high schools reported whether their counselors and teachers met with their middle school counterparts to plan transitions for incoming ninth graders. They also reported whether their schools had parent orientations and parent–teacher meetings for the parents of these incoming students. Clearly, the available data in NELS88 are weighted toward school-initiated communication, which is regrettable given that parents often are active initiators of family–school partnerships. Still, the focus

Figure 9.1. Breakdown of Family–School Partnerships in NELS88

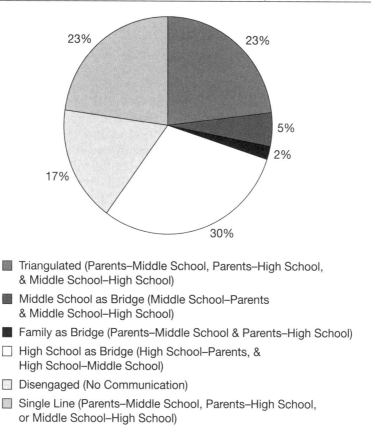

■ Triangulated (Parents–Middle School, Parents–High School,
  & Middle School–High School)

■ Middle School as Bridge (Middle School–Parents
  & Middle School–High School)

■ Family as Bridge (Parents–Middle School & Parents–High School)

☐ High School as Bridge (High School–Parents, &
  High School–Middle School)

☐ Disengaged (No Communication)

▨ Single Line (Parents–Middle School, Parents–High School,
  or Middle School–High School)

in NCLB and other educational policies that emphasize family–school partnerships is on what schools can do. Thus, the breakdown of lines of communication in Figure 9.1 is useful from a policy perspective.

Slightly less than one quarter of the students (23%) fit the triangulation profile—they had parents who had communicated with their middle school personnel and attended high schools with policies of coordinating with the middle schools of incoming students and making connections with the parents of incoming students. At the same time, no links among families, middle schools, and high schools existed for 17% of the students (disengaged). Smaller percentages (5% and 2%, respectively) were in situations in which middle school personnel were in contact with their parents and high schools (middle school as bridge) or in situations in which their parents were in contact with their middle schools, and their high schools had policies of outreach to parents (family as bridge). A larger bloc of students, 30%, attended high schools that had policies for coordinating with the middle schools and parents of incoming students (high school as bridge). The remainder experienced only one of the three possible linkages.

On average and without taking into account anything else, students in triangulated family–school partnerships scored higher than others on indicators of academic performance, including in math and science, before and after the transition from middle school to high school. Moreover, this achievement trend was more pronounced in groups targeted by NCLB for special attention. For example, in the full NELS88 sample, the students in triangulated partnerships had a significantly higher group average on math/science tests than students in disengaged partnerships. This test score advantage of the triangulated over disengaged categories was bigger in the subsample of NELS88 consisting of students from low-income families, and even bigger in the subsample of consisting of English language learners. In other words, the benefits of multiple lines of communication appeared to be greater in segments of the population widely considered to be at risk academically. Thus, cultivating a specific kind of family–school partnership during a particular period of schooling has the potential to be a policy lever for raising performance levels and reducing performance disparities in a specific domain of education.

FAMILY–SCHOOL PARTNERSHIPS
AND THE LATINO/A POPULATION

Above I discussed in general terms a step-by-step framework for approaching family–school partnerships in evidence-based, policy-oriented ways, but I realize that a specific application will better illustrate the value of this approach. Asking the where, when, and how questions led me to focus on the three-way linkage among the math/science pipeline, the transition from middle school to high school, and communication about coursework among parents, middle school personnel, and high school personnel. Focusing on that three-way linkage, in turn, brings the Latino/a population in the United States into the research and policy spotlight. Indeed, understanding what is going on among Latino/a youth has been a major pursuit of mine (Crosnoe, 2006; Crosnoe, Lopez-Gonzalez, & Muller, 2004), and I have learned through this experience that family–school partnerships are integral to serving their educational interests.

Family and School Patterns Among Latino/as in the United States

The exponential growth of the Latino/a population in the United States is one of the most dramatic demographic trends in recent history, and it is writ large in the education system. Especially in traditional entry-point states like California, Florida, and Texas, Latino/a youth represent a primary constituency for public schools (Bean & Stevens, 2003; Stanton-Salazar, 2001; Valenzuela, 1999). As a group, they rate lower than peers on standardized test performance, graded achievement, school completion, activity participation, and other markers of academic performance (Gándara, Rumberger, Maxwell-Jolly, & Callahan, 2003; Glick & White, 2003; Kao & Thompson, 2003; Reardon & Galindo, 2007; Romo & Falbo, 1998). Consequently, Latino/a youth often are considered academically at risk and are explicitly labeled as such in educational policy.

Three factors make this population more relevant than many other similar populations to look at in terms of math/science coursework and family–school partnerships during secondary school. First, the general trend of academic underperformance just noted extends to the math/science pipeline, in terms of coursework and achievement (Crosnoe et al., 2004). Second, the high rates of socioeconomic disadvantage in this population make the education system a crucial vehicle for social mobility (Suárez-Orozco & Suárez-Orozco, 1995), meaning that their low persistence in math and science is especially problematic in the long term. Third, many factors have been implicated in the academic disparities between Latino/a youth and their peers, including language barriers, the aforementioned socioeconomic disadvantages (e.g., poverty, low parent education), segregation, and discrimination. One frequently cited factor concerns the psychological distance between Latino/a families and the schools that Latino/a youth attend (Crosnoe, 2006; Suárez-Orozco & Suárez-Orozco, 1995; Valenzuela, 1999).

Importantly, however, understanding the link between family–school partnerships and the academic performance of Latino/a youth—including the math/science pipeline during the transition from middle school to high school—also requires a careful consideration of the incredible heterogeneity of the Latino/a population. Two important dimensions of heterogeneity, national origin and immigration status, condition the general at-risk label applied to Latino/a youth. Consider the different regions of Latin America from which Latino/a families originate. Cuban American youth, who historically have had greater access to financial capital and been more accepted by Whites, typically have done better in American schools. On the other hand, Puerto Rican and Mexican American youth historically have had high rates of poverty and linguistic isolation, and therefore have had more pronounced academic struggles (Oropesa & Landale, 2000; Portes & Stepick, 1993; Valenzuela, 1999; Velez, 1989). Now consider the different stages of immigration and assimilation among Latino/a families. Youth born outside of the United States typically have much stronger ties to their families and communities, whereas U.S.-born youth are more likely to be absorbed into an American youth culture that downgrades academic success. Consequently, academic problems appear to become more common with time in the United States once socioeconomic status is taken into account (Hirschman, 2001; Zhou, 1997).

In summary, three-way communication among families, middle schools, and high schools may be a more powerful lever for producing change in math/science trajectories for Latino/a youth than for their peers. Yet, the added value that Latino/as derive from this policy lever likely varies across subsets of this heterogeneous population.

An Investigation of Family–School Communication Among Latino/a Youth

Of the 2,041 Latino/as in NELS, 65% were Mexican origin; 10% traced their roots to Puerto Rico, 5% to Cuba, and the remaining 20% to other regions of Latin America. In all, 12% were foreign born (first-generation immigrants), 31% were U.S. born with foreign-born parents (second-generation), and 57% were U.S. born with U.S.-born parents (third-plus generation).

Compared with the rest of the NELS88 sample, Latino/a youth had relatively low averages on math/science indicators before and after the transition from middle school to high school. For example, they scored about 5–10 points lower, on average, on standardized math and science tests in middle school than White and Asian American students. As another example, their average starting level in high school was prealgebra and a noncore science, compared with algebra and a core science among White and Asian American students. A first glance at their distribution across the family–school partnership typology suggests a reason for these academic patterns that extends beyond the obvious socioeconomic, language, and school organization explanations. Compared with others in NELS88 (and especially White and Asian American youth), Latino/as were underrepresented in the triangulated, middle school as bridge, and family as bridge family–school partnerships (17%, 3%, and 1%, respectively) and overrepresented in the high school as bridge and disengaged partnerships (33% and 23%, respectively).

To go deeper, I estimated multilevel models predicting Latino/as' math/science coursework level at the start of high school. Full details of the analyses can be obtained by contacting me, but I will highlight three details here. First, these models took into account the many NELS88 design effects. Second, these models followed NELS88 convention (e.g., Stevenson, Schiller, & Schneider, 1994) by using an eight-point categorization scheme for math coursework (0 = none, 1 = remedial math, 2 = general math, 3 = prealgebra, 4 = algebra I, 5 = geometry, 6 = algebra II, 7 = advanced math, such as trigonometry, 8 = calculus) and a three-point scheme for science coursework (0 = none, 1 = noncore science, such as earth science, 2 = core science, such as biology or chemistry, 3 = advanced science, such as physics). Third, these models controlled for several demographic characteristics (e.g., age, gender), family circumstances (e.g., SES, parents' marital status, home language use), and school characteristics (e.g., location, region, sector) as well as middle school standardized test scores.

Overall, Latino/a youth had the highest level of math coursework at the start of high school when in triangulated and family as bridge family–school partnerships, net of the other important factors, including middle school test scores. They also had the highest level of science coursework when in the triangulated and high school as bridge family–school partnerships.

Recall, however, all of the heterogeneity in the Latino/a population. Based on a multilevel model that included markers of national origin and immigration status but did not take into account family SES or middle school test scores, Cuban American students were the Latino/a subgroup with the highest level of math/science coursework at the start of high school. Mexican American students had the lowest, and Puerto Ricans and other Latino/as fell in between. Furthermore, first-generation Latino/as had higher coursework levels than their third-generation counterparts, with second-generation Latino/as significantly different from neither. Yet, almost all of these national origin and generational differences vanished when family SES and middle school test scores also were included in the model.

What *did* differ across subsets of the Latino/a population was the link between family–school partnerships and early high school coursework, more specifically, science coursework. What I describe below are statistically significant findings from multilevel models, including all controls, in which the markers of the family–school partnerships were interacted with the markers of national origin and immigration status, respectively. For science, the associations of the triangulated and high school as bridge partnerships with coursework level were conditioned by third-generation status, net of all other factors. These patterns are presented in Figure 9.2. The science coursework level of the average first- and second-generation Latino/a did not differ across types of family–school partnerships, but

**Figure 9.2. Initial High School Science Coursework Level,
by Family–School Partnership and Immigration Status**

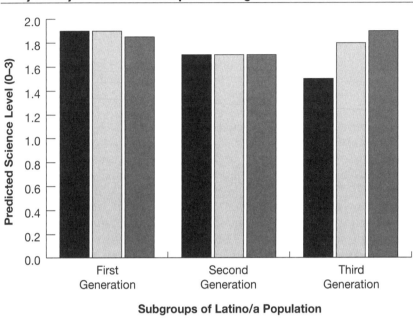

it did for the average third-generation Latino/a. Specifically, the average third-generation Latino/a had a slightly but significantly higher level of science coursework at the start of high school when in the high school as bridge partnership and an even higher level when in the triangulated partnership. A similar pattern was found when national origin was considered. The increase in science coursework level associated with being in a family as bridge partnership or a high school as bridge partnership, compared with a disengaged partnership, was greater for Puerto Rican students than for their peers of other national origins.

In summary, almost any link between families, middle schools, and high schools was related to higher level math coursework during the transition from middle school to high school among Latino/as of similar family backgrounds and middle school test profiles. Moreover, all Latino/as had higher science coursework levels when in family–school partnerships characterized by triangulation or schools acting as bridges. In general, these science benefits were more pronounced for third-generation Latino/as and Puerto Rican students.

CONCLUSION AND RECOMMENDATIONS

The topic of family–school partnerships illustrates how the link between science and policy is both tenuous and important. The value of these partnerships seems intuitive, but the actual evidence about their benefits for individual students and the larger system is quite nuanced and highly conditional. Unfortunately, the educational policy that takes up family–school partnerships—and there is a lot of it—tends to reflect a rather one-size-fits-all picture of this potentially valuable resource, typically paying little attention to how family–school partnerships may differ in meaning, implementation, and focus across stages of schooling and diverse groups.

My argument here is that we need to push an agenda for family–school partnerships that is tailored to specific windows of opportunity in which the payoff will be maximized. As noted earlier, I am interested in informing exchanges among researchers, policymakers, and school personnel. The latter two groups of actors can identify a general goal, typically addressing some challenge facing educators. Researchers can then provide useful information on how to get started on or make progress toward that goal by applying the simple where, when, and how questions to the issue at hand and coming up with evidence-based answers about what policy levers to target and when. In this chapter, I have offered one example of such an exchange by focusing on two general goals of educational policy (raising overall performance rates and reducing major disparities in these rates) and then demonstrating how these goals can be advanced by targeting communication among families, middle schools, and high schools about math/science coursework as young people from different segments of the American student population transition from middle school to high school.

This domain-specific, period-specific, and timely agenda for family–school partnerships potentially has more value, I have argued, when thinking about the challenges and opportunities that the growing Latino/a population presents the American education system. Applying this agenda to this population leads to a few recommendations.

- This population is vulnerable to slippage, or being enrolled in high school math and science classes incommensurate with their middle school coursework and achievement. Dialogue among parents, middle school personnel, and high school personnel about coursework options is a potential policy lever for reducing this vulnerability. Building lines of communication could be explicitly worked into the family–school compacts currently required by NCLB.
- If three lines of communication cannot be achieved during this transition, getting parents to talk to both middle school and high school personnel would serve a similar purpose for slippage in math, and getting high school personnel to talk to both parents and middle school personnel would serve a similar purpose for slippage in science.
- Middle school and high school counselors should coordinate to develop a detailed but accessible report covering the high school's coursework requirements for graduation and the formal and informal (e.g., skill level) prerequisites for each coursework level. This report also should cover the average graduation and college-going (2-year, 4-year, elite) rates for recent students who have reached each coursework level in that school, as well as similar national data made public by the National Center for Education Statistics. This report should be distributed to all exiting middle school students and their parents through multiple venues, including mailings, school-based gatherings, parent–teacher meetings, community groups, and Web sites.
- Such efforts should begin with targeted interventions for third-plus generation Latino/as and those of Puerto Rican origin, who face special academic risks but also may derive greater benefit from communication among families and schools as they transition to high school.
- Bilingual school personnel and document translation would greatly facilitate—or make possible—this type of parental involvement.

These recommendations flow from analyses of a nationally representative data set. Of course, statistical analyses do not always reflect real life. For example, poverty and language status cannot be simply controlled when dealing with actual people in actual schools. As another example, available survey questions might be incomplete in ways that affect what conclusions can be made, such as the tendency in NELS to emphasize school-initiated communication over parent-initiated communication. The research that scientists produce, therefore, is a foundation for what comes next. Policymakers have the training and experience to assess the feasibility and cost-effectiveness of the recommendations that come out of what researchers do. Much as the education of young people is a partnership between families and schools, deriving value from family–school relations on a large scale is a partnership between researchers and policymakers.

ACKNOWLEDGMENTS

Direct correspondence to the author at the Department of Sociology and Population Research Center, University of Texas at Austin, 1 University Station A1700, Austin, TX 78712-1088 (crosnoe@austin.utexas.edu). The research was supported by a Faculty Scholar Award from the William T. Grant Foundation, a Changing Faces of America Young Scholar Award from the Foundation for Child Development, and a center grant (R24 HD042849) from the National Institute of Child Health and Human Development to the Population Research Center.

REFERENCES

Adelman, C. (1999). *Answers in the toolbox: Academic intensity, attendance patterns, and bachelor's degree attainment.* Washington, DC: U.S. Government Printing Office.

Arum, R. (2000). Schools and communities: Ecological and institutional dimensions. *Annual Review of Sociology, 26,* 395–418.

Barber, B. K., & Olsen, J. A. (2004). Assessing the transitions to middle and high school. *Journal of Adolescent Research, 19*(1), 3–30.

Bean, F., & Stevens, G. (2003). *America's newcomers and the dynamics of diversity.* New York: Russell Sage.

Bernhardt, A., Morris, M., Handcock, M. S., & Scott, M. A. (2001). *Divergent paths: Economic mobility in the new American labor market.* New York: Russell Sage.

Coleman, J. S. (1990). *Foundations of social theory.* Cambridge, MA: Harvard University Press.

Crosnoe, R. (2006). *Mexican roots, American schools: Helping Mexican immigrant children succeed.* Palo Alto, CA: Stanford University Press.

Crosnoe, R., & Huston, A. (2007). Socioeconomic status, schooling, and the developmental trajectories of adolescents. *Developmental Psychology, 43*(5), 1097–1110.

Crosnoe, R., Lopez-Gonzalez, L., & Muller, C. (2004). Immigration from Mexico into the math/science pipeline in American education. *Social Science Quarterly, 85*(5), 1208–1226.

Dornbusch, S., Glasgow, K., & Lin, I. (1996). The social structure of schooling. *Annual Review of Psychology, 47,* 401–429.

Eccles, J. S. (2004). Schools, academic motivation, and stage-environment fit. In R. M. Lerner & L. D. Steinberg (Eds.), *Handbook of adolescent psychology* (2nd ed., pp. 125–153). Hoboken, NJ: Wiley.

Epstein, J. L. (2005). Attainable goals? The spirit and letter of the No Child Left Behind Act on parental involvement. *Sociology of Education, 78*(2), 179–182.

Epstein, J., Sanders, M. G., Simon, B. S., Salinas, K. C., Jansorn, N. R., & Van Voorhis, F. L. (2002). *School, family, and community partnerships: Your handbook for action.* Thousand Oaks, CA: Corwin Press.

Fischer, C. S., & Hout, M. (2006). *Century of difference: How America changed in the last one hundred years.* New York: Russell Sage.

Gamoran, A. (2007). *Standards-based reform and the poverty gap: Lessons for No Child Left Behind.* Washington, DC: Brookings Institution Press.

Gándara, P., Rumberger, R., Maxwell-Jolly, J., & Callahan, R. (2003). English learners in California schools: Unequal resources, unequal outcomes. *Education Policy Analysis Archives, 11*(36). Retrieved June, 2008, from http://epaa.asu.edu/epaa/v11n36/

Glick, J. E., & White, M. J. (2003). The academic trajectories of immigrant youths: Analysis within and across cohorts. *Demography, 40*(4), 589–603.

Hirschman, C. (2001). The educational enrollment of immigrant youth: A test of the segmented-assimilation hypothesis. *Demography, 38*(3), 317–336.

Huston, A. C. (2005). Connecting the science of child development to public policy. *SRCD Social Policy Report, 19*(4), 3–18.

Kao, G., & Thompson, J. (2003). Race and ethnic stratification in educational achievement and attainment. *Annual Review of Sociology, 29,* 417–442.

Labaree, D. (1997). Public goods, private goods: The American struggle over educational goals. *American Educational Research Journal, 34*(1), 39–81.

Lee, V., Smith, J., & Croninger, R. (1997). How high school organization influences the equitable distribution of learning in mathematics and science. *Sociology of Education, 70*(2), 128–150.

Oropesa, R. S., & Landale, N. (2000). From austerity to prosperity? Migration and child poverty among mainland and island Puerto Ricans. *Demography, 37*(3), 323–338.

Portes, A., & Stepick, A. (1993). *City on the edge: The transformation of Miami.* Los Angeles: University of California Press.

Reardon, S., & Galindo, C. (2007). Patterns of Hispanic students' math skill proficiency in the early elementary grades. *Journal of Latinos and Education, 6*(3), 229–251.

Romo, H. D., & Falbo, T. (1998). *Latino high school graduation.* Austin: University of Texas.

Schiller, K. S. (1999). Effects of feeder patterns on students' transition to high school. *Sociology of Education, 72*(4), 216–233.

Schneider, B. (2007). *Forming a college-going community in U.S. schools.* Seattle: Bill and Melinda Gates Foundation.

Shettle, C., Roey, S., Mordica, J., Perkins, R., Nord, C., Teodorovic, J., et al. (2007). *The nation's report card: America's high school graduates* (NCES 2007-467). Washington, DC: U.S. Government Printing Office.

Stanton-Salazar, R. D. (2001). *Manufacturing hope and despair: The school and kin support networks of U.S.–Mexican youth.* New York: Teachers College Press.

Stevenson, D. L., Schiller, K. S., & Schneider, B. (1994). Sequences of opportunities for learning. *Sociology of Education, 67*(3), 184–198.

Suárez-Orozco, C., & Suárez-Orozco, M. (1995). *Transformations: Immigration, family life, and achievement motivation among Latino adolescents.* Stanford: Stanford University Press.

Thurston, D. (2005). Leveling the home advantage: Assessing the effectiveness of parental involvement. *Sociology of Education, 78*(3), 233–249.

Valenzuela, A. (1999). *Subtractive schooling: U.S.–Mexican youth and the politics of caring.* Albany: State University of New York Press.

Velez, W. (1989). High school attrition among Hispanic and non-Hispanic white youths. *Sociology of Education, 62*(2), 119–133.

Xie, Y., & Shauman, K. (2003). *Women in science: Career processes and outcomes.* Cambridge, MA: Harvard University Press.

Zhou, M. (1997). Growing up American: The challenge confronting immigrant children and children of immigrants. *Annual Review of Sociology, 23,* 63–95.

10

Opportunities for Moving Family Involvement Research Into Policy and Practice

HOLLY KREIDER
SUZANNE M. BOUFFARD

IN THE PAST FOUR DECADES, MUCH RESEARCH attention has been paid to aspects of family status and process, including family educational involvement, in predicting student success. Research has found that family involvement is associated with higher GPAs and test scores, enrollment in more challenging academic programs, more classes passed and credits earned, better attendance, improved behavior at home and at school, and better social skills and adaptation to school (Caspe, Lopez, & Wolos, 2006, 2007; Henderson & Mapp, 2002; Weiss, Caspe, & Lopez, 2006). The benefits of involvement for adolescents is no exception (Kreider, Caspe, Kennedy, & Weiss, 2007); indeed, there is evidence that positive effects hold true across most types of involvement and for students from all ethnic backgrounds (Jeynes, 2005, 2007).

Yet educational policy and practice have yet to fully realize the promise of family–school partnerships, especially at the middle and high school level where few family involvement policies and programs exist. In this chapter we consider the challenges to and opportunities for bridging family involvement research with educational policy and practice, especially in secondary schools. This exploration is framed by three research-based premises about effective family involvement: (1) it occurs across ages but changes as children mature; (2) it occurs across the varied contexts in which children and youth live and learn; and (3) it must be co-constructed and a function of shared responsibility among all stakeholders.

THE RESEARCH–POLICY–PRACTICE GAP

Family support for and involvement in learning have played some role in policy for decades, but it has been a shifting and often limited one, which has not reflected research on how and through what mechanisms family involvement benefits students. School practices also have not reflected family involvement research—a disconnection likely interrelated with the policy trend.

Due in large part to shifting political ideologies over time, today many family involvement provisions exist on the books in federal policy, including the No Child Left Behind Act (U.S. Department of Education, 2001), but few incentives or sanctions exist to ensure that these provisions are implemented in states, districts, and schools. Historically, most policy attention has focused on parent advisory committees and other school committees, even though research suggests that such roles are not associated with benefits for individual students (D'Agostino, Hedges, Wong, & Borman, 2001; Henderson & Mapp, 2002). Other legislative provisions call for district- and school-level family involvement policies, compacts, and communication with families, but these also are disconnected from research: (1) Most communication is one-way and not tied to specific instructional strategies or student progress (Public Education Network, 2007), and (2) research has not found that parent–school compacts alone can improve student outcomes (D'Agostino et al., 2001; Funkhouser, Stief, & Allen, 1998). Since NCLB, family involvement provisions have focused on a consumer model, requiring that parents be notified about school performance and options to transfer children to other schools. However, many families are not notified of their options until after the start of the school year, if at all, and receive notification in language or jargon that they cannot understand (Coleman, Starzynski, Winnick, Palmer, & Furr, 2006; U.S. Department of Education, 2007; U.S. General Accounting Office, 2006). Furthermore, no research to date suggests that this consumer model benefits students.

A gap also exists between research and practice. Teachers play a critical role in engaging families for student success (e.g., Hoover-Dempsey & Sandler, 1997; Weiss, Dearing, Mayer, Kreider, & McCartney, 2005). In high schools, teacher outreach positively predicts parents' involvement in parenting activities, volunteering, and home-learning activities across student backgrounds and achievement levels (Simon, 2004). However, outreach and opportunities are inequitably distributed. Parents of adolescents report receiving less outreach from schools (Herrold & O'Donnell, 2008). Disadvantaged and minority families also report receiving less outreach from schools, even though educators report equal outreach to all families (Chen, 2001; Vaden-Kiernan & McManus, 2005). The reason for this difference in perception is not clear, but it underlines differences in how families from different backgrounds experience the education system, and documents that educational practice is not living up to the potential of outreach to and involvement of families.

CHALLENGES TO
MOVING RESEARCH INTO POLICY AND PRACTICE

Several realities make it challenging to bridge these gaps. First, family involvement tends to be narrowly defined, especially the involvement of families of adolescents. NCLB has contributed to this reality, according to family involvement experts, by focusing on instruction with accountability and teacher quality as primary ingredients, while family involvement is only modestly emphasized and, even then, is defined primarily as parents' right to receive and act on information about their child's school. Districts also tend to focus on family involvement narrowly, as compliance with policies rather than a statement of belief that family involvement is integral to learning (Bouffard & Weiss, 2008). As other authors in this volume attest, the discourse on family involvement strategies only recently has broadened to include a more nuanced understanding of multiple critical forms of engagement, such as academic socialization, expectations, and other aspects of parenting and parent–youth relations. A related challenge is the prevalent view of family involvement as an "add-on" to educational practice. Experts use words like "peripheral" to describe how family involvement typically is perceived in relation to schools' main purpose. In an interview with parental involvement experts, Karen Mapp explains, "There hasn't been a whole-hearted acceptance of the fact that family involvement is a strategy that must be seen as part of the instructional core and not something that's separate" (Caspe, 2008, p. 6).

Second, many educators still receive little preparation and professional development on how to engage families (Epstein & Sanders, 2006; Hiatt-Michael, 2004). Teachers, especially those just entering the profession, often report that working with families is a key challenge (Markow & Martin, 2005; Public Education Network, 2003). This appears to be even more salient for teachers of adolescents. When surveyed about the effectiveness of their preservice and inservice preparation to collaborate with families, middle and high school teachers report being less well prepared than teachers of young children (Wright, Daniel, & Himelreich, 2000). Faculty in colleges of education confirm that teacher preparation is especially important for those entering secondary schools, where lack of staff outreach, school structures, and adolescent desire for autonomy pose added challenges to family involvement (Flanigan, 2007). School administrators also need to work with families and set the tone and expectations for teachers' interactions with families. Yet, while most higher education faculty believe that administrators need knowledge about working effectively with families (Epstein & Sanders, 2006), few states expect principals to demonstrate or train for such skills (Radcliffe, Malone, & Nathan, 1994), and little research exists on whether administrator training programs offer or require family involvement courses.

Most families also report a desire to be involved, but many, particularly lower SES and minority families, face logistic challenges to involvement and want guidance from schools on why and how to be involved, particularly when they do not have the same cultural and social capital as school personnel (Eccles & Harold, 1996). Parents of high school students in particular are also much less satisfied with their children's schools than parents of younger children, most importantly in the way school staff interact with parents. This further reinforces the need for preservice and professional development of secondary school teachers in how to engage families, as well as the need for parents to learn engagement and advocacy skills for negotiating with secondary school environments (Herrold & O'Donnell, 2008).

Third, family involvement suffers from limited investments in research-based interventions and high-quality evaluation. This trend is evident at the levels of both national or large-scale demonstration programs and local programs. Although research demonstrates the influence of family involvement on student achievement, by and large this research has not informed family involvement interventions. And rigorous impact evaluations of family involvement programs—a form of research that can have the most direct implications for practice—are few and far between. The evaluation data that do exist on family involvement programs are often limited methodologically, producing uneven evidence about program success (Mattingly, Prislin, McKenzie, Rodriguez, & Kayzar, 2002). Furthermore, those evaluations and demonstration programs that do exist focus mainly on early childhood or elementary school; for example, see the national evaluations of Head Start, Early Head Start, and other early childhood programs as well Nye, Turner, and Schwartz's (2006) meta-analysis of involvement programs for parents of elementary school children. The limitations of the evaluation base make it difficult for researchers and advocates to present an evidence-based case about effective interventions to educators and policymakers.

Finally, educational practice and policy are peppered with sporadic and often disconnected practices and programs to involve families, rather than systemic, sustained efforts. Historically and currently, programs and policies have been disconnected from one another. At the federal level, family involvement initiatives and mandates are disconnected across agencies, including the Department of Education, the Department of Health and Human Services, and the Office of Juvenile Justice and Delinquency Prevention, and even within departments and legislation such as the Elementary and Secondary Education Act (currently known as No Child Left Behind). This disconnection has been exacerbated by the separate congressional committees that authorize the funding, as well as by the splintering of parent interest groups, which represent populations such as special education and Title I students (Fege, 2006). There have been few efforts to integrate all of these strands and groups (Fege, 2006; Palanki & Burch, 1992).

A SYSTEMATIC APPROACH TO FAMILY INVOLVEMENT IN ADOLESCENCE

To address these challenges and move research into policy and practice, the conceptualization of family involvement needs to be reframed to acknowledge that families must be part of a holistic system to promote children's learning and development. This reframing underscores the concomitant need for a more systemic approach to involving families of adolescents, by embedding family involvement in the instructional core, strengthening federal policies and local practices, investing in building the capacity of educators and parents for involvement, engaging all stakeholders concerned, and using data and evaluation to strengthen family involvement programs and inform policies.

Redefining Family Involvement Within a Complementary Learning Framework

Researchers and education leaders alike are calling for a more holistic approach to education that integrates both school and nonschool supports to ensure that all children succeed in school and in life (Bouffard, Malone, & Deschenes, n.d.). Research and practice increasingly demonstrate that opportunities that extend beyond the school building and the traditional school day confer academic and social benefits, ranging from enhanced literacy skills to emotional and physical readiness to learn, especially for the most at-risk youth (Weiss, Coffman, Post, Bouffard, & Little, 2005). These nonschool supports include the critical involvement and support of families, as well as after-school programs and other youth development settings, health and social services, and community-based institutions such as libraries, museums, and universities. When linked with one another and with schools, these supports form a network that works toward consistent learning and developmental outcomes. The Harvard Family Research Project refers to this system of linked supports as *complementary learning* (Weiss, Coffman, et al., 2005). Within a complementary-learning framework, effective family involvement is understood according to three key premises, described below.

Family Involvement Across Contexts

First, a complementary learning approach introduces points of entry for family involvement beyond the school and its staff, for example, an after-school program and its providers who often have relationships with both families and school personnel, and can serve as liaisons between the two (Kakli, Kreider, Little, Buck, & Coffey, 2006). A pilot evaluation of the Family PLUS (Parents Leading, Uniting, Serving) initiative, for example, revealed strategies for supporting and connecting families that build from the strengths inherent in youth development settings. Family PLUS is a 5-year initiative of the Boys & Girls Clubs of America, which has provided youth development clubs in schools and communities across the country for over 100 years. Family PLUS provides seed grants to clubs to support families through activities focused on outreach, economic opportunity, male involvement, kinship care, and FAN Club (an evidence-based family support program).

As one Boys & Girls Clubs leader noted, club staff members are often experts at both forming meaningful, positive relationships with families and youth, and collaborating with outside agencies. Schools, on the other hand, have ready access to many parents through existing groups like parent–teacher associations. One club with a Family PLUS grant brought together the best of both of these worlds to better serve youth by hosting family social nights in a club site located at a middle school, piggybacking off school PTA meetings. This served to encourage PTA parents to enroll their children in the club and to encourage club parents to get involved in the PTA. Eventually other parents with children in the school also were drawn in to these double meetings (Kreider & Raghupathy, 2009).

Family Involvement as a Continuous
Process from Birth Through Adolescence

Second, complementary learning provides a way to address developmental changes in family involvement. Research demonstrates that the amount and types of family involvement needed by youth change as they get older (Eccles & Harold, 1996; Kreider et al., 2007). These changes reflect youth's increasing needs for autonomy, changes in schoolwork and projects, and parents' own competing responsibilities. As a result, effective family involvement changes from a focus on cognitive stimulation and social skills in the early years, to a focus on involvement in the school and PTA/PTO organizations in the elementary school years, to a focus on helping with homework in the middle school years, and finally to a focus on conveying expectations and discussing postsecondary plans in the high school years. Complementary learning highlights how the importance of different settings shifts at different developmental stages, and provides a variety of entry points for involvement; for example, prekindergarten programs in the early years, community-based institutions such as after-school programs and libraries in the elementary school years, and university-access programs in the high school years. Family involvement programs at the high school level often focus on college preparation, with some showing success and innovation in engaging low-income and ethnic minority parents, many of whom have children who will be the first generation of college goers in their families. These programs utilize counselors and parent panels with similar backgrounds to those of parent participants to give parents who never went to college critical information about the application and financial aid process, and to inspire them with role models from their own community (Auerbach, 2004; Gándara & Moreno, 2002).

Family Involvement as Mutually Constructed

Third, complementary learning underscores the need to engage a broad range of stakeholders as allies in a mutual effort to support children. In the realm of policy, this means acknowledging the fact that families are part of a dynamic system that supports or constrains their involvement. Social policies and workplaces affect the basic conditions of economic well-being and the affordances for involvement (Heymann & Earle, 2000; Rothstein, 2004). Schools influence family involvement via outreach, opportunities, and expectations (Sheldon, 2005; Simon, 2004), while community-based institutions provide additional entry points for families.

In the realm of practice, this means co-constructing involvement among all stakeholders, including parents, teachers and school leaders, community members, and especially in adolescence, the students themselves. For example, family involvement efforts at the Boston Arts Academy high school succeed by having a clear vision with buy-in from school staff, parents, and students. This is achieved through intentional hiring of a committed staff, clearly communicated expectations via parent orientation, and a contract that parents and students sign at the start of the year. Parent–teacher–student conferences, dubbed family narratives at the school, serve as a centerpiece of the program. Teachers present students' learning strengths and weaknesses to both the students and parents, creating a sense of shared accountability for student success (Ouimette, Feldman, & Tung, 2006).

Thinking Systemically About Family Involvement in Policy and Practice

This broader conceptualization of family involvement must be paired with policies and practices that support its occurrence, prevalence, and impact across the developmental continuum from early childhood through late adolescence. Here we describe a set of key principles derived from research that should underlie future policies and practices going forward. Embedding them in coordinated ways across national, state, and district levels can better ensure that family involvement is sustained, systemic, and an everyday "way of doing business" for schools and families alike. To realize this vision, family involvement must be: (1) integrated into the instructional core; (2) carried out by educators and families whose individual capacities for building partnerships have been fully supported; (3) inclusive of all stakeholders; and (4) informed by data and evaluation.

Make Family Involvement Part of the Instructional Core

A broader definition of family involvement as extending across contexts, ages, and stakeholders must be accompanied by a sharper definition of involvement as an endeavor clearly linked to student learning. As Henderson and colleagues (2006) discovered, high-achieving districts tend to connect family–school partnerships to the district's school improvement initiative and performance goals for students. They argue that by linking family involvement to the school improvement process, visibility and understanding of how families fit into the larger school improvement picture increase. Epstein and Sheldon (2006) also found a focus on increased student learning as a key ingredient of successful partnership programs. This extends to adolescence, where effective and sustainable partnership programs in middle and secondary schools include action plans that are linked to goals for student success and consider involvement that occurs outside the school building (Epstein, 2007).

Embedding family involvement as an integral strategy for learning has implications for how educators involve families in practice (e.g., prioritizing communication about student progress and how to help at home over

186 PART II—Facing the Challenges

volunteering) and also for the composition and focus of policies. For example, in 2007, the Kentucky Commissioner's Parents Advisory Council, a statewide group of family involvement leaders that advises the commissioner, proposed a set of family involvement standards clearly tied to student learning. Their report delineates six overarching goals for family involvement, a set of detailed recommendations, and a set of benchmarks for assessing progress—all of which are clearly tied to learning goals. As another example, the Iowa State Parental Information and Resource Center worked with the School Administrators of Iowa to ensure that one of the statewide standards for school administrators focuses on building family involvement in order to improve student learning.

Build Capacity for Family Involvement Among Both Educators and Families

Building family involvement is not about checklists or programs, but about fundamental attitudes and beliefs about the roles and importance of families in learning (McLaughlin & Shields, 1987). Therefore, for family involvement practices to take hold systematically in secondary schools and the policies pertaining to them, both educators and the families of adolescents must have the knowledge, skills, and attitudes necessary to carry out effective family–school partnerships. Opportunities to build such capacities can occur through preservice teacher and administrator education and professional development, and parent education and leadership efforts.

Researchers concur that aspiring, new, and veteran teachers and school leaders need concrete skills, knowledge, and positive attitudes about family involvement in order to carry it out effectively (Burton, 1992; Davies, 1991; Edwards & Jones Young, 1992). Specifically, they need access to the latest research-based knowledge about the benefits of family involvement, barriers to it, types of activities, and effective strategies for engaging families. The developmental period of adolescence—in which youth desire more autonomy from parents, yet still need parental guidance and support—poses special involvement challenges for parents and the educators who wish to encourage them. Educators need to know how to support the parents of adolescents in monitoring students' academic and social lives, offering meta-strategies for successfully completing homework, and discussing expectations and plans for college (Kreider et al., 2007).

Preservice preparation also should draw from appropriate methods for transfer of learning. "Knowledge-in-action" models view practice as an arena not only for applying scientific knowledge but also for generating knowledge (Barr & Tagg, 1995). This approach stresses what students can know and do as a result of a learning process rather than what faculty impart to students, which is the approach of many traditional methods of instruction. For example, field experiences can allow for rehearsal of research-based involvement strategies, as well as action research projects that generate new knowledge. Mentoring and coaching can help new teachers adapt research lessons to their current context. The case discussion method can be utilized to help educators frame problems, analyze solutions, and construct generalizations, in part through the application of theory and research. These approaches serve to convey research to aspiring educators through varied pedagogies that afford clear connections to educational practice.

Even with appropriate preservice training, school and district leaders and staff need resources and information to help them engage families. An ongoing process of professional development is needed, with inservice training for customizing plans to specific schools and families, and technical assistance to increase and advance skills (Epstein, 2006). Such ongoing training may be particularly important for middle and high school educators, given the fact that they are less likely to engage families (Herrold & O'Donnell, 2008). The state-level Parental Information and Resource Centers (PIRCs), funded by the U.S. Department of Education, are a resource for building the capacity of schools, districts, and states to engage families. Representing the only major federal funding stream for family involvement, PIRCs are designed to be statewide leaders that coordinate involvement efforts in their states (e.g., from Title I, the State Education Agency, the state PTA, and other stakeholders and leaders) and that also work with districts and schools to build capacity for family involvement.

Parents, too, need the knowledge and skills to be involved with learning in effective ways. Although families from all backgrounds want to be involved in their children's education, some may not know how to do so, particularly during adolescence, when school policies and procedures become more complex and critically important for postsecondary plans. Parents who did not attend high school, or who did not attend school in the United States, may be unfamiliar with course selection procedures, examination requirements, the college application process, and expectations for their involvement at the middle and high school levels. Rudy Crew, former superintendent of several large urban school districts and 2008 Superintendent of the Year, articulates the school's role in building parent capacity: "We're walking out halfway and extending an institutional hand . . . we're making a big, wide bridge to connect [parents] to us, with handrails so they feel safe" (Crew & Dyja, 2007, p. 165).

To help build parents' capacity, schools, districts, and states around the country are taking a range of approaches. One model is the parent leadership training model, exemplified by Kentucky's Commonwealth Institute for Parent Leadership (CIPL). CIPL trains parents to become advocates for their own children and for collective educational reform, through a series of workshops and a parent-led project to put their new skills into practice. "Parent academies" represent another increasingly common approach. For example, Miami–Dade's Parent Academy is a multifaceted and community-wide initiative that helps parents learn about their roles, rights, responsibilities, and opportunities to support learning. To date, the Parent Academy has worked with community partners to reach over 85,000 parents through workshops, educational and cultural events, resource sharing, and referrals on a wide variety of topics. At the school level, parent liaisons and family resource centers present additional opportunities, by helping to bridge communication between homes and schools and sharing information either one-on-one or through group workshops, trainings, and events.

Engage all stakeholders in family involvement efforts. With a broadened definition of family involvement as a process occurring across the many contexts in which youth traverse, comes the corollary that multiple institutions and the adult actors who carry out their missions all have a role to play in family–school–community partnerships. As previously discussed, youth development contexts represent a recent addition to the discourse on important partnership players beyond parents and classroom teachers. The Family PLUS initiative described earlier offers many examples of youth development leaders advancing family–school–community connections. One urban club houses a charter high school on its premises, providing the club with substantial unrestricted revenue each year through rental income. The club's parents and youth enjoy first priority for coveted school enrollment, as well as the informal assessment of and motivational influence on youth's school performance that club staff supply. Parents, school staff, and club staff also benefit from aligned expectations about parent volunteering (which is required at both the club and the school) (Kreider & Raghupathy, 2009).

School and district leaders and policymakers at all levels also shape partnership possibilities (e.g., Epstein, 2006), especially in secondary school contexts where school structures, staff outreach, parent hesitance, and adolescent developmental needs pose special challenges for engaging families. And perhaps most relevant to adolescence, youth themselves have an obvious stake and active role to play in initiating and sustaining connections, as the family narratives at the Boston Arts Academy described earlier illustrate so well. To ensure active engagement of all of these stakeholders, an array of opportunities for engaging families in adolescents' learning must be proffered.

Use data and evaluation for learning and continuous improvement. A stronger and more extensive foundation of program evaluation data and expertise is a critical way to increase knowledge for family involvement policy and practice. Program evaluations can provide information about the impact of programs, their successful implementation, and what it is about programs that helps them work. In particular, evaluations are needed that target those families most in need of supports—including families of adolescents. Promising evaluation findings for programs that engage parents in their teens' learning are beginning to point the way. For example, Teachers Involve Parents in Schoolwork is an interactive homework process in which the assignments require 6th- to 8th-grade students to share their work with someone at home. Parents are invited to pose questions to teachers and offer comments and feedback on the assignments (Van Voorhis, 2003). Such findings can provide guidance to other educators wishing to effectively engage similar populations.

The individual evaluation capacity of schools and community-based organizations implementing family involvement programs also must be built up. Educators are often unfamiliar with the importance and methods of conducting evaluation and have competing responsibilities that limit time for evaluation. One evaluation method consistent with an ethos of family–school partnership engages youth and families in the evaluation process itself. Thomas and LaPoint (2005) describe their use of the Talent Development evaluation framework to co-construct an evaluation of a family–school–community partnership program with the culturally diverse adolescents it serves. Likewise, Parent Services Project, in conjunction with its evaluator, Sociometrics Corporation, is evaluating its parent leadership institutes in part by training a core group of parent alumni to help design, collect, and interpret evaluation findings (Ocón, 2008). The evaluation also includes a database for easy data entry and at-a-click analysis so that program staff and parent leaders can have ready access to basic evaluation results to inform their future programming. Efforts by evaluation researchers to share their evaluation processes, measures, and analysis tools with family involvement program staff, parents, and youth can go a long way toward building local evaluation capacity. With such knowledge, local stakeholders can collect and use evaluation data for continuous improvement and learning related to family involvement efforts that directly affect them. Besides small-scale evaluation programs like these, high-quality, large-scale evaluations also are needed for informing federal and state policies.

CONNECTING THE DOTS:
ADOLESCENT FAMILY INVOLVEMENT IN CONTEXT

Policies and practices to promote family involvement in adolescence cannot be isolated from those in other developmental periods. At the same time, concerted efforts must be made to reverse the trend of decreasing focus on family involvement at the middle and high school levels, and to do so in developmentally appropriate ways. What is needed is a systemic effort to promote family involvement as a continuous and evolving process that is an integral part of larger educational reform. The reframing of family involvement and the principles for effective policy and practice laid out here can help to drive meaningful change at all levels. Policies and practices at the national, state, and local levels are interdependent and must fit together in a cohesive way. Integrating these strands will require bringing together many sectors and stakeholders, including policies that span many different levels and departments, diverse program models, parent groups representing different interests, and researchers from many disciplines. Making a true commitment to family involvement requires acknowledging that the whole is greater than the sum of its parts, and promoting mutual responsibility so that family educational involvement is part of the day-to-day work of all schools, communities, and families.

ACKNOWLEDGMENTS

We would like to thank Heather Weiss, Abby Weiss, Ellen Mayer, and M. Elena Lopez from the Harvard Family Research Project for feedback on earlier drafts of this manuscript.

REFERENCES

Auerbach, S. (2004). Engaging Latino parents in supporting college pathways: Lessons from a college access program. *Journal of Hispanic Higher Education, 3*(2), 125–145.

Barr, R. B., & Tagg, J. (1995). From teaching to learning—A new paradigm for undergraduate education. *Change, 27*(6), 12–25.

Bouffard, S. M., Malone, H. J., & Deschenes, S. (n.d.). *Complementary learning: Recommended and related readings*. Cambridge, MA: Harvard Family Research Project.

Bouffard, S., & Weiss, A. (2008). Family involvement policy: Past, present, and future. *Evaluation Exchange, XIV*(1/2), 16.

Burton, C. B. (1992). Defining family-centered early education: Beliefs of public school, child care, and Head Start teachers. *Early Education and Development*, 3(1), 45–59.

Caspe, M. (2008). Building the field. *Evaluation Exchange, XIV*(1/2), 6.

Caspe, M., Lopez, M. E., & Wolos, C. (2006/07). *Family involvement in elementary school children's education* (Family involvement makes a difference: Research Brief No. 2). Cambridge, MA: Harvard Family Research Project.

Chen, X. (2001). *Efforts by public K–8 schools to involve parents in children's education: Do school and parent reports agree?* (NCES 2001-076). Washington, DC: U.S. Government Printing Office.

Coleman, A. L., Starzynski, A. L., Winnick, S. Y., Palmer, S. R., & Furr, J. E. (2006). *It takes a parent: Transforming education in the wake of the No Child Left Behind Act*. Washington, DC: Appleseed.

Crew, R., & Dyja, T. (2007). *Only connect: The way to save our schools*. New York: Farrar, Strauss and Giroux.

D'Agostino, J. V., Hedges, L. V., Wong, K. K., & Borman, G. D. (2001). Title I parent-involvement programs: Effects on parenting practices and student achievement. In G. D. Borman, S. C. Stringfield, & R. E. Slavin (Eds.), *Title I: Compensatory education at the crossroads* (pp. 117–136). Mahwah, NJ: Erlbaum.

Davies, D. (1991). Schools reaching out: Family, school, and community partnerships for student success. *Phi Delta Kappan, 72*(5), 376–382.

Eccles, J. S., & Harold, R. D. (1996). Family involvement in children's and adolescents' schooling. In A. Booth & J. F. Dunn (Eds.), *Family–school links: How do they affect educational outcomes*? (pp. 3–34). Mahwah, NJ: Erlbaum.

Edwards, P. A., & Jones Young, L. S. (1992). Beyond parents: Family, community, and school involvement. *Phi Delta Kappan, 74*(1), 72–80.

Epstein, J. L. (2006). Links in a professional development chain: Preservice and inservice education for effective programs of school, family and community partnerships. *The New Educator, 1*(2), 125–141.

Epstein, J. L. (2007). Improving family and community involvement in secondary schools. *Principal Leadership, 8*(2), 16–22.

Epstein, J. L., & Sanders, M. G. (2006). Prospects for change: Preparing educators for school, family, and community partnerships. *Peabody Journal of Education, 81*(2), 81–120.

Epstein, J. L., & Sheldon, S. (2006). Moving forward: Ideas for research on school, family and community partnerships. In C. F. Conrad & R. Serlin (Eds.), *SAGE handbook for research in education: Engaging ideas and enriching inquiry* (pp. 117–138). Thousand Oaks, CA: Sage.

Fege, A. F. (2006). Getting Ruby a quality public education: Forty-two years of building the demand for quality public schools through parental and public involvement. *Harvard Educational Review, 76*(44), 570–586.

Flanigan, C. (2007). Preparing preservice teachers to partner with parents and communities: An analysis of college of education faculty focus groups. *School Community Journal, 17*(2), 89–109.

Funkhouser, J. E., Stief, E. A., & Allen, S. E. (1998). *Title I school–parent compacts: Supporting partnerships to improve learning* (Final report). Washington, DC: U.S. Department of Education.

Gándara, P., & Moreno, J. F. (2002). Introduction: The Puente Project: Issues and perspectives on preparing Latino youth for higher education. *Educational Policy, 16,* 463–473.

Henderson, A., & Mapp, K. (2002). *A new wave of evidence: The impact of school, family, and community connections on student achievement.* Austin, TX: Southwest Educational Development Laboratory.

Henderson, A., Mapp, K. L., Johnson, V. R., & Davies, D. (2006). *Beyond the bake sale: The essential guide to family–school partnerships.* New York: The New Press.

Herrold, K., & O'Donnell, K. (2008). *Parent and family involvement in education, 2006–07 school year, from the National Household Education Surveys Program of 2007* (NCES 2008-050). Washington, DC: U.S. Government Printing Office.

Heymann, S. J., & Earle, A. (2000). Low-income parents: How do their working conditions affect their opportunity to help school-age children at risk? *American Educational Research Journal, 37*(4), 833–848.

Hiatt-Michael, D. (2004). Preparing teachers for parental involvement: Current practices and possibilities across the nation. *Thresholds in Education, 30*(2), 2–10.

Hoover-Dempsey, K. V., & Sandler, H. M. (1997). Why do parents become involved in their children's education? *Review of Educational Research, 67*(1), 3–42.

Jeynes, W. (2005). Parental involvement and secondary school student educational outcomes: A meta-analysis. *Evaluation Exchange, X*(4), 6.

Jeynes, W. H. (2007). The relationship between parental involvement and urban secondary school student academic achievement: A meta-analysis. *Urban Education, 42*(1), 82–110.

Kakli, Z., Kreider, H., Little, P., Buck, T., & Coffey, M. (2006). *Focus on families! How to build and support family-centered practices in after school.* Cambridge, MA: Harvard Family Research Project and Build the Out-of-School Time Network.

Kreider, H., Caspe, M., Kennedy, S., & Weiss, H. (2007). *Family involvement makes a difference: Family involvement in middle and high school students' education* (Vol. 3). Cambridge, MA: Harvard Family Research Project.

Kreider, H., & Raghupathy, S. (2009, April). *Engaging families in boys & girls clubs: An evaluation of the Family PLUS pilot initiative.* Paper presented at the annual meeting of the American Educational Research Association, San Diego.

Markow, D., & Martin, S. (2005, December 22). The Metlife survey of the American teacher: Transitions and the role of supportive relationships. *Childhood Education* (ERIC Document Reproduction Service No. EJ726595). Retrieved March 9, 2009, from ERIC database.

Mattingly, D. J., Prislin, R., McKenzie, T. L., Rodriguez, J. L., & Kayzar, B. (2002). Evaluating evaluations: The case of parent involvement programs. *Review of Educational Research, 72*(4), 549–576.

McLaughlin, M. W., & Shields, P. M. (1987). Involving low-income parents in the schools: A role for policy? *Phi Delta Kappan, 69*(2), 156–160.

Nye, C., Turner, H. M., & Schwartz, J. B. (2006). *Approaches to parental involvement for improving the academic performance of elementary school children in grades K–6.* London: The Campbell Collaboration. Available from http://campbellcollaboration.org/doc-pdf/Nye_PI_Review.pdf

Ocón, J. (2008). Upcoming evaluations: Parent Services Project's parent leadership institutes. *Evaluation Exchange, XIV*(1&2), 29.

Ouimette, M. Y., Feldman, J., & Tung, R. (2006). Collaborating for high school student success: A case study of parent engagement at the Boston Arts Academy. *The School Community Journal, 16*(2), 91–114.

Palanki, A., & Burch, P. (1992). *Mapping the policy landscape: What federal and state governments are doing to promote family–school partnerships.* Washington, DC: U.S. Department of Health and Human Services, Office of Educational Research and Improvement.

Public Education Network. (2003). *The voice of the new teacher.* Washington, DC: Author.

Public Education Network. (2007). *Open to the public: How communities, parents, and students assess the impact of the No Child Left Behind Act.* Washington, DC: Author.

Radcliffe, B., Malone, M., & Nathan, J. (1994). *Training for parent partnership: Much more should be done.* Minneapolis: University of Minnesota, Hubert H. Humphrey Institute of Public Affairs, Center for School Change.

Rothstein, R. (2004). *Class and schools: Using social, economic, and educational reform to close the black–white achievement gap.* Washington, DC: Economic Policy Institute.

Sheldon, S. B. (2005). Testing a structural equation model of partnership program implementation and parent involvement. *The Elementary School Journal, 106*(2), 171–187.

Simon, B. S. (2004). High school outreach and family involvement. *Social Psychology of Education, 7*(2), 185–209.

Thomas, V., & LaPoint, V. (2005). Blending evaluation traditions: The talent development model. *Evaluation Exchange, 10*(4), 7.

U.S. Department of Education. (2001). *Public Law PL 107-110. The No Child Left Behind Act of 2001.* Retrieved December 22, 2008, from http://www.ed.gov/policy/elsec/leg/esea02/index.html

U.S. Department of Education. (2007). *State and local implementation of the No Child Left Behind Act: Vol. I. Title I school choice, supplemental educational services, and student achievement.* U.S. Department of Education Office of Planning, Evaluation and Policy Development, Policy and Program Studies Service. Retrieved September 5, 2008, from http://www.ed.gov/rschstat/eval/choice/implementation/

U.S. General Accounting Office. (2006). *No Child Left Behind: Education actions needed to improve local implementation and state evaluation of supplemental education services* (GAO Rep. No. 06-758). Washington, DC: Author.

Vaden-Kiernan, N., & McManus, J. (2005). *Parent and family involvement in education: 2002–2003* (NCES 2005-043). Washington, DC: U.S. Government Printing Office.

Van Voorhis, F. L. (2003). Interactive homework in middle school: Effects on family involvement and science achievement. *The Journal of Educational Research, 96*(6), 323–338.

Weiss, H., Caspe, M., & Lopez, M. E. (2006). *Family involvement makes a difference: Family involvement in early childhood education.* Cambridge, MA: Harvard Family Research Project.

Weiss, H. B., Coffman, J., Post, M., Bouffard, S. M., & Little, P. (2005). Beyond the classroom: Complementary learning to improve achievement outcomes. *Evaluation Exchange, XI*(1), 2–3.

Weiss, H., Dearing, E., Mayer, E., Kreider, H., & McCartney, K. (2005). Family educational involvement: Who can afford it and what does it afford? In C. R. Cooper, C. T. García Coll, W. T. Bartko, H. M. Davis, & C. Chatman (Eds.), *Developmental pathways through middle childhood: Rethinking context and diversity as resources* (pp. 17–40). Mahwah, NJ: Erlbaum.

Wright, K., Daniel, T., & Himelreich, K. S. (2000). *Preparation for building partnerships with families: A survey of teachers, teacher educators, and school administrators.* Cambridge, MA: Harvard Family Research Project.

Recommendations for Developmentally Appropriate Strategies for Parental Involvement During Adolescence

RUTH K. CHAO
NANCY E. HILL

T HIS VOLUME HAS DOCUMENTED the various reasons or arguments for further investigation and consideration of the need for guidelines or recommendations for building family–school relationships in our secondary schools. These reasons or arguments are based both on prior research that demonstrates the positive effect of parental involvement in education on academic outcomes for adolescents (Catsambis, 2001; Chao, 2000; Hill et al., 2004) and on the call from policymakers and practitioners to close achievement gaps across elementary and secondary schools through engaging families (Dearing, Kreider, Simpkins, & Weiss, 2006; Hampton, Mumford, & Bond, 1998). Based on this prior research and policy agenda, this edited volume set as its goals to identify developmentally appropriate strategies to maintain effective parental involvement in middle and high schools. The identification of such strategies has taken account of how policies at the federal and local levels may be informed by research on the plausible mediators or processes by which parental involvement in education matters, and by teacher and school-level practices and intervention programs. In this final chapter, we first highlight key themes or findings common across chapters, studies, samples, and ethnicities on the most developmentally effective strategies for parental involvement in education during middle and high school. Second, based on these strategies and their associations with achievement, we highlight how programs and policies should broaden their thinking about developmentally appropriate and meaningful outcomes for adolescents. Third, we highlight how policies at the federal, state, and local levels can be informed by existing research and be more developmentally and culturally inclusive. Finally, we highlight next stages of research that are necessary in order to more fully understand the underlying processes of parental involvement in education and its relation with achievement.

DEVELOPMENTALLY APPROPRIATE
STRATEGIES FOR ADOLESCENCE: A CONSENSUS

Prior research demonstrates that parental involvement as typically defined (e.g., involvement at the school and helping with homework) declines in amount and effectiveness during adolescence (Hill & Tyson, in press; Seginer, 2006; Singh et al., 1995; Stevenson & Baker, 1987). As found by Chao and colleagues in Chapter 6 of this volume, the management of homework declined especially for Asian Americans. In this volume, collectively, we found that effective parental involvement includes additional practices (e.g., planning for college or post-high-school) that are most effective in supporting achievement. In the context of these declines in home- and school-based involvement, however, we found that parents increased their involvement in four broad ways not accounted for in studies of elementary school students.

Communicating Expectations

Although research with elementary school children has found that communicating expectations is positively associated with achievement (Fan & Chen, 2001), many chapters in this volume, that is, those of deCastro and Catsambis, Hill and colleagues, and Hoover-Dempsey and colleagues, found or explained that such expectations were important for fostering adolescents' future goals and plans after high school. By communicating educational expectations to their children, parents provide them not only with clear standards for their behavior or effort in school, but also with a sense of possibilities for the future.

Planning Beyond or After High School

Related to communicating expectations is the increased importance of actively planning for post-high-school and college during middle and high school. As reported by Chao and colleagues and Hoover-Dempsey and colleagues, as youth make the transition to middle school, parents need to be very proactive and think ahead in terms of their eventual entrance to college. This includes parents' willingness to learn about college opportunities (deCastro & Catsambis), providing materials to assist with preparing for the SAT test (Chao et al.), and discussing the value or utility of a college education for adolescents' future careers (Hill et al.; Hoover-Dempsey et al.; Jones & Schneider). This type of planning during the transition to middle school also includes knowledge about courses and extracurricular activities that represent the opening or foreclosure of future educational opportunities (Eccles & Harold, 1996). Further, because parents' knowledge about and efficacy in actively planning for college often are linked to parents' own educational attainment and social capital (Lareau, 1987), it is particularly important for theories and policies to recognize such involvement so that this knowledge can be provided to all families.

Augmenting or Supplementing Instruction

The third type of involvement that may be unique to adolescence and that is not included in prevailing theories of parental involvement in education is families' *augmenting or supplementing instruction*. Chao and colleagues described how Asian American families often provide additional textbooks and study materials to supplement the instructional materials received in school. Further, parents may enroll their adolescents in extracurricular activities, study groups, and classes to augment or support the instruction provided in school or to provide additional opportunities for adolescents' learning experiences (Chao et al.; Jones & Schneider). Although ideally all schools would provide a challenging curriculum that prepared students for college and math- and science-based occupations, schools in higher SES communities are more likely to do so. Concomitantly, families from higher SES backgrounds are much more likely to engage in these activities than are families from lower SES backgrounds, thereby exacerbating economic gaps in achievement (Jones & Schneider, this volume; Lareau, 2003).

Fostering Adolescents' Management of Their Schoolwork

Fourth, because adolescence is a period marked by youths' increasing independence, autonomy, and cognitive abilities for planning and decisionmaking, parents should play more of a supportive than a supervisory role in their schoolwork. Adolescents need experiences with managing their own schoolwork. Parents may need to provide some *scaffolding* or gradual increase in the level to which adolescents are expected to accomplish such management without the supervision of parents. This process includes responding to adolescents' requests for assistance with organizing projects, rather than taking a more direct managerial approach to homework help (Chao et al.; Hoover-Dempsey et al.), and monitoring homework, rather than actively checking or engaging in homework (Hill et al.; Hoover-Dempsey et al.). Building on such independence in adolescence also includes linking schoolwork to current events and students' interests (Hill et al.) and providing activities that guide and support students' decisionmaking abilities (deCastro & Catsambis). Such guidance and support for students' decisionmaking do not preclude setting some boundaries around time use, particularly leisure time (Jones & Schneider), and also monitoring friendships (Hill et al.). Although these strategies are also important during elementary school, they become even more significant during adolescence.

In considering the implementation of these developmentally appropriate strategies, Bouffard and Crosnoe (Chapters 8 and 9, respectively) outline the importance of communication between schools and families, and overcoming potential barriers in communication. Crosnoe describes the need for the transference or sharing of information between middle schools, high schools, and families for facilitating the transition between middle schools and high schools. Transference of basic information on students' school records and performance across this transition allows for more expedient identification of where students are at academically and what they need. This information shared between schools is especially important for students whose families or parents may not be knowledgeable about or efficacious in advocating for their adolescents' schooling and performance. For example, as Crosnoe has pointed out, change or improvement for Latino students in courses (i.e., math and science) critical for the pipeline to college is more likely when middle schools and high schools work together than when these schools work only with parents. Similarly, Kreider and Bouffard document how after-school programs and other community organizations for youth can work with schools to support adolescents' learning. In addition to broadening the frameworks that guide parental involvement in education during adolescence, this set of chapters highlighted the need to broaden our thinking about appropriate educational outcomes.

BROADENING OUR UNDERSTANDING OF "OUTCOMES" IN DEVELOPMENTALLY APPROPRIATE WAYS

With the introduction of NCLB and its focus on accountability, indicators of academic progress are focused largely on test scores, especially in mathematics, science, and English language arts. The chapters in this volume point to a broader range of outcomes for defining academic success in adolescence. Part of the goal of middle and high school is to prepare students for success in college and in the workplace after high school. Although competence in academic subjects is essential for achieving such goals, internalized values and motivation for learning, and a strong work ethic are also markers of occupational and educational success. DeCastro and Catsambis (Chapter 5), Hoover-Dempsey and colleagues (Chapter 1), Jones and Schneider (Chapter 4), and Mandara (Chapter 7) identified other more proximal or mediating aspects of learning that are also important in explaining just how parental involvement leads to academic success and are critical outcomes in and of themselves. They include academic engagement, self-regulation, self-efficacy, academic self-concept, internalized motivation to learn, social self-efficacy (i.e., appropriate help seeking), and time management. The significance of many of these proximal outcomes or learning processes was identified in multiple chapters in this volume, attesting to their validity or generalizibility. Because there is often less individual attention and monitoring from teachers in secondary schooling, these independent or self-motivated learning processes are essential to the development of adolescents' psychosocial resources for achieving in both school and the workplace. Thus, in addition to examining the direct relation between parental involvement and distal outcomes, such as grades, test scores, and graduation rates, adolescents' future success is equally likely to be dependent on these proximal learning outcomes, as demonstrated in three of the chapters in this book (deCastro & Catsambis; Hill et al.; Jones & Schneider).

IMPROVING POLICIES AND PROGRAMS
AT THE FEDERAL, STATE, AND LOCAL LEVELS

Federal Level

NCLB, under Part A of Title I, "Improving the Academic Achievement of Disadvantaged Students," lays out basic program requirements that include a focus on parents' involvement in schools, that is, Section 1118, Parental Involvement. This section allows for educational agencies to receive funding contingent on their offering programs and activities for the involvement of parents. The components of this section require that schools not only provide parents of participating children a written parental involvement policy, but also develop such policies in conjunction with parental input and direction. Another component of Section 1118 includes general guidelines for the content of such policies, as well as specifications for how educational agencies or schools can build upon these guidelines "to ensure effective involvement of parents and to support a partnership among the school involved, parents, and the community." In addition to these recommendations, which are delineated below, two additional components attempt to (1) provide greater accessibility for parents with limited English proficiency, and (2) inform parents of the existence and purpose of a resource developed through the U.S. Department of Education, the Parental Education and Resource Centers.

Recommendations identified under subsection (e) of Section 1118 of NCLB

1. helping parents to understand state academic content standards, achievement standards, assessments, and how to monitor children's progress
2. providing materials and training to help parents in working with children to improve academics
3. educating teachers and other school staff in how to assist parents; communicate, implement, and coordinate programs; build ties
4. coordinating and integrating PI programs with other existing activities or programs
5. ensuring that information related to school and PI programs is disseminated to parents in understandable language
6. involving parents in development of training of teachers and other school educators
7. providing necessary literacy training
8. paying reasonable and necessary expenses allowing parents to participate in school-related activities and trainings
9. training parents to enhance involvement of other parents
10. arranging school meetings at a variety of times and even at homes of parents who are unable to attend school meetings
11. adopting and implementing model approaches to improving PI
12. establishing district-wide parent advisory council
13. developing appropriate linkages with community-based organizations
14. providing other reasonable support for PI activities

NCLB revisited for middle and high school students. It is particularly urgent and necessary to address these recommendations for secondary schools because, as this volume attests, this formally marks the beginning of the pipeline to college. We know from research presented in this volume not only that some parents increase their focus on planning for college (see Chao et al.; deCastro & Catsambis), but that such strategies (including specifically communicating their aspirations to their teens, encouraging their teen to prepare for SATs, and holding frequent discussions with them about taking the SAT/ACT and about applying to colleges) are related to students' school motivation and plans for college. However, as Hill and colleagues have demonstrated, such efforts are less efficacious for parents of lower socioeconomic status than parents of higher status.

Parents need to know college requirements, in addition to state requirements, including the required assessments for performance. NCLB recognizes the importance of sharing information about state academic standards and assessments, and many schools have workshops or orientations for disseminating and explaining this information. Schools need to include information on college requirements in conjunction with state requirements, specifically the types of courses needed, additional advanced placement and honors courses, and extracurricular activities that are necessary and beneficial for applying to college. Currently this information is disseminated primarily to students on an individual basis through a school or college counselor based on their current academic performance. In other words, counselors are selectively conveying information to students whom they judge are academically capable. Although research has shown that prior grades and performance are important indicators of the likelihood of attending college, this does not empower students, or their families, to change or improve their academic preparation in ways that increase their chances of pursuing and succeeding in higher education.

This system of information dissemination needs to move beyond a reliance on school counselors as the gatekeepers to higher education or knowledge about higher education. Instead, this knowledge should be provided to all families, regardless of their children's academic performance. Hill and colleagues found with middle school students that parents are very desirous of such information and are motivated to be involved. In particular, as Hill and colleagues have cited, parents reported that they are looking for information about effective strategies for promoting academic achievement and navigating pathways to college (Hill & Torres, in press; Lareau & Horvat, 1999). Hoover-Dempsey and colleagues provide additional evidence that parents' perceptions of their role in their children's schooling are formed in part by schools' willingness to involve parents. Their notions of "parental role construction for involvement," and their "sense of efficacy for helping adolescents succeed in school" involve the idea that these are social constructions that are largely open to school influence. Schools then need to reinforce parents' role constructions and show their support by also espousing these same beliefs and acting in accordance with them.

State Level

Looking across schools and districts, disadvantaged and minority parents receive less outreach than other parents (Herrold & O'Donnell, 2008). Whereas inequities are often difficult to track and manage at the local or district level, often the inequities are most prominent across districts, rather than within districts. Comparisons across districts for determining the schools with the greatest inequities can be made more effectively at the state level. With this comparative information, states can provide funding to increase staff across districts for supporting parental involvement and the provision of information to families to support involvement. Whereas information to families about the progress of individual students happens at the level of schools and teachers, other information about how parents can support their adolescents' education can be developed at the state level and disseminated through schools. Further, because some information that parents need is common across districts, such as elucidating pathways from middle school to college, linking this information to state institutions of higher education can be done at the state level.

Although additional funding for increasing staff is essential to effectively disseminating information to parents, such dissemination depends on other factors as well. These factors include professional development (e.g., sensitivity training) of school staff at both the school and district levels to ensure that all families are treated equally with respect to information dissemination, and any other needs of families to facilitate their involvement. In addition, states need to set the tone for parental involvement by stating clearly that schools should assume that all students are bound for higher education or occupational training, and should make concrete efforts to involve all parents.

Local Level

As families and schools are situated in communities, schools and school personnel should understand the local context—at both district and school levels. That is, local policies should focus on the local context. Rodríguez (Chapter 2) demonstrated that the amount and effectiveness of parental involvement for supporting academic outcomes among Latino families were dependent on characteristics of the school and the community, which is likely true for other ethnic groups as well. These characteristics include the size of the school, the numerical size and status of the ethnic group, parents' and students' perceived power and influence in the school, and intergroup contact. Similarly, Hill and colleagues described how beliefs about involvement, how adolescents learn, and implicit world views within the school vary by culture and ethnicity, and may influence how parents become involved and how effective they are. Because there is tremendous variation across and within communities, these issues cannot be addressed at the federal or state level, but must be understood at the local level. Policies at the district and school level should be informed by the local cultural context.

Barriers to parental involvement or family–school relations that may exist at the community level also can be addressed through local policies that encourage the use of technology, especially email, Web sites, and e-bulletin boards (see Chapter 8 by Bouffard). Further, as studies have shown, adolescents often are not comfortable with their parents showing up at their school (Stevenson & Baker, 1987). Communicating through the Internet or other technology allows parents access to their adolescents' schooling without having to be physically present at the school. Finally, there is also evidence that the use of technology to support parental involvement is effective—such involvement is associated with achievement across high school (Chapter 8). Although initially equipping schools and families with such technology, particularly computers, is expensive, such expenses may be more cost effective in the long run as the technology may provide a platform for effective dissemination of information to parents *and* students. That is, through innovations in the development of software programs, it may be possible in the not too distant future for teachers to disseminate homework assignments to students and even to have homework graded and recorded by computer programs, with students accessing their homework through the Internet.

Another consideration in this volume for the building of family–school linkages at the local level is through the integration of parental involvement programs with other existing programs and/or with other settings beyond the school. There also may be other existing programs in schools that could be linked to or fed into parental involvement programs or activities in schools. Some examples of existing programs provided in NCLB do not apply to secondary schools (e.g., Head Start). There are, however, community-based programs that do target or include secondary school students or adolescents. Kreider and Bouffard (Chapter 10) highlight how the Family PLUS initiative, after-school programs sponsored by the Boys & Girls Clubs of America, offer examples of youth development leaders advancing family–school–community connections. As Kreider and Bouffard illustrate through the complementary-learning model (Weiss, Coffman, Post, Bouffard, & Little, 2005), effectively supporting parental involvement in education can be done through a system of linked supports across contexts to already existing after-school programs, and building such linkages is a continuous process that is developmental in nature (i.e., it changes with the needs of the students). The onus, or burden, of building family–school linkages or relationships does not rest just on the shoulders of schools and families, but on all of the agencies that engage children and families.

NEXT STAGES OF RESEARCH

The consistency in findings about the nature of parental involvement during adolescence and the programs and policies that support effective parental involvement in middle and high schools across the chapters of this book are a large first step in making sure that families and schools effectively work together to ensure that adolescents reach their potential. Next steps in research should focus on identifying the processes through which involvement makes a difference. As Crosnoe (Chapter 9) indicates, families are not always appropriate or amenable targets for policy intervention, because their involvement depends on other factors, including family circumstances (e.g., socioeconomic status or lack of financial and social resources or capital) that may limit their capacity for change; therefore, identifying the underlying processes of the effects of involvement will assist in designing programs to support students whose parents are unable to be effectively involved. In addition, research is needed to better identify policy levers or areas of change for students that may make the difference between succeeding in a college preparatory curriculum and being unaware of its existence or importance, resulting in lost potential. As Crosnoe has elucidated, identification of dilemmas or areas in need of the greatest change involves addressing the following questions: (1) where is action on this dilemma likely to make a difference, (2) when are the critical points of intervention, and (3) how can family–school partnerships serve as a lever of action in such intervention? Crosnoe specifically targeted math/science courses in secondary schools for Latino/a students as an effective point of entry for addressing the educational inequities and disparities of this group relative to Whites. Family–school partnerships that were most effective in increasing enrollment in math and science courses among these students involved communication between middle schools, high schools, and families. Finally, research is needed that empirically evaluates programs and interventions to support families of adolescents and their achievement so that program and policy dollars are most effectively utilized.

Putting a Human Face on Research and Policymaking

In making recommendations for future research and educational policies geared toward fostering family–school partnerships, we would be remiss if we did not remind ourselves and our readers of the experiences and concerns of families in the United States today that limit and hinder the capacity for change. Although the use of or reference to family–school partnerships as "parental involvement in school" implies that parents are the primary agents of responsibility for their children's academic achievement, all research and recommendations for educational policy ultimately must recognize that the onus of such relationships should rest more with schools, districts, communities, and local, state, and federal lawmakers. It cannot be overstated that families today, particularly ethnic minority and immigrant families, are struggling under the pressure of many burdens or demands, including, on the most basic level, how to parent adolescents, and concerns that increases in their adolescents' independence and autonomy also may bring increases in risk taking or exposure to risk or even danger. Also, parenting in today's dire economic conditions not only creates increased feelings of anxiety and uncertainty, but also results in increased work hours and shifts not amenable to attendance at parent–teacher conferences or other types of involvement at school. Needless to say, the financial difficulties created by the current economic crisis have exacerbated the uncertainties among many families as to whether they can even provide adequate meals and pay their bills. These are the current conditions that many families in the United States are facing or experiencing.

Additional barriers to school involvement are experienced by immigrant families. These involve not only the linguistic and cultural barriers mentioned throughout many of the chapters in this volume, but also policies targeting immigrants and the curtailing of immigration, particularly across the U.S.–Mexican border. One example of a policy that targets immigrants involves Proposition 187 passed in California by voters in 1994, which basically attempts to deny undocumented immigrants access to public services such as healthcare, welfare benefits, and even education. In denying access to education, it specifically requires school personnel to report to state authorities those children or parents that are in the United States illegally. Such policies are particularly damaging and antithetical to the spirit of family–school partnerships. Many immigrant families, even documented immigrants, may feel that schools are not safe places for them and that school personnel may be hostile to them. Although many portions of the initiative have been struck down by rulings from U.S. district courts, the initiative nonetheless created a climate or message of hate, exclusion, and deprivation of the basic right of access to public schools intended for all families. Although families are often the agents who assume much of the burden for advocating for children's education and academic achievement, this is a responsibility that should not rest solely on their shoulders.

REFERENCES

Catsambis, S. (2001). Expanding knowledge of parental involvement in children's secondary education: Connections with high school seniors' academic success. *Social Psychology of Education, 5*(2), 149–177.

Chao, R. K. (2000). Cultural explanations for the role of parenting in the school success of Asian American children. In R. W. Taylor & M. C. Wang (Eds.), *Resilience across contexts: Family, work, culture, and community* (pp. 333–363). Mahwah, NJ: Erlbaum.

Dearing, E., Kreider, H., Simpkins, S., & Weiss, H. B. (2006). Family involvement in school and low-income children's literacy: Longitudinal associations between and within families. *Journal of Educational Psychology, 98*(4), 653–664.

Eccles, J. S., & Harold, R. D. (1996). Family involvement in children's and adolescents' schooling. In A. Booth & J. F. Dunn (Eds.), *Family–school links: How do they affect educational outcomes?* (pp. 3–34). Mahwah, NJ: Erlbaum.

Fan, X., & Chen, M. (2001). Parental involvement and students' academic achievement: A meta-analysis. *Educational Psychology Review, 13*(1), 1–22.

Hampton, F. M., Mumford, D. A., & Bond, L. (1998). Parental involvement in inner city schools: The project FAST extended family approach to success. *Urban Education, 33*(3), 410–427.

Herrold, K., & O'Donnell, K. (2008). *Parent and family involvement in education, 2006–07 school year, From the National Household Education Surveys Program of 2007* (NCES 2008-050). Washington, DC: U.S. Government Printing Office.

Hill, N. E., Castellino, D. R., Lansford, J. E., Nowlin, P., Dodge, K. A., Bates, J. E., & Pettit, G. (2004). Parent academic involvement as related to school behavior, achievement, and aspirations: Demographic variations across adolescence. *Child Development, 75*(5), 1491–1509.

Hill, N. E., & Torres, K. (in press). Negotiating the American dream: The paradox of Latino students' goals and achievement and engagement between families and schools. *Journal of Social Issues.*

Hill, N. E., & Tyson, D. F. (in press). Parental involvement in middle school: A meta-analytic assessment of strategies that promote achievement. *Developmental Psychology.*

Lareau, A. (1987). Social class differences in family–school relationships: The importance of cultural capital. *Sociology of Education, 60*(2), 73–85.

Lareau, A. (2003). *Unequal childhoods: Class, race, and family life.* Berkeley: University of California.

Lareau, A., & Horvat, E. M. (1999). Moments of social inclusion and exclusion: Race, class, and cultural capital in family–school relationships. *Sociology of Education, 72*(1), 37–53.

Seginer, R. (2006). Parents' educational involvement: A developmental ecology perspective. *Parenting: Science and Practice, 6*(1), 1–48.

Singh, K., Bickley, B. G., Trivette, P. S., Keith, T. Z., Keith, P. B., & Anderson, E. (1995). The effects of four components of parental involvement on eighth grade student achievement: Structural analysis of NELS88 data. *School Psychology Review, 24*, 299–317.

Stevenson, D. L., & Baker, D. P. (1987). The family–school relation and the child's school performance. *Child Development, 58*(5), 1348–1357.

Weiss, H. B., Coffman, J., Post, M., Bouffard, S. M., & Little, P. (2005). Beyond the classroom: Complementary learning to improve achievement outcomes. *Evaluation Exchange, XI*(1), 2–3.

About the Editors
and Contributors

Nancy E. Hill, Ph.D., is a professor at Harvard University, Graduate School of Education and the Suzanne Young Murray Professor at Radcliffe Institute of Advanced Study, Harvard University. She was an associate professor in the Department of Psychology and Neurosciences at Duke University until 2009. She received her Ph.D. in developmental psychology from Michigan State University. Dr. Hill's research focuses on how cultural, economic, and community contexts influence family dynamics and family socialization patterns and in turn shape children's academic achievement and other developmental outcomes. Specifically, her work examines how parenting and family–school relations vary across ethnicity and socioeconomic status, and the ethnic and economic variations in the relationship between family processes and children's developmental outcomes, especially among African American and Latino families. Dr. Hill has published her work in top journals in the field such as *Child Development, Developmental Psychology, Journal of Educational Psychology, Applied Developmental Science,* and *Journal of Family Psychology.* In addition to journal articles, she co-edited *African American Family Life: Ecological and Cultural Perspectives* (2005). She served as associate editor of *Child Development* from 2003–2007 and on the editorial boards for several developmental, family, and education journals. In addition, she served on the Committee on Children, Youth, and Families of the American Psychological Association (2003–2006, as chair 2006). She is currently a member of the Governing Council of the Society for Research in Child Development.

Ruth K. Chao, Ph.D., is an associate professor in the Department of Psychology at the University of California, Riverside. She received her Ph.D. from the University of California, Los Angeles. Her research interests include sociocultural perspectives of parenting and the family, focusing on Asian immigrants. She has just completed a 5-year, longitudinal study funded by the National Institute of Health, examining the effects of parental control, warmth, and parental involvement in school on adolescents' school performance and behavioral adjustment. Her research also includes studies of the language acculturation of Asian immigrant families across time and its effects on adolescents' adjustment.

Christine Aque completed her third year in the Developmental Psychology graduate program at the University of California, Riverside. Her research interests include mental health outcomes among Asian American adolescents and how they may be impacted by parenting. For her master's thesis, she examined the effects of the affective interpretations of parental control on adolescent outcomes. She currently works as a research analyst and conducts evaluation studies on children's programs.

Suzanne M. Bouffard, Ph.D., is a project manager and researcher at the Harvard Family Research Project (HFRP) at Harvard University, Graduate School of Education. She has an extensive background in family involvement research and evaluation and also has worked in the fields of out-of-school time, developmental psychology, and the arts. She specializes in communicating about research for practitioners and policymakers, through both written publications and speaking at national and local conferences and workshops. Her work has appeared in such diverse publications as *New Directions for Youth Development*, *The Journal of Youth Development: Bridging Research and Practice*, *Merrill Palmer Quarterly*, and *Social Psychology of Education*. She also has edited several issues of HFRP's periodical *The Evaluation Exchange*. Her recent work includes a policy paper on family involvement for the Campaign for Educational Equity, writing about family involvement for secondary school principals, and providing technical assistance and evaluation support to the national Parental Information and Resource Centers program. She earned a Ph.D. in developmental psychology from Duke University, where she was a J.B. Duke Fellow and a University Scholar. She won an Outstanding Dissertation Award from the American Educational Research Association for her work on the role of Internet and voicemail technology in promoting family involvement.

Lea Bromell graduated from Duke University in 2004 with a B.A. in psychology and a certificate in human development. Currently, she is a graduate student studying developmental psychology in the Department of Psychology and Neuroscience at Duke University.

Sophia Catsambis, Ph.D., received her doctorate from New York University. She is a professor of sociology at Queens College and the Graduate Center, City University of New York. She brings equity concerns into the arena of educational research through the analysis of major longitudinal survey data. She currently is studying influences of disadvantaged neighborhoods on the educational opportunities of at-risk students as well as the use and effects of ability grouping in the early elementary grades.

Robert Crosnoe, Ph.D., is an associate professor of sociology and a faculty associate in the Population Research Center at the University of Texas at Austin. His main field of interest is the life course and human development, with a special emphasis on how the education and health of young people are connected to socioeconomic, racial/ethnic, and immigration-related stratification.

Belkis Suazo deCastro, Ph.D., is a senior research associate at the Community College Research Center, Teachers College. Dr. deCastro's research explores the social mechanisms that affect the educational resources necessary for successful transition into 2- or 4-year colleges. Central to her analysis is the role that familial, peer, and school support plays in understanding racial/ethnic and gender differences in education. This program of research is part of her current study on race/ethnicity and gender differences in access to and attainment of a postsecondary education using the National Education Longitudinal Study of 1988 and Educational Longitudinal Study of 2002.

Kathleen V. Hoover-Dempsey, Ph.D., is an associate professor of psychology and human development at Peabody College, Vanderbilt University. Her model of the parental involvement process, developed with colleagues, offers a theoretically and empirically grounded understanding of why parents and families become involved in their children's education, and how their involvement influences students' learning and achievement. She and her colleagues also have developed and evaluated school-based interventions designed to increase the effectiveness of school invitations to involvement. At Vanderbilt, she teaches courses in developmental and educational psychology in the undergraduate and graduate programs.

Christa L. Ice, Ph.D., is a research instructor with the Department of Pediatrics at West Virginia University, Health Sciences Center. She received her doctorate in psychology from Vanderbilt University, focusing on parental involvement among public school and home-school families. She currently is assisting the Coronary Artery Risk Detection in Appalachian Communities (CARDIAC) project with methodological issues and statistical analyses. As part of this collaboration, her recent epidemiological research efforts have led her to examine obesity rates among West Virginia schoolchildren and the influence on children's cardiovascular risk factors. In addition, her research program focuses on the effects of parental involvement on many facets of children's development, including health and academic achievement.

Nathan Jones is a doctoral candidate in the Education Policy program at Michigan State University. His research focuses on teacher quality and the sociology of education, particularly related to the role of colleagues in influencing the practices, beliefs, and commitment of early-career teachers. Much of this work has explored variation in the experiences of special education teachers and their general education colleagues. He also has conducted research looking at the impact of family characteristics and experiences on educational outcomes of adolescents.

Akira Kanatsu is a doctoral student at the University of California, Riverside, in the developmental psychology area. He received his bachelor's degree in psychology from California State University, Northridge, in 2003, where he conducted research on the effects of perceived racial climate on college students' academic achievement and well-being. He also received his master's degree in psychology from the University of California, Riverside, in 2006. His research interests include academic achievement and well-being of ethnic minority students in relation to parenting behaviors and family relationships. He is also interested in the levels and effects of parental involvement among Asian immigrant fathers. He currently is working on his dissertation, which examines the longitudinal trajectory patterns of high school academic achievement among Asian immigrant and European American students, and how different trajectory patterns are associated with individual and family characteristics.

Holly Kreider, Ed.D., is vice president at Sociometrics Corporation, where she leads federally funded and private-sector research and evaluation projects pertaining to child and adolescent health, mental health, and development; family support and parent leadership; and professional development and training of health educators. She also oversees corporate outreach and dissemination efforts for major science-based resources. Prior to joining Sociometrics, she spent 15 years as an applied researcher at the Harvard Family Research Project, where she managed child development research studies focused on the multiple contexts and relationships supporting children's successful development, with an emphasis on family–school–community relations. She is co-founder of an online national network of over 8,000 educators committed to family–school–community partnerships (www.finenetwork.org); has published articles in *Journal of Educational Psychology, Review of Marriage and Family,* and *Urban Education.* In addition, she co-edited *From Theory to Practice: Preparing Educators to Involve Families* (2005). She earned her doctorate in human development and psychology from Harvard University, Graduate School of Education in 1997.

Jelani Mandara, Ph.D., is an assistant professor in the Program of Human Development and Social Policy at Northwestern University. His interdisciplinary research program integrates developmental, family, and educational domains and is concerned primarily with understanding the nature and effects of socialization, fathers' involvement, and identity development on youths' behaviors and academic achievement. His current research projects examine the effects of parenting styles on Black, Latino, and White American youth's academic achievement. As part of his focus on translating basic research into empirically based prevention interventions, he regularly conducts parenting workshops for parent groups and teachers.

Inna Padmawidjaja, Ph.D., received her doctoral degree in human development and family studies from the University of Rochester, Rochester, New York. She spent 4 years as a postdoctoral fellow at the University of California, Riverside, studying multicultural families and adolescents. Her main fields of interest are (1) investigating cultural factors that promote family self-sufficiency and well-being among youth and families receiving cash aid from U.S. government welfare programs, with a special focus on immigrant youth community services; (2) studying parental influences on career development among immigrant youth; (3) exploring relationships between parental beliefs, practices, and academic achievement with respect to immigrant youth adjusting to living conditions in the United States; (4) testing Western psychological and sociological theories that claim universal applicability to social programming; and (5) studying parental functioning on child and adolescent mental health across cultures and across ethnic groups in the United States.

James L. Rodríguez, Ph.D., is an associate professor of child and adolescent studies at California State University, Fullerton. He received his undergraduate degree in psychology from Pomona College and a Ph.D. in education, with a specialization in child and adolescent development, from Stanford University. Prior to joining the Department of Child and Adolescent Studies, he was an associate professor of education at San Diego State University. His research is focused on the psychological development and education of Latino children, adolescents, and families. His publications have appeared in educational and psychological journals, including *Applied Developmental Science, Child Development, Early Childhood Research Quarterly, Equity and Excellence in Education, High School Journal, Hispanic Journal of Behavioral Sciences, Review of Educational Research*, and *Theory Into Practice*.

Barbara Schneider, Ph.D., is the John A. Hannah Chair University Distinguished Professor in the College of Education and Department of Sociology at Michigan State University. She worked for 18 years at the University of Chicago, holding positions as a professor in sociology and human development and a senior researcher at the National Opinion Research Center (NORC). She continues to hold an appointment as a university faculty research associate at the University of Chicago and as senior fellow at NORC, where she is the principal investigator of the Data Research and Development Center. She also directs the Alfred P. Sloan Center on Parents, Children, and Work at Michigan State University, an initiative that began at the University of Chicago where she was co-director. She uses a sociological lens to understand societal conditions and interpersonal interactions that create norms and values that enhance human and social capital. Her research focuses on how the social contexts of schools and families influence the academic and social well-being of adolescents as they move into adulthood. She has published 12 books and over 100 articles and reports on family, social context of schooling, and sociology of knowledge. Presently, she is the editor of *Sociology of Education*. She received her bachelor's and master's degrees from National-Louis University and her Ph.D. from Northwestern University.

Nicole Stanoff is a doctoral student at the University of California, Riverside, in the developmental psychology area. She received her bachelor's degree in psychology and child development from California State University, Chico, in 2004, where she conducted research on romantic relationship satisfaction among gay, lesbian, and heterosexual college students. She also received her master's degree in psychology from the University of California, Riverside, in 2006. Her research interests include the quality and openness of parent–adolescent communication, parental influences on adolescent sexual behavior and contraceptive use, and cultural and ethnic group differences in adolescent reproductive behavior and pregnancy risk. She currently is beginning work on her dissertation, which examines the association between parent–child sexual communication and adolescents' decisionmaking skills and engagement in sexual intercourse and contraceptive use.

Diana F. Tyson, Ph.D., is a Society for Research in Child Development (SRCD) Executive Branch Fellow at the Department of Health and Human Services in the Child and Youth Policy Division, Office of the Assistant Secretary for Planning and Evaluation (ASPE). Prior to her selection as an SRCD Fellow, she completed her doctoral degree in developmental psychology at Duke University's Department of Psychology and Neuroscience. She is a former Spencer Education Fellow and a Sulzberger Family Social Policy Research Fellow with Duke's Center for Child and Family Policy, where she explored the role of parental involvement in education and the development of student motivation. In her dissertation work, she focused on the manner in which these factors combine to influence the academic achievement of middle school students. She also has conducted focus groups with adolescents, parents, and teachers to improve family–school relations during the transition into middle school. Additionally, she has worked in collaboration with Duke's Interdisciplinary Initiative in Social Psychology to examine the role of emotion regulation during test taking among college and middle school populations, in order to identify the physiological factors associated with challenging classroom experiences. She graduated from Columbia University with a bachelor's degree in psychology.

Manya C. Whitaker is a doctoral student at Vanderbilt University. She received her bachelor's degree from Dartmouth College, where she conducted research on adolescents and interracial social skill development. As the only graduate student in the Family–School Partnership Lab at Vanderbilt, her research interests are extensive, including social and cultural capital, the development of parental role construction beliefs, and parental involvement in marginalized populations. She currently is working on her dissertation, which investigates factors contributing to children's invitations to parental involvement.

Index